RE-STATING SOCIAL
and POLITICAL CHANGE

SOCIOLOGY *and* SOCIAL CHANGE

Series Editor: *Alan* **Warde, Lancaster University**

Published titles

Gail **Hawkes** – *A* **Sociology** *of* **Sex** *and* **Sexuality**

Colin **Hay** – **Re-stating Social** *and* **Political Change**

RE-STATING SOCIAL
and POLITICAL CHANGE

Colin **Hay**

Open University Press
Buckingham · Philadelphia

Open University Press
Celtic Court
22 Ballmoor
Buckingham
MK18 1XW

and
1900 Frost Road, Suite 101
Bristol, PA 19007, USA

First Published 1996

A catalogue record of this book is available from the British Library

ISBN   0 335 19386 2 (pb)   0 335 19387 0 (hb)

Library of Congress Cataloging-in-Publication Data
Hay, Colin, 1968–
    Re-stating social and political change / Colin Hay.
      p.   cm.
    Includes bibliographical references and index.
    ISBN 0-335-19387-0. — ISBN 0-335-19386-2 (pbk.)
    1. State, The.   2. Social change.   3. Political science.
  I. Title.
JC131.H39   1996   95–24919
320.1′01—dc20   CIP

Typeset by Graphicraft Typesetters Ltd, Hong Kong
Printed in Great Britain by Biddles Ltd, Guildford and King's Lynn

For Elspeth

A Klee painting named 'Angelus Novus' shows an angel looking as though he is about to move away from something he is fixedly contemplating. His eyes are staring, his mouth is open, his wings are spread. This is how one pictures the angel of history. His face is turned toward the past. Where we perceive a chain of events, he sees one single catastrophe which keeps piling wreckage upon wreckage and hurls it in front of his feet. The angel would like to stay, awaken the dead, and make whole that which has been smashed. But a storm is blowing from Paradise; it has got caught in his wings with such violence that the angel can no longer close them. This storm irresistibly propels him into the future to which his back is turned, while the pile of debris before him grows skyward. This storm is what we call progress.

Walter Benjamin

Contents

Series editor's preface

In response to perceived major transformations, social theorists have offered forceful, appealing but competing accounts of the predicament of contemporary Western societies. Key themes emerging have been frequently condensed into terms like postmodernism, postmodernity, post-Fordism, risk society, disorganized capitalism, the post-welfare state, post-industrialism, the information society. These have important and widespread ramifications for the analysis of all areas of social life and personal well-being. The speculative and general theses proposed by social theorists must be subjected to evaluation in the light of the best available evidence if they are to serve as guides to understanding and modifying social arrangements. One purpose of sociology, among other social sciences, is to marshal the information necessary to estimate the extent and direction of social change. This series is designed to make such information, and debates about social change, accessible.

The focus of the series is the critical appraisal of general, substantive theories through examination of their applicability to different institutional areas of contemporary societies. Each book introduces key contemporary debates and surveys current sociological argument and research about institutional complexes in advanced societies. The integrating theme for the series is the evaluation of the extent of social change, particularly in the past twenty years. Each author offers explicit and extended evaluation of the pace and direction of social change in his or her chosen area.

If asked to identify important recent institutional change, many people would include the institutions of party, government and state. Comparison between the 1990s and the first two decades after the Second World War has generated theories of crisis and decline. Major adjustments were required, first by the passing of Empire, then by the collapse of the post-war economic boom and subsequently by the end of the Cold War. The very role of the nation-state has come into question in the face of European political integration and enhanced global economic competition. In domestic politics, reaction was mediated in Britain by the Governments of Margaret Thatcher, the ultimate effects of whose policies remain a matter of controversy. Through legislative programmes, management of state organizations and enterprises, and the battle of ideas, Thatcherism created a distinctive party politics.

Whether reflecting a change in the balance of domestic social forces, or a reaction to external pressures, or an adaptation to a more volatile, diverse and disenchanted electorate, the Conservative years after 1979 require appraisal to determine whether they have caused a lasting transformation of British social life.

This book, a decisive history of change in the operation of the British political system since the Second World War, offers an answer. Intellectually anchored in debates about theories of the capitalist state, it explores key phases in the development of the British case. Colin Hay reviews debates about many of the most contentious issues of interpretation – about economic policy, party programmes and welfare provision. These in turn are used to introduce more abstract conceptual debates about how to understand theoretically the role of the nation-state in an increasingly global order. His analysis is clear, his conclusion about recent transformation firm and distinctive, his theoretical reflections instructive. Some may disagree with his substantive interpretation of political change or his preferred theoretical approach; but the breadth of coverage and fluent argument make the kind of fresh contribution that the series is designed to promote.

Alan Warde

Preface

The contemporary state is something of a paradox. On the one hand it is seemingly all-pervasive, shaping and reshaping the landscape of social and political life. Yet at the same time it is apparently intangible, elusive and almost impossible to pinpoint finely and specify tightly. Its boundaries are blurred and constantly shifting; its responsibilities multiple, contested and variable; its form and function the complex outcome of a multitude of processes, struggles and strategies operating over differing time horizons and at different spatial scales. If we wish to consider what is at stake in *re-stating* social and political change, then, it is instructive to reflect upon the extent to which our daily routine experiences and mundane rituals are deeply influenced, punctuated and at times even structured by the uninvited interventions of the state.

We wake at a preordained hour in a national context which shares a common time. We may be summoned from sleep by an alarm clock to the dulcit tones of a state radio station, be it Radio 1's *Morning Show* or Radio 4's *Today Programme*. In our condition of semi-slumber we are bombarded with today's newsworthy events in the British nation-state and stories from 'elsewhere' which have significance for 'us', the national community of British people. Should we listen to a private radio station then that too is heavily regulated by the state. If we find ourselves tuned into a pirate channel, the likelihood is that as we doze, state officials are monitoring the broadcast, tracking down the signals or on their way to apprehend the culprits.

Having showered, bathed or washed with privatized water regulated (we are led to believe) by Ofwat, we may adorn ourselves in the uniforms or 'costumes' considered appropriate within this national setting for the tasks we are to perform in the hours ahead. In so doing we orient ourselves towards a 'working day', whether of paid employment, unpaid domestic labour or 'jobseeking'. Our taken-for-granted routine assumptions about the day to come in turn reflect the capitalist and patriarchal state and society within which we have been, and continue to be, socialized. Our intuitive actions and routine practices display: (a) our internalization of dominant conceptions of gender roles, and family responsibilities; (b) our understanding of the need to work, in turn to earn, in turn to live; and (c) our orientation towards symbolic codes of dress, taste and demeanour. Though the product of complex, conflicting and contested processes to which we are differentially exposed, such socialization reveals the extent of the state's reach into the seemingly 'private' sphere of the home and the supposedly autonomous arenas of civil society.

Once dressed we may descend the stairs in a home or flat perhaps built and subsequently sold off by the state and on which we are currently receiving mortgage interest tax relief. Whether or not our house was built by the state, one thing is almost certain – it was constructed to state-regulated British building standards. We may make our way to the kitchen to prepare a 'full *English* breakfast', some '*Scottish* porridge oats', or merely a bowl of cereal. As we contemplate the day ahead we may stare ruefully at the box of corn flakes on which, it is stipulated, must be printed a list of ingredients.

Suitably nourished, we may leave the house on our way to work, the supermarket or the state benefits agency. We may travel by car, in which case we rely upon the assumption that at least within this particular nation-state everyone will drive on the left-hand side of the road, stop at red lights and negotiate roundabouts in a clockwise direction. When we step into our car we enter into an intensely state-regulated space. Not only must we abide by the 'highway code', we must also be in possession of a valid driving licence in a vehicle for which there is insurance certification, a tax disc and, if appropriate, a current MOT. Should we traverse the bounds of such legal stipulation then we expose ourselves to the legitimate sanctions of the state's juridical authority. And furthermore, we do so in the almost certain knowledge that the state's surveillance and policing apparatuses are, however sporadically and inefficiently, honing in on our waverings from the 'straight and narrow'. Should we decide to travel by public transport (scared off perhaps by this degree of influence behind the steering wheel), then we hardly escape the institutional reach of the state. For even as we step on to a private double-decker on a deregulated bus route we enter, once again, into an arena thoroughly infiltrated and deeply structured by legal regulation. And all this before we even begin our day's work.

Clearly this diary could be extended. The crucial point, however, is made. There is scarcely any aspect of our daily rituals and routine experiences that is not thoroughly influenced and profoundly shaped by the interventions of the state. It is this 'state', which makes so many unacknowledged and uninvited appearances into our lives, that is the subject of this book. If we wish to consider processes of social and political change, and we concede that the state is indeed able to shape the very contours of social and political life as demonstrated above, then we cannot avoid the imperative to *re-state social and political change*. It is to this task that the rest of this text is devoted.

In writing this book I have had the very enjoyable experience of incurring a great number of personal and intellectual debts. I must begin by thanking Bob Blackburn and Tom Ling, without whose advice, encouragement and infectious enthusiasm I would probably never have found myself in the position of being able to 'make a career' out of doing what I enjoyed. Though others might hold them culpable for putting this dastardly thought into my head, I can only express my immense and eternal gratitude.

A very large number of colleagues and friends have commented at
various stages upon draft chapters and papers whose contents have found
their way in some form into this text. Though they can be held in no way
responsible for the errors and omissions that no doubt remain, they have
certainly kept me somewhat closer to the theoretical straight-and-narrow
than might otherwise have been the case. In alphabetical order, these in-
clude (for I'm sure I have forgotten someone): Nick Abercrombie, Barbara
Adam, Paul Bagguley, Ted Benton, Pete Burnham, Kevin Bonnett, Simon
Bromley, Alan Cochrane, Davina Cooper, George DeMartino, Norman
Fairclough, Allan Finlayson, David Forgács, Mariam Fraser, Andrew Gamble,
Till Geiger, Mark Gillard, Paul Ginsborg, Piyel Haldar, Wayne Hope, John
Hughes, Ray Jobling, Peter Kerr, Des King, Les Levidow, Tom Ling (again),
John Lovering, Gordon MacLeod, Dave Marsh, Doreen Massey, Michael
Moran, Jim O'Connor, Martin O'Connor, Jamie Peck, Mark Poster, Trevor
Purvis, Andrew Sayer, Ingrid Scheibler, Caroline Schwaller, Martin Smith,
Gerry Stoker, John Thompson, Adam Tickell, Nick Tiratsoo, John Urry and
Alison Young.

More formally, I must extend my thanks to the numerous anonymous
referees of the following journals (in which earlier versions of some of the
arguments presented here were first published): *Arena*; *Capital & Class*; *Capitalism, Nature, Socialism*; *Common Sense*; *Economy & Society*; *Futur Antérieur*;
Political Studies; *Rethinking Marxism*; *Ricerche di Storia Politica*; *Social and Legal
Studies*; *Sociology*; and *Transformations*.

I must also express my immense gratitude to Bob Jessop and Alan
Warde who provided invaluable comments on an earlier version of the entire
manuscript, and to Nick Evans, Jacinta Evans and Claire Hutchins at Open
University Press for their amazing efficiency and friendly enthusiasm. Together they have made the writing of this book a much less fraught process
than I believe it often is. The other factor that has made this book easier to
write than it might otherwise have been is the unique atmosphere that
suffuses the corridors of the Department of Sociology at Lancaster University.
For providing such a conducive environment in which to work I must thank
all of my friends and colleagues in Sociology, and particularly the hub of the
department – Cath, Diane, Karen, Maeve and Pennie – the best support team
in the business.

This book could not have been written were it not for the (apparent)
willingness of the students on 'Socl 325: State and Society' over the past
three years to indulge my proclivity for theory, and to come back for more.
They have provided the most important sounding-board for the ideas con-
tained in the chapters that follow. I am still convinced that the only way to
discover whether you have an argument or not is to try teaching it!

This leaves my most important debt of all. Without the enthusiasm
and encouragement of Bob Jessop this text could simply not have been
written. His own work continues to represent the greatest single influence
over my thinking about the state (an influence it established when I first
read it as an undergraduate). The analytical and theoretical rigour of his own
writing provides a model that I can only aspire to emulate. As a supervisor,
colleague and friend Bob has devoted an immense amount of effort and time

in talking through my ideas at every stage of their development. Though the position I express in this book clearly departs, at times quite significantly, from his own, I can only hope that the Jessopian influence is still clear to see.

Finally, I owe an immeasurable debt to Elspeth, my parents and my brother, Mark. Over the past few years they have heard rather more about the state, Thatcherism and social and political change than even the most enthusiastic of state theorists might have cared for. It is, above all, their support and love that has made the writing of this book possible.

Part I
STATING *the* OBVIOUS

1 What is *the* state *and* why do we need *a* theory *of* it?

State-ing the obvious

The modern state is ... an amorphous complex of agencies with ill-defined boundaries performing a great variety of not very distinctive functions.

(Schmitter 1985: 33)

It might seem somewhat strange, if not downright defeatist, to begin a text on the state with this comment. For if the state is indeed so fragmented, so elusive and so intangible an object what can possibly be gained by developing a theory of it? The purpose of this text is to provide some answers to this question. In fact, it will be the argument of this chapter that it is precisely *because* of, and not in spite of, the difficulty of framing any simple conception of the state that such a theory is so important. Schmitter's observation is, at least in one sense, a particularly appropriate place to begin. For there is no more arduous a task in the theory of the state than that of defining this notoriously illusive and rapidly moving target. We begin then with perhaps the most difficult and sadly neglected questions in the theory of the state. What is the state? And why do we need a theory of it?

In what follows I hope to show that there is something distinctive about the *state* (however apparently intangible such an object might be) that necessitates a theory of it (whatever form that might take) in order that we may better understand the changing social, political, cultural and economic context we inhabit.

The theory of the state, perhaps more than most branches of social and political theory, does require some justification. For, on the face of it, the 'state' is not a directly apparent *material object*, and it is difficult to see what an analysis of this somewhat vague, even abstract, notion can contribute to an understanding of the political process, the economy and the internal structuring of society. Yet state theorists would claim to offer new insights which might supplement and at times even transcend those of the disciplines traditionally associated with such issues: political science; economic theory; and industrial, economic and political sociology.

The purpose of this chapter is to evaluate this claim – to consider what it is that state theory can offer us that conventional or mainstream political science and sociology cannot, and to argue that this 'extra insight' sheds an important new light upon the processes of social, political, cultural and economic change.

However, before we can even begin to do this we must have some working definition of the 'state'. For clearly, if we haven't got a clue what the state actually is, it is very difficult to make a case for arguing that we need a theory of it, let alone that this theory is capable of transcending the limitations of conventional political sociology, political science and political economy.

Defining the state: stating the obvious

Drawing boundaries around 'the state' is not easy; taxation departments and courts are obviously state institutions, but are medical associations? universities? unions? The problem is compounded by the fact that the realm of the state as well as the form of the state changes historically.

(Connell 1990: 509)

A moment's foray in the substantial archives of state theory will immediately reveal that while theorists of the state may well rely *implicitly* upon certain conceptions and understandings (however idiosyncratic) of the nature of the state, they are notoriously bad at consigning these to the page. This makes it somewhat difficult to identify any analytically precise definition of the state as an object of inquiry, let alone one that is commonly agreed upon. This is partly for some very good reasons that we will return to later. Yet although there are mitigating circumstances, it is still something of an indictment of state theorists that they are apparently so loath to tell us what this 'state' is that they spend so much time thinking about.

Among those brave or perhaps foolhardy enough to try to specify what it is that we are talking about when we refer to the state are John Hall and John Ikenberry. Compelled perhaps by the title of their book, *The State*, into providing something of a definition, they make the somewhat surprising claim that 'there is a great deal of agreement amongst social scientists as to how the state should be defined' (1989: 1). If only this were so. They elaborate by mapping out a 'composite definition' comprising three elements. The state, they suggest, giving voice to this spurious consensus, is

- a set of institutions operated by the *state's own personnel* (the most important of which are the means of coercion and violence);
- these institutions lie at the 'centre of gravity' of a geographically bounded territory;
- the state monopolizes rule-making within its territory, leading to the creation of a common culture shared by all of its citizens (1989: 1–2).

In its emphasis upon the state as a territorially bounded and sovereign administrative institution, this is a classically Weberian conception of the state.[1] However, quite apart from the fact that this definition would not be accepted by all neo-Weberians, let alone all state theorists, *far less all social scientists*, it is, like most succinct definitions, somewhat problematic. Yet it does loosely fix a *subject matter* and it does give us an idea as to the nature of the state, the essence of 'stateness'. The state is basically a set of institutions, unified in some way (the definition tells us little about how), that retains a certain monopoly over the legitimate use of organized violence and rule-making within a geographically bounded society (the Weberian aspect). Although different state theorists would chose to emphasize different characteristics of the state, and this would be reflected in their different definitions, few would argue with the suggestion that the object of this particular neo-Weberian definition is the same 'state' that they themselves study. We do at least appear to be making some progress.

Before we can proceed further, however, it is necessary to qualify this somewhat overgeneralized and grandiose definition. For it is in problematizing the ease with which we may 'fix' the state as an object of analysis that much theoretical progress in understanding the state is made. The state is a highly complex, differentiated and variable set of apparatuses, institutions and practices, so why should its definition be simple and homogeneous? As John Hoffman notes, the definition of the state necessarily embodies a certain irony since the importance of defining the state in the first place 'arises from the fact that this is the only way to highlight, in an intelligible and critical fashion, its problematic and ambiguous character' (1995: 33). If the central theme of this text is the re-stat(e)ing of the obvious, then a second is the demystification of the state.

The first point to note is that Hall and Ikenberry define the state *institutionally*, and hence *structurally*: the state is a set of institutions, a set of structures. This, on the face of it, doesn't really tell us very much. The crucial question of *which* institutions comprise the state is, at least for the moment, sidelined. Yet it is very difficult to be more precise. For, state structures vary *between* societies. The set of institutions that characterize an advanced capitalist state such as Britain today is clearly very different to those, say, of Chinese state socialism or the post-socialist societies of Eastern Europe. Furthermore, as R. W. Connell's comment cited at the beginning of this section rightly emphasizes, state structures also change with time. The set of institutions that characterized the British state in the seventeenth century, or even in the immediate post-war period, do not correspond terribly closely to those today.

Thus, although a basic set of core *practices*, or perhaps better still *functions*,[2] can be specified, their means of delivery and the precise boundaries of the state and society are historically variable and, indeed, in almost constant flux. This tends to render institutional definitions either notoriously imprecise, or, where a more specific institutional 'laundry list' is provided, extremely limited in their historical and geographical scope.

This is not the end of the problem, however. For even at a particular moment for a particular state formation, different theorists will argue about which institutions belong to the state apparatus, which to civil society. None the less, as R. M. MacIver noted as early as 1926, 'it is easier to agree on the nature of a particular state than on the nature of *the* state' (MacIver 1926:

4). The subsequent history of state theory would appear to bear out this perceptive observation.

In a famous essay written in 1968 the French Marxist philosopher Louis Althusser provocatively suggested that within capitalist societies the family was an ideological apparatus *of the state* (Althusser 1968/71). Perry Anderson (1977) replied that it was only under fascism that the family was subsumed within the structures of the state and that Althusser's analysis was thus dangerous in its effective conflation of liberal democracy and fascist dictatorship.[3] Most other commentators seemed to agree that the family had never been, nor was ever likely to become, an institution of the state. None the less, although Althusser's argument might seem somewhat counterintuitive (there is, apparently, no more private an institution than the family), what he was identifying is the pervasive and often extremely covert influence of the state upon such taken-for-granted institutions of the 'private' sphere as the family. In a sense, he was *'re-stating'* the obvious (a central theme of this text).

What the above brief discussion illustrates is the difficulty of formulating a precise and unambiguous definition of the *boundaries* of the state. Perhaps the best we can do is to agree upon a set of core institutions of the state, and be clear, for the purpose of a particular analysis, about where we will take the blurred boundary between state and civil society to lie.

In certain contexts, for instance, it is extremely useful to think of the family as a state institution or at least as an 'adjunct of the state' (Elliott 1989; cf. McIntosh 1978; Cooper 1994). This is especially so if we wish to consider the role of the state in the reproduction of patriarchal forms of domination through the legal regulation of sexual relations, the juridical construction of the family and the reliance of the welfare state upon the unpaid domestic labour of women in an assumed 'nuclear family' setting (see Chapter 4). As Zillah Eisenstein (1980: 61) perceptively notes, through 'the legal formulation of the sex-gender system, through marriage law, divorce law, abortion law, day care law, etc., [the state] monitors the relations of familial patriarchy'.

A further weakness of Hall and Ikenberry's institutional definition of the state is that it provides no analysis of what holds this loose aggregation of structures and apparatuses together. If they have no *common essence* and no *unity*, then they do not constitute a state. The problem, however, is once again that what unites these disaggregated institutions varies with time within specific states, and varies at the same time between different states. Unity, in as much as it exists, must be worked at and achieved. It is not a universal, trans-historical property of states (Hay 1994b; cf. Schmitter 1985). As a consequence, an abstract definition is not much use here, and a more concrete 'shopping list' of state institutions is likely to prove extremely limited in its applicability. To say that *state institutions are those run by state personnel* doesn't actually help. We get stuck in the eternal tautological circle. How do we know an institution is a state institution? State personnel administer it. How do we know they're state personnel? They work for a state institution.

Finally, the idea that the existence of a state really gives rise to a *common political culture* must be seriously questioned. This is perhaps the most dubious aspect of Hall and Ikenberry's definition and the one that most *critical* state theorists (be they neo-Marxists, feminists or those engaged in anti-racist struggles) would most want to dissent from. In fact, a near universal property of the state is its systematic exclusion from full citizenship (and hence full participation in the dominant political culture) of certain groups (by virtue of their class, gender, ethnicity, family type, age and so forth). The exclusion or 'expurgation' of such marginalized others (as we will see in later chapters) often becomes the basis for the unification of those granted 'full citizenship' of the state, helping in the cementation of the state as a national community – predominantly of white, middle-class, heterosexual males.

If the above discussion reveals anything, it is perhaps that we shouldn't put too much emphasis upon tightly delineating the state, since what we are generally interested in is the state's *variability*: its dynamic nature as a condensation of power relations within society, and the various forms it takes in different historical and geo-political contexts. Clearly if we wish to make a case for re-stating social and political change, we cannot afford to begin with a static and invariant conception of the state. None the less we can tidy up the above Weberian definition so that it at least reflects the abstract object of scrutiny of various theories of the state. If we were to do so we might get somewhat closer to the definition provided by Michael Mann in *States, War and Capitalism* (1988). The state, for Mann, comprises:

- a *differentiated set of institutions* and personnel embodying
- *centrality* in the sense that political relations radiate outwards from the centre to cover
- a *territorially demarcated area* over which it exercises
- a *monopoly of authoritatively binding rule-making*, backed up by a monopoly of the means of physical violence (1988: 4).

What such a definition emphasizes is that the theoretical notion of the state embodies far more than the popular notion of 'government'. It refers to the whole apparatus of rule within society: government, army, judiciary, nationalized industries and so forth; in fact, to the very *context* inhabited by government and inherited by incoming regimes. Furthermore, it suggests that the state has a unity, essence and power over-and-above that of the specific apparatuses that give effect to this 'primary societal authority'. The whole is, at least in some sense, greater than the sum of its component parts. The unity of the state resides in the constellation of constraint and opportunity that it imposes upon the strategies of government, bureaucracy and civil service alike. As Bob Jessop (1990: 129) notes, 'the form of the state is the crystallization of past strategies as well as privileging ... [certain] ... current strategies'. This introduces the important idea that the state, and the institutions that comprise it, are *strategically selective*. Its structures, practices and *modus operandi* are more amenable to some types of political strategy and certain types of intervention than others. The state constitutes an uneven playing field which privileges some forces and interests while proving less accessible to others.

As we said earlier, different state theorists frame different conceptions (and thus definitions) of the state because they are interested in different aspects of its form, function, structure and action – the concept of the state does different types of theoretical work for different theorists. The Weberian definition is particularly useful as a basis from which to consider the legitimacy of the state and its repressive or coercive arm.

An alternative, though not incompatible, framework is provided by Marxist and neo-Marxist conceptions of the state, of which inevitably there are several (for useful reviews see Gold *et al.* 1975/6; Jessop 1982; Carnoy 1984; Barrow 1993). A simultaneously clear yet sophisticated Marxist definition of the state is provided by Jessop. The core of the state apparatus, he argues, 'comprises a distinct ensemble of institutions and organisations whose socially accepted function is to define and enforce collectively binding decisions on the members of a society in the name of their common interest or general will' (Jessop 1990: 341). The strength of this definition is that it puts the contradictions and dilemmas of the state at the heart of its analysis. What is more, Jessop, unlike the other theorists we have so far considered, recognizes the inherent limitations of attempts to 'fix' the state by definition, insisting on several qualifications:

1 States never achieve complete separation from society – the specific nature of the boundary is blurred and constantly in doubt (cf. Bertramsen *et al.* 1991: 20–4; Mitchell 1991; Hay 1994b).
2 The means by which the legitimacy of the state is secured varies; indeed, it is periodically threatened, and is dependent upon the social and historical context in which it is constructed.
3 Though coercion is the state's ultimate sanction, it has other means of enforcement and influence that it can deploy (such as surveillance, moral appeal, privilege or nepotism).
4 The common interest or general will in whose name the state claims to act is always illusory, asymmetrical and marginalizing of certain groups.

Thus far we have focused on the generic properties of the state, seeking to provide an answer to the question, 'if we were to come across a state, how would we recognize it *as a state*?'. We have emphasized the difficulty of tightly specifying the state as an object of investigation and the impossibility of formulating a hard and fast, trans-historical definition of what is an inherently unstable and constantly evolving set of apparatuses and practices.

This establishes a point of departure for what is to follow. Instead of seeking to 'fix' the state as a relatively static object of inquiry which can then be exposed to a detailed structural and institutional interrogation, our strategy will be to treat *the essential dynamism and complexity of the state as integral to its very nature*. Accordingly, we will focus upon the state as a series of dynamic and complexly interwoven *processes* and *practices* (occurring within specific institutional settings), and hence upon the state as a dynamic and evolving system. Accordingly, we must reject the prevalent notion that the definition of the state may be used as means to 'fix' and thereby render static what is, in fact, a constantly changing network of relationships and institutional practices and procedures. In defining the state, then, we should not place too much emphasis upon tightly delineating its structural form, function, content or boundaries. Indeed what might be taken as a characteristic, even defining, trait is the essential variability of the state – its dynamic nature as a condensation of power relations within society (Poulantzas 1973, 1978; Resnick and Wolff 1987). This is reflected in the sheer diversity of forms it takes in different historical and geo-political contexts. Our conception of the state must prove sufficiently flexible to accommodate this diversity, complexity and variability: from seeking to 'fix' the state we must move towards a conception which allows us to 'follow' a constantly (and often rapidly) moving subject. In place of a series of instantaneous and static 'snapshots' we must seek to develop a 'panning shot' of the state *in motion*. Thus far we have tended to assume that in defining the state we are searching for a single, elusive, essence of 'stateness'. In fact, as we shall see in the next section, a number of different moments of 'stateness' can be identified.

Moments of stateness: other states and the state's others

These various senses of stateness are revealed in sharp relief if we consider the *processes* by which the state is constituted *as a state* through the identification and maintenance of its various *boundaries*. Through the procedures and practices of boundary-maintenance, the state defines itself in contrast to its multiple 'others'. These are, variously: other (nation-)states; the institutions of the economy, civil society and the private sphere (considered as that which is not the state, and hence the state's 'other'); and those excluded from full citizenship of the state (or upon whom the obligations of citizenship fall disproportionately), who are thus similarly defined as 'other' (through the practices of racism, patriarchy and homophobia, for instance).

We can then fairly readily differentiate between three moments of stateness (which have tended to become elided in much state theory):

1 The *state as nation*, the state as an 'imagined' national community (cf. Anderson 1983; Hoffman 1995: 67–8).
2 The *state as territory*, the state as a strictly bounded sovereign terrain (cf. Tilly 1973; Shaw 1984; Giddens 1985; Mann 1985, 1988; Agnew and Corbridge 1995: 78, 80–100).
3 The *state as institution*, the state as a set of apparatuses and practices unified through some form of centralized coordination (cf. Weber 1978).

The state as nation

The sense of stateness encapsulated in this conception is that of the state as a community, the state as a national 'people'. The boundary of the state is thus *symbolic* or *discursive*. It is manifest in inclusions and exclusions from participation in a collective national culture and common identity (cf. Schlesinger 1987: 245). This conception of stateness stresses the constitution of the state through the mobilization of a sense of belonging to a national collectivity: through national identity, nationalism and loyalty to a sovereign authority (be it monarchy or republic).[4] Though the boundary of the state as nation is primarily discursive as opposed to material or physical, it is none the less very real in the sense that it is linked to the distribution of the material advantages accruing to those possessing the status of full *citizenship* (Marshall 1950: 18, 24; see Chapter 4). The boundary of the state as an imagined national community is particularly blurred. Indeed, despite the inclusive rhetoric of universal citizenship, the state as nation is a highly contoured terrain within which different social groupings experience different degrees of inclusion and exclusion by virtue of their gender, sexuality, ethnicity, home country,[5] religion, age and so forth (Turner 1990; Yuval-Davis 1990; Balibar 1991; Anthias and Yuval-Davis 1992; Roche 1992; Small 1994). The resulting pattern of inclusion and exclusion is reflected in the very real distribution of rewards, obligations, responsibilities and life chances within civil society.

Moreover, the state as nation, and the sense of nationhood through which it is imagined, is constructed and sustained through a series of very real practices, symbolic rituals and ceremonies. It is reflected in symbolic representations of the state, such as: the 'portrait of the king' on coins and bank notes (Marin 1988); ceremonial crests, flags and costumes (Dillon and Everard 1992); national anthems; and emblems such as Britannia or the 'plucky' British (English?)[6] Bulldog (Nairn 1988; Billig 1992). The latter are presented as symbols of stateness, and as unambiguously representative of a collective and unified 'national interest' (threatened by the tyranny of the Russian Bear or the sign of the Swastika, for instance). This imagery of nationhood and stateness can be seen as a resource in the legitimation of: (a) the *state as territory*, as the 'national people' is mobilized in defence of the realm, for instance; and (b) the *state as institution*, as the practices and procedures of state administration are justified in terms of the 'national-popular' interest (Gramsci 1971: 131).

The state as territory

A further 'moment' of stateness is the territorial: the state as territory, the state as a strictly bounded sovereign terrain. Yet, although we might identify this as an *analytically* separable sense of stateness, it is hard to escape the obvious relationship between the state as nation and the state as territory. This becomes immediately apparent if we consider the process of crossing a national/territorial boundary. Here the state effectively recruits or 'interpellates' its 'national' subjects (those subject to its authority) at its administrative frontier. The physical boundary of the state's terrain and the custodial and military practices which enforce it help to sustain the state's discursive construction as a people, as a nation, as a national community with a common heritage. As Louis Marin (1988: 5) perceptively notes,

> by the representation of one's passport at the border [representation both in the sense of *re*-presenting oneself and of being represented by the passport itself], the bearer not only presents himself [*sic*] really but also his legitimate presence by the sign or title that authorises or permits, not to say compels, his presence.

Yet if these twin moments of stateness are mutually reinforcing, they cannot simply be conflated. The state as territory and the state as nation are not the same thing, as a momentary reflection on the question of Scottish nationhood (yet territorial stateless-ness) quickly reveals (Nairn 1976, 1981; McCrone 1992; Harvie 1994). Moreover, the state as defined territorially exercises jurisdiction over those excluded from 'belonging' to the state as nation (by virtue of their 'foreign' status) or from full citizenship (by virtue of their gender, class or ethnicity), as much as if not more than it does over those on whom such status is confirmed. One does not need to belong to the symbolic community of the national state to suffer the power of its territorially administered authority, its sovereign claim to legitimate violence, as ethnic minorities, 'illegal aliens' and civil rights demonstrators find to their cost. The state as territory thus refers to a geo-politically bounded area of administrative sovereignty, and is associated with such practices of boundary maintenance as border controls, passport checks, the 'defence of the realm', military aggression and international diplomacy.

The state as institution

A third sense of stateness is that of the state as institution. A moment's reflection reveals that it is in fact the very condition of the other two. For, without an apparatus of state it is impossible to conceive of the mobilization of perceptions of belonging to a national community with a common tradition and heritage in a complex and differentiated society,[7] far less the maintenance, policing and defence of a geo-politically demarcated sovereign terrain. Yet, once again, this is an analytically separable moment of stateness. Clearly, for instance, it means something entirely different to speak of the unity of the state with reference to the state as nation and the state as institution. One is certainly not the condition of the other. It is possible to conceive of a state unified as nation, yet fundamentally fragmented at an institutional level, or indeed vice versa.

By referring to the administrative and organizational dimension of stateness, the emphasis is placed on the state as an assemblage of more-or-less centrally coordinated apparatuses, institutions and practices. The boundaries of stateness are practical as much as physical or discursive and concern the 'institutional reach' of the state – the extent of its intervention into the private sphere (of the home and family), the economy and civil society. The state as institution can thus be categorized (at a particular moment, in a particular national setting) in terms of: (a) its distinctive *modes of intervention* within such spheres; (b) the extent of state regulation; and (c) the degree of administrative centralization or decentralization. It is important to stress that forms of intervention within civil society, the private sphere and the economy may be overt and obvious, such as legal regulation or policing, or more covert, such as the subterranean activities and practices of state surveillance.

As the above discussion should make clear, in identifying these different moments of stateness, I do not want to suggest that they are unrelated, or easily separable. Thus as Timothy Mitchell (1991: 94) notes, 'by establishing a *territorial boundary* and exercising absolute control over movement across it, state practices define and help constitute a *national* entity' (emphasis added; cf. Marin 1988: 5). It is precisely the state's existence as territory that allows it to constitute itself as nation. Similarly, we might argue, it is the institutions, apparatuses and practices of the state (the state as institution) that allow it to establish and police a physical boundary or to mobilize popular perceptions of national identity in the first place. These, then, are three *senses* of 'stateness' necessarily bound together in the practices and processes of specific state forms (see Table 1).

Levels of stateness: from abstract to concrete

If we can distinguish between different *senses* of stateness, then we can equally easily specify different *levels* of stateness, by identifying various degrees of concreteness at which we might specify the institutions, practices and structures of the state. Moving progressively from the generic to the concrete, we can consider:

1 The *state as category* at the most general and abstract level: that which allows us to identify a political system as a state, that which allows us to say 'this is a state' – the presence in articulation of the three moments of stateness identified above.[8]
2 The *state form*: the specific type of state we are referring to (be it capitalist, feudal or patriarchal).
3 The *state regime*: a particular stage in the evolution of a state form, and hence a more concrete and specific level of stateness.
4 The *state structure*: the state in its institutional specificity, the particular structures and institutions of a specific state formation at a specific moment in time – the most concrete and specific level of stateness.

The identification of a hierarchy of levels of stateness allows us to retain an abstract and generic definition of the state, yet simultaneously to proceed towards a progressively more complex and concrete specification of the state apparatus itself (this process is schematically outlined in Figure 1).

Applying the distinctions formulated above, we can now move to a specification of the state apparatus in post-war Britain. In so doing we might refer to various aspects of state power: its capitalist, patriarchal, racist, homophobic or environmentally unsustainable nature to identify merely five. However, for the purpose of what is to follow in Parts II and III it will prove instructive to consider the capitalist and patriarchal character of the post-war British state in more detail (see Figure 2).

At the most abstract and generic level we can first reiterate that the political system in Britain throughout the post-war period is indeed a state. It can be interpreted as the complex and dynamic articulation of the three moments of stateness identified above. Moreover, its core would seem to comprise 'a distinct ensemble of institutions and organizations whose socially accepted function is to define and enforce collectively binding decisions on the members of a society in the name of their common interest or general will' (Jessop 1990: 341). Moving to a lower level of abstraction and generality we can further categorize this state as both capitalist and patriarchal.

Table 1 The state as nation, territory and institution

	Sense of 'stateness'	Boundary	Practices	'Others'	Key processes
State as nation	State as a community; state as a national 'people'	Discursive: 'belonging'; communal or shared national identity	Inclusion/exclusion from full citizenship; national ceremony	Women; ethnic and religious minorities; 'partial' citizens	Citizenship; nationalism; racism; patriarchy; incarceration
State as territory	Geo-politically bounded area of administrative sovereignty	Physical: administratively policed political frontier/border	Border controls; customs; defence; maintenance of a standing army	Other nation-states; other foreign offices; 'foreign' citizens	Geo-politics; diplomacy; war (hot and cold); defence; immigration
State as institution	State as an assemblage of coordinated apparatuses, institutions and practices	Practical: institutional reach into the private sphere, the economy and civil society	Mode of intervention; extent of state regulation, surveillance and funding	Apparatuses of the private sphere (family); civil society (church, media); and the economy (firms)	Bureaucracy; legal and economic regulation; surveillance; taxation and subsidization

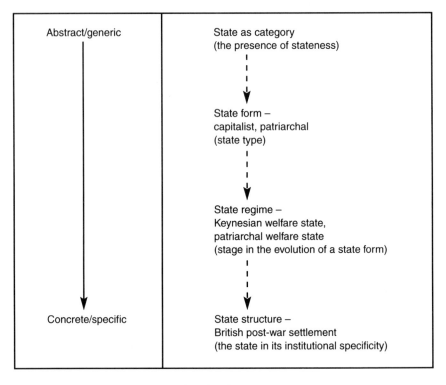

Figure 1 Specifying the state: levels of stateness.

Its capitalist nature does not necessarily imply its patriarchal form, and its patriarchal nature does not necessarily imply its capitalist form, though in practice the two are intertwined in complex ways and are mutually reinforcing. Hence we can speak of the capitalist and patriarchal state forms in post-war Britain (as elsewhere) as 'contingently articulated' (as interrelated but not in some necessary and invariant way), and as thereby comprising a dualism (both characteristics are present though one does not imply the other). Moving to a lower level of abstraction and generality still, we can identify the British state in the post-war period as a Keynesian welfare state (see Chapter 3), and as a patriarchal welfare state (Pateman 1989b; see Chapter 4). These are state regimes: stages in the evolution of the capitalist and patriarchal states respectively. They are necessarily related – the Keynesian welfare state is inherently patriarchal (embodying a structurally inscribed patriarchy in its reliance upon a feminized public/private distinction and the unpaid domestic labour of women). Accordingly, we can speak of these state regimes as comprising a 'duality', as necessarily related and as implying one another. Finally, moving to the level of the state structure itself we can begin to identify the specific apparatuses, institutions and practices through which the patriarchal-welfare and Keynesian-welfare aspect of the state are effected, reproduced and sustained.

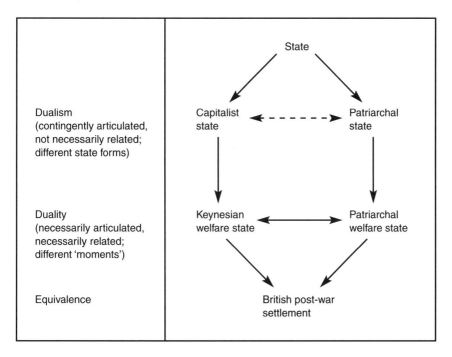

Figure 2 Specifying the state in post-war Britain.

What the above analysis demonstrates is that we can retain the universality, abstractness and generality of the term 'state', while still acknowledging and reflecting theoretically the historical and geo-political variability of specific state forms, regimes and structures.

Re-stating the obvious

So far we have loosely established what it is that we are talking about when we refer to the state; suggested that precisely what we chose to include in our working definition of the state depends upon the specific questions we are asking; and noted the variability in the structures of the state between different societies and across time. However, we still haven't addressed the fundamental question: *why do we need a theory of the state in the first place?*

Sadly this question has scarcely if ever been addressed by state theorists. It is immensely difficult to answer in the abstract. Indeed, probably the only satisfactory response to such a question is to *demonstrate* for particular contexts, and particular problems, the extra theoretical insights that can be gleaned by recasting orthodox questions of social and political change in terms of a political sociology of the state. In the chapters that follow, my aim is to make a case for re-stating social and political change in post-war Britain in precisely these terms.

In Chapter 2 we move from abstract and theoretical reflections on the nature of 'stateness' to the concrete realities of wartime Britain, considering the threat posed by the war to the territorial integrity of the state. The impact of total war upon the subsequent nature and trajectory of social, political and economic change is assessed by examining the influence of the *experience* of the Second World War upon the *process* of Britain's post-war reconstruction. It is argued that the structures of the state were significantly transformed in the initial post-war period, yet that the blueprint for this restructuring was effectively formulated between 1942 and 1944. This in turn suggests that the experience of total war itself, and the need for (near) total mobilization that it engendered, are crucial to an understanding of the pace, process and trajectory of post-war reconstruction. Indeed it becomes apparent that the recognition of the need for total mobilization in conditions of total war led to attempts to extend the state's basis of legitimacy during the war years and to significant structural change in the initial post-war period. The promise of a universal welfare state and the commitment to full employment after the war were effectively offered in return for the collective altruism required for the successful prosecution of the war effort. This notion of a wartime sacrifice to be rewarded through the building of the 'New Jerusalem' in the post-war period is well captured by Robert E. Goodin and John Dryzek in their notion of 'justice deferred' (1995). The very legitimacy of the Attlee government from 1945 became dependent upon its ability to bring to fruition this vision of the New Jerusalem.

The implications of this argument are considered further in Chapter 3, in which the emergent structures of the post-war state regime (the British variant of the Keynesian welfare state) are examined in more detail. The widely observed period of consensus and harmony is seen to be characterized by a series of internal tensions and contradictions, and the articulated commitment to a variety of rather conflicting imperatives and objectives. The contradictions of the state regime can usefully be mapped by identifying two *antagonistic* domestic post-war settlements: (a) a politico-economic settlement reflecting the imperatives of capitalist accumulation; and (b) a welfare settlement reflecting those of societal legitimation. Moreover, consensus there may well have been. Yet, contrary to the political science orthodoxy, this consensus was not particularly Keynesian, not particularly interventionist and not particularly social democratic.

In Chapter 4 we consider further the contradictions of the welfare settlement identified in the previous chapter, by turning our attention to the promise of universal citizenship that the Keynesian welfare state was held to embody. In so doing we examine T. H. Marshall's highly influential account of the gradual extension since the eighteenth century of the rights of citizenship, culminating in the granting of the universal right to social welfare in the post-war period (Marshall 1950). We contrast this somewhat abstract and idealized picture of the progressive evolution of the 'citizenship contract' with the realities of a welfare state deeply implicated in the reproduction of the inequalities of class, gender and ethnicity.

In Part III we move from the internal contradictions of the post-war settlement(s) to its disintegration in the crisis of the mid to late 1970s. In

Chapter 5 we concentrate upon the two most prominent diagnoses of the condition afflicting the British state and economy in this period: (a) the new right's overload or ungovernability thesis; and (b) the new left's thesis of legitimation crisis. Despite the considerable influence of the former, and despite the similarities between the two, we see that the overload thesis is in fact irretrievably flawed, while the theory of legitimation crisis is at least salvageable in some form. In Chapter 6 we return to the structural and ideological contradictions of the twin settlements identified in Chapter 3, arguing that such tensions, steering problems and conflicting imperatives can be seen as providing portents of the eventual crisis to come. Given the structural contradictions that characterized Britain's post-war settlement, it is perhaps remarkable that this state regime was to remain largely intact for thirty years. The onset of state crisis was initially postponed by virtue of Britain's comparative economic strength in the early post-war period at a time of comprehensive continental European reconstruction. Yet by the mid-1960s the structural frailty of the British economy was starkly exposed. State crisis was now postponed only by virtue of a second factor – the use of voluntary and subsequently statutory incomes policies to pass the costs of state and economic failure on to labour.

The exhaustion of this last and most desperate attempt at crisis management and the resulting precipitation of a crisis of the state regime is the subject of the second half of Chapter 6. The Winter of Discontent emerges as a moment of crisis, an 'epoch-making' moment of transition marking the dawning of a new period of political-historical time. For Thatcherism as a state project, though conceived long before, was born in the ideological contestation that surrounded the moment of crisis – a crisis that was to become 'lived' in the terms provided by the new right.

In Chapter 7 the impact of the Thatcherite state and hegemonic project is assessed in the light of the events of the Winter of Discontent. Contrary to an ever more popular tendency within mainstream political science (see, for instance, Riddell 1983, 1991; Hogwood 1992; Marsh and Rhodes 1992),[9] it is argued that Thatcherism does indeed represent a profound social, political, economic and indeed cultural break with the discourses, practices and 'invented traditions' (Hobsbawm and Ranger 1983) of the post-war settlement. This is not to suggest, however, that the consequences of this 'Thatcherite revolution' are not deeply contradictory and damaging to Britain's economic competitiveness and social stability; nor that the Thatcher Governments have proved successful in pursuit of all of their stated ambitions. Thatcherism, it is argued, is best conceptualized as a regressive and primarily neo-liberal project *camouflaged* in the rhetoric of moral conservatism. Stuart Hall's description of it as an 'authoritarian populism' is thus revealed as only appropriate to its initial mobilization of popular support. This in turn necessitates a more differentiated periodization of Thatcherism such as that provided by the self-styled alternative 'gang of four' (Jessop *et al.* 1988). Such a periodization (suitably extended and updated) reveals the cumulative and strategic transformation of the institutions, practices, boundaries and perceived responsibilities of the state; a significant recasting of the very nature of the 'political'; and perhaps even a certain enduring impact upon the 'hearts and minds' of the electorate. The Thatcher Governments, it would seem, presided over a period of profound structural transformation perhaps unprecedented in the post-war period, and certainly comparable in scope to that of the Attlee Governments.

It is this legacy, in the form of an emerging post-Thatcher settlement, that is the focus of Chapter 8. Here it is argued that Major's Thatcherite inheritance is considerable, and that many of the changes of the Thatcher years are likely to prove irreversible in the medium to long term regardless of the political complexion or will of the incumbent administration. Thus although we have entered an era that is chronologically post-*Thatcher*, we cannot yet speak of a context that is substantively post-*Thatcherite*. Indeed, at the time of writing we are witnessing the emergence of a deeply contradictory post-Thatcher settlement to which all the principal parties have now accommodated themselves, yet which is likely to prove fundamentally damaging for Britain's economic competitiveness within the global political economy, and for continued social and political stability at home. I conclude by considering the similarities between the current context, a 'catastrophic equilibrium' in which the old is dying and yet the new cannot be born (Gramsci 1971: 276), and that of the late 1970s, suggesting that there is much that the left can learn today from the origins of Thatcherism in the contradictions of the post-war settlement.

Notes

1 Weber argues that the state is characterized by the possession of 'an administrative and legal order subject to change by legislation, to which the organised activities of the administrative staff, which are also controlled by regulations, are oriented. This system of order claims binding authority, not only over the members of the state, the citizens, most of whom have obtained membership by birth, but also to a very large extent over all action taking place in the area of jurisdiction. It is thus a compulsory organisation with a territorial basis ... the use of force is regarded as legitimate only so far as it is either permitted by the state or prescribed by it ... The claim of the modern state to monopolise the use of force is as essential to it as its character of compulsory jurisdiction and of continuous operation' (1978: 56).

2 Specifying functions of the state, it must be emphasized, is no guarantee of their delivery. But, in as much as a set of basic functions is delivered, we might talk of the existence of a 'state'.

3 Here it is important to note that Althusser's argument has tended to be somewhat misrepresented. Althusser was in fact referring less to the family as a set of social relationships between individuals in a domestic setting, than to the 'institution' of the family, which he viewed as an *ideological* support to capitalist society.

4 Here it is important to note that such an appeal to a 'sovereign authority' need not be recognized within international law (by the 'community of states') for it to have the effect of instilling a sense of belonging within an 'imagined' national community.

5 This raises the difficult issue of the United Kingdom as a 'multi-nation state'. Despite the complexities this necessarily introduces, we can still refer to the UK state as an imagined (multi-)national community, albeit one in which 'national identity' is likely to become an axis of inclusion and exclusion. Put simply, the Welsh, the Scottish and the Northern Irish do not experience full citizenship within the UK as a 'multi-national state' (cf. McCrone 1992).

6 It is difficult to think of an example of the 'British' Bulldog being used as a symbol of popular political mobilization north of Hadrian's Wall or west of the Severn Bridge, as distinct from Unionist Northern Ireland (part of the United Kingdom but not Britain) or England.

7 Though this is not to imply that 'non-state' agencies do not play a highly significant part in the reproduction of such a sense of 'national' belonging.

8 A variety of para-state and non-state agencies can be identified which are characterized by the articulation of two moments of the stateness in the absence of the third. The European Union, for instance, though it cannot (yet) be considered an 'imagined national community', does possess the institutional and territorial aspects of stateness. Similarly, the Palestine Liberation Organization might be considered to possess the national and institutional characteristics of stateness while lacking sovereign territoriality. Moreover, Scotland, a 'stateless nation' (McCrone 1992), might be regarded as an 'imagined national community' with only partially developed territorial and institutional characteristics of stateness.

9 Although Marsh and Rhodes's work is often cited as emblematic in accounts which downplay the significance of the Thatcher years, their aim was in fact merely to provide a corrective to those accounts which seem to posit an almost one-to-one correspondence between Thatcherite ideology and government policy since 1979. For an important clarification of their position see Marsh and Rhodes (1995).

Part **II**

STATING SOCIAL *and* POLITICAL CHANGE

2 War *and* social change: building *the* New Jerusalem

> War is the greatest of all agents of change. It speeds up all processes, wipes out minor distinctions, brings reality to the surface. Above all it brings home to the individual that he [*sic*] is not altogether an individual.
>
> (Orwell 1941: 117)

In Part I we concentrated upon *re-stat(e)ing* social and political change. We saw that if we are fully to grasp the complexity of social and political dynamics, it is imperative to consider the central mediating role of the state. Yet, if Orwell is correct, it would seem time to turn the tables on such an approach. For if war is indeed the greatest agent of social change, then surely we must consider the processes through which such social change itself becomes reflected in transformations in the structures, boundaries and responsibilities of the state. Instead of re-stating social change, should we not be *re-socializing the transformation of the state*? In fact, as we shall see, social change and the evolution of the state cannot be so easily disentangled. If war is the greatest agent of social change, then it is perhaps also the greatest agent of state transformation. It is to these issues that this chapter is devoted.

In assessing the impact of the war upon the nature of the state regime that was to emerge in post-war Britain we can usefully ask ourselves a series of questions which might frame our investigation.

- To what extent were the structures of the state in post-war Britain different from those of the inter-war and war years?
- Can the experience of war itself help to account for the transformation of the state and its basis of legitimacy in the immediate post-war period?
- Would *any* post-war government (regardless of political creed) have been constrained to pursue policies similar to those of the Attlee Government?

Now, these, though perhaps obvious questions to ask, are not easy questions to answer. Indeed, they continue to divide historians, political scientists, political sociologists and even state theorists. Intense and continuing controversy surrounds each one. In this chapter we cannot hope to provide final answers. We can, however, begin to consider what answering such questions might entail.

War: the catalyst of social and political change?

If we are to evaluate the impact of war upon the evolution of the state in post-war Britain, then it is first crucial that we consider the distinctiveness, indeed uniqueness, of the situation which faced the Attlee Government in 1945. Britain was victorious, triumphant and in optimistic mood. Her near total mobilization in a time of total war had apparently been vindicated. She was the only one of the European allies to have avoided Nazi occupation,[1] and as a consequence her political system had remained intact, if not wholly unscathed, throughout the war years. This institutional continuity, as we shall see, was to prove highly significant in determining the extent, nature and pace of Britain's post-war reconstruction when contrasted to that of her European allies, and particularly to that of her former aggressors.[2]

Moreover, of all the European participants in the war, with the exception of Sweden, the extent of the physical destruction of manufacturing capacity in Britain was the least (Hobsbawm 1993: 20). Indeed, in its assessment of the impact of the war, the UN was to dismiss war damage to industry in Britain as 'negligible' (Armstrong *et al.* 1991: 8). Post-war reconstruction in Britain was to be less concerned with the physical reconstruction (and the associated modernization) of her manufacturing base than it was with the realization of the aspirations mobilized during the war for wide-scale social reform (Mercer 1991).

Before we can assess the links between war, social change and the transformation of the state, it is first important that we consider *what is to be accounted for*. For we may well argue that the experience of war was indeed the key determinant of social and political change in post-war Britain. Yet if at the same time we suggest that the extent of such change was in fact minimal, then this is scarcely a significant observation. We must then address the question of what, if anything, changed in post-war Britain, before we consider how we might account for any such changes.

Here, at least, there is some degree of consensus. Though they can agree on little else, most of the historians, political scientists and political sociologists who have focused on this period do seem to share the view that the initial post-war reconstruction ushered in an enduring post-war consensus. This 'consensus on consensus' (Lowe 1990: 153; Kavanagh 1992: 175) is in turn premised upon the widely shared assumption that the structures and perceived responsibilities of the state were profoundly transformed in the immediate post-war period. Yet even this sacred cow is not unassailable. For, as we shall see in the next chapter, there are those who challenge the notion of consensus (Taylor-Gooby 1985: 53–70; Harris 1986; Jeffreys 1987; Pimlott 1988, 1989), and even those who challenge the very idea that the structures of the state were significantly transformed in the post-war period (Nairn 1964; Blackwell and Seabrook 1988; Saville 1988; Anderson 1992a). So although much of the literature we shall consider reflects this apparent orthodoxy, we should try to keep these questions open at this stage.

Coercion and consent in contemporary capitalism

The 'consensus on consensus' would suggest that the experience of total war[3] was a crucial turning point in the development of a more consensual form of capitalism in the post-war period. Here it will prove instructive to engage in a brief theoretical detour to reflect on the work of the Italian Marxist, Antonio Gramsci (1891–1937). Though he could not possibly have anticipated what was to transpire in the years following his death, it is testimony to Gramsci's theoretical brilliance that his ideas should have proved so influential in informing many of the most telling observations on the transformation of the state in post-war Western Europe (see, for instance, Hall *et al.* 1978; Scase 1980; Hall 1988; for an excellent review see Forgács 1989).

In his *Prison Notebooks* (1971: 158–73, 210–76) Gramsci developed a highly innovative and influential analysis of the maintenance of class domination and social stability within civil society through the interventions of the state (see also Anderson 1977: 18–35; Buci-Glucksmann 1980; Sassoon 1980: 109–231). In so doing he elaborated upon the crucial distinction between coercion and consent present in Italian social thought since Machiavelli (Gramsci 1971: 125–205). The state, he argued, may secure social cohesion by relying upon either one of two strategies:

1 The systematic and routine repression and physical *coercion* of groups within civil society considered subversive to the dominant mode of production. This strategy is effected through the deployment of the state's coercive apparatus, which comprises such institutions as the military, the police and the secret service (Gramsci 1971: 56n; Poulantzas 1978: 28–53; Jessop 1982: 147–8).
2 The mobilization of societal *consent*. This the state must work to maintain by constructing a legitimating dialogue with civil society, by channelling and responding to societal expectations and aspirations and by satisfying material interests (see Hay 1992a). The institutions primarily involved here are what Althusser (1968/71) somewhat contentiously terms the 'ideological state apparatuses': education, the media, the church, the family (Poulantzas 1978: 28–53).[4] The principal mechanisms for maintaining legitimacy and societal consent are democratic representation and the granting and extension of the rights of citizenship (see Chapter 4).

In practice coercion and consent are often mutually reinforcing strategies. Most contemporary states rely upon a combination of the two in their attempt to maintain social stability. Indeed, at times and within certain sections of the population, consent can in fact be secured through the systematic and public repression of populations defined as deviant or 'other' (by virtue of their sexuality, ethnicity, political conduct and so forth). Here we need only think of the mass mobilization of 'Aryan' Germany around the repression, torture and extermination of the Jews; the fervour 'whipped up' in certain sections of society by the tabloid media's construction of the image of the 'folk devil' as the enemy within society (Hall *et al.* 1978; Cohen 1980; Hay 1995a); or Thatcherite 'authoritarian populism' (Hall 1979a, 1985; cf. Jessop *et al.* 1984; see Chapter 7).

As the modern state has developed, the resources at its disposal to secure the wide-scale consent of civil society have been progressively enhanced. As a consequence, coercion has tended to be relegated to a secondary and more covert function, reserved for dealing with the periodic, though now rarer and more localized, breakdown of consent. None the less, the state's repressive arm is periodically unleashed in the policing of forms of civil disobedience such as the Poll Tax riots. As this example would suggest, coercion is now a sign of governmental or state failure (see Butler *et al.* 1994). It has been subordinated to consent as the primary means through which societal stability is maintained. None the less, we should be wary of overstating either the extent or the irreversibility of the transition from coercive to consensual capitalism. For, coercion and consent remain inextricably interwoven within modern societies (Hay 1992a: 41–3). The systematic repression of those sections of the population defined (often by the state) as 'deviant' is at times crucial to the maintenance of consent and legitimacy within contemporary capitalism. Moreover, the state's capacity for the unseen and covert surveillance and repression of those cast as 'subversive' has been enhanced by technological developments (Cohen 1985; Cohen and Scull 1985; Lyon 1988, 1994: 91–4; Dandeker 1990; Poster 1990: 69–98). Although consent has certainly supplemented repression as a strategy for securing social stability, the state is still essentially a coercive apparatus.

None the less, the state's ability to mobilize consent and to secure continued legitimacy has been massively enhanced by technological developments (many of them spin-offs from military research conducted during 'the century of total war'[5] and the ensuing Cold War period). The effect of such technological innovation has been to extend significantly: (a) the state's surveillance capacity (something Gramsci could scarcely have contemplated); (b) its ability for mass dissemination through the media and educational institutions (itself a condition for an effective legitimating 'dialogue' with civil society); and (c) the state's bureaucratic power of coordination.

This in turn has had the effect of enhancing the capacity of the state to monitor, respond to, influence and, to a limited extent, even construct societal perceptions. None the less, it is important to note that this capacity or potentiality is precisely that: a capacity, a potential. Consent is not necessarily secured.

Those authors who have sought to apply this type of analysis to the development of the capitalist state form have observed a generalized tendency towards consensual as opposed to coercive capitalism throughout Western Europe and North America (for emblematic British statements see Marshall 1950; Crosland 1956; cf. Hindess 1987: 12–48). In apparent confirmation of this thesis they point to the gradual extension of the franchise in the nineteenth century, the granting of a modicum of social welfare in the early twentieth century and the development of a more comprehensive welfare state in the post-war period (see, for instance, Marshall 1950; Turner 1990; Pierson 1991: 21–4, 196–208; Roche 1992; see Chapter 4).

Comforting though this gradual evolutionism might be, however, a quick glance at the present rapidly tempers such optimism. The contemporary experience of the 'rolling back of the welfare state' initiated under

Thatcher and Reagan, but now consolidated by Major, Bush and even Clinton (Fraser 1993; Skocpol 1995: 228–312; see also Gingrich *et al.* 1994), should make us wary (if we were not already) of a single universal historical dynamic. For while the twentieth century may well be interpreted as marking a general movement towards a more consensual period of capitalist accumulation, this does not necessarily imply a benevolent form of capitalism, as a moment's reflection on the patriarchal character of the post-war welfare state, or on the politics of Thatcherism and Reaganism, clearly reveals (see Chapters 7 and 8). Moreover, as the above discussion suggests, it is important to ask 'whose consent?'. If post-war British politics was until the 1970s characterized by the attempt to secure a broad and inclusive 'social contract' (albeit one still premised upon a differential apportionment of the rights and obligations of citizenship), then the policies of successive Thatcher governments seemed to reflect a deeply held conviction that, in a two-party, first-past-the-post electoral system, the consent of the entire population is not only unnecessary, but is in fact something of a constraint upon government autonomy.[6] Though an obvious point, then, it is surely worth emphasizing the need to distinguish between the *potential* for society-wide consent on the one hand, and the extent to which this is realized in practice on the other.

None the less, the contemporary capitalist state is generally accorded a degree of operational legitimacy by its 'citizens' – the massive majority of the population does not actively desire or even contemplate an alternative. Furthermore, within capitalist social formations this has not always been the case (see, for instance, Foster 1974; Stedman-Jones 1983; Mooers 1991). This would in turn lend credence to the view that structural changes in the nature of the capitalist state form have occurred, bringing with them the potential for increased societal legitimation and consent.

This, however, does not tell us very much about what those changes are, or why they were brought about. To answer those questions we have to recast and update the Gramscian problematic.

Total war . . . and total mobilization? From Bovril to Beveridge

If we are to extend the Gramscian perspective developed above, then we might suggest that there are times when the state is more reliant upon consent and legitimacy than others – times when consent cannot simply be subordinated to coercion in securing continued social and system stability. Chief among these is *war*.

The external challenge to the sovereign territorial claim of the state represents perhaps the greatest threat to its stability. Quite simply, invasion or defeat in war threatens to destroy the institutional, national and territorial basis of state power. War poses in some sense the ultimate question of the state: can it preserve its very continuity in the face of an external challenge to its sovereign authority, territorial integrity and institutional existence? Thus war, and in particular *total war*, provides an 'audit' of the state (Barnett 1986; Edgerton 1991: 361), revealing the full range of strategic, technical and social resources that can be mustered in its defence. The state's capacity to mobilize a population in 'defence of the realm'; the relative technological superiority and 'competitiveness' of its military–industrial complex; the military–strategic innovation and resolve of its leaders; and the bureaucratic power of coordination of the state apparatus are all exposed to rigorous scrutiny.

Above all, the successful prosecution of the war effort requires a considerable degree of altruism and self-sacrifice on the part of the direct participants, whether military or civilian (Marwick 1968; Wright 1968: 264).[7] Moreover, it is often those sections of society who consistently benefit the least from continued capitalist accumulation (the unemployed and the working class in particular) on whom the state calls to make the greatest sacrifice. There is a limit to how effective strategies of coercion and repression are likely to prove in producing a successful war effort. War requires mobilization, and *total war requires total mobilization*.[8]

As we noted in Part I, the state can be viewed as the complex and dynamic articulation of three 'moments of stateness': the state *as institution* (the state as a set of apparatuses and practices); the state *as nation* (the state as an imagined national community, and a collective national identity); and the state *as territory* (the state as a sovereign administrative terrain). During times of war, in which the territorial integrity of the state is *directly* threatened (and as a consequence the continuity of the state as both nation and institution is *indirectly* threatened),[9] the state is re-unified under the dominance of the territorial imperative of stateness. In such strategic moments the prosecution of the war effort and the defence of the territorial integrity of the sovereign state assume priority over all other political and economic imperatives, with little regard to the consequences for the subsequent evolution (in the post-war period) of the state as institution or nation. War, particularly total war, may thus emerge as a 'tipping point' in the institutional transformation of the state.

It is not then surprising to find a close correspondence between total war and extensions in political and social welfare.[10] The conditions of social deprivation and mass unemployment that had predominated in Britain during the inter-war years were incapable of generating the level of spontaneous self-sacrifice on the part of the industrial working class necessary to prosecute successfully a total war to defend them (Miliband 1970; Bagguley 1991).[11] By May 1940 the government was only too well aware of this fact (Addison 1977: 103–26; Cronin 1991). From Dunkirk onwards, the ideological struggle on the home front became as significant for the outcome of the war as the physical battles raging on foreign soil (Maier 1987: 153–84). As James Cronin (1991: 131) perceptively notes, social reform, which has scarcely been conceivable before, 'became now a matter of national survival. What had seemed beyond the capacity of the state now became feasible, indeed essential objects of public policy.'

Thus, although different strategies of mobilization *could be*, and to a certain extent *were*, adopted (such as the counterposing of democracy and totalitarianism, friend and enemy), the war effort required the mobilization of a collective perception of 'something worth fighting for'. The expressed aim of winning the war to build the 'New Jerusalem' was to provide the ideological site around which this unity might be forged (Barnett 1986; Stevenson 1988).

This allows us to propose two initial hypotheses:

Hypothesis 1: The successful prosecution of a total war required a degree of mobilization that simply could not be secured within the structures of the state regime inherited from the inter-war years.

Hypothesis 2: The promised creation of the welfare state in the post-war period was tied to the need to enhance the legitimacy of the state during the war years.

In other words, the extension of citizenship *obligations* during the war was to be rewarded by the extension of social citizenship *rights* in the post-war period (Hay 1994a: 39). As Robert Goodin and John Dryzek (1995: 66) note,

> the principle at work is indeed that of paying off a debt. It is truly a matter of justice being deferred. The poor are asked to make wartime sacrifices for which they simply cannot be compensated during the war itself. Their pay off can come only later – by which time, of course, their contribution has already been made. Still it would be imprudent in some extended sense to renege on that debt.

To evaluate these *theoretically derived* hypotheses we need to move from the abstract and theoretical to the concrete reality of the British wartime experience. A number of specific factors widely identified in the historiographic record can be pointed to which would support these hypotheses.

The impact of the Beveridge Report

In 1942 William Beveridge, a liberal civil servant, presented his report on social insurance to Arthur Greenwood's Reconstruction Committee of the Cabinet. The report proposed the provision of universal insurance against sickness, old age, widowhood and unemployment, and a system of family allowances. Beveridge, much to the irritation of civil servants and ministers alike, orchestrated a massive public relations campaign on its behalf. He could scarcely have anticipated the public reaction that it was to generate. His proposals were to take on vast symbolic significance as they came to be seen as a 'preview' of the post-war British 'dream'. The Beveridge Report was to become the best-selling bureaucratic memo in British history (over half a million copies were purchased). The fervour with which it was received clearly reflected a deep societal appetite for wide-scale social reform. Yet whether it provided such a vision is more debatable. For as Cronin (1991: 138) observes,

> it was not a particularly profound document, it articulated no new philosophy of the state and no grand vision of the relationship between citizenship and welfare, but it was sufficient to capture and channel the popular desire for change and to reshape the wartime discourse on social policy.

Thus, although it is tempting to concur with Colin Leys when he suggests that the Beveridge Report 'gave concrete expression to what most people wanted' (1989: 65), we should perhaps be somewhat more sceptical. First, it is important to note that Beveridge, as his official biographers make clear (Beveridge 1954: 101–13; Harris 1977: 378–418), made no attempt in writing his report to express or indeed solicit the views of the population. He was in fact scarcely willing to discuss his ideas for social reform with the members of his committee on Social Insurance and Allied Services (Harris 1977: 385; Barnett 1986: 26–7). In fact, as José Harris (1977: 413) observes, 'many of Beveridge's ideas had been formulated and much of his report drafted before more than a fraction of evidence had been received.' Indeed, as Janet Beveridge notes, many of her husband's proposals expressed deeply held social convictions that pre-dated the war (Beveridge 1954: 75–89). Moreover, as Master of University College, Oxford, and as a senior civil servant, Beveridge can hardly be regarded to have had his finger on the pulse of public opinion (a point well made by Barnett 1986: 26–31). If Beveridge did indeed give 'concrete expression to what most people wanted', then this could only have been a fortuitous coincidence. Second, Leys assumes that by 1942 public opinion on post-war reconstruction was already well established and that there was a popular vision of social reform that Beveridge could reflect. What scant historiographic evidence is available would certainly suggest that this was far from being the case – a general if vague desire for social reform there certainly was, but prior to the publication of the Beveridge Report there was little popular sense of what tangible form such reforms might take (Mason and Thompson 1991; Morgan and Evans 1993a, b).

More convincing is the view that Beveridge effectively defined what civil society could legitimately expect. Rather than reflecting the aspirations of civil society, the report and the extensive publicity which surrounded it was to mould and channel a generic but still vaguely formulated desire for social reform. As Ian Taylor (1991: 10) notes, the proposals of the Beveridge Report were in fact extremely conservative when contrasted to prior Labour, TUC and Fabian Society documents which had not received wide-scale public dissemination. Thus, although there is little evidence of a 'mass radicalization' during the war (Mason and Thompson 1991; Tiratsoo 1991b: 5; cf. Schwarz 1991), the context was one in which a more genuinely leftist series of proposals might well, given a similar degree of publicity prior to the publication of the Beveridge Report, have proven equally capable of finding resonance with people's, at that stage, still loosely articulated aspirations (cf. Fielding 1991: 120–1).

The significance of the Beveridge Report is thus unquestionable. Indeed, it emerges as symptomatic of what Gramsci terms a *passive revolution*, limiting the extent of potential radicalism, preventing a more fundamental break with the legacy of the inter-war years and perhaps even forestalling the potential for wide-scale social transformation orchestrated from below (Gramsci 1971: 115–20; cf. Buci-Glucksmann 1980: 54–63, 291–324; Sassoon 1980: 204–17). This ties in closely with Stuart Hall and Bill Schwarz's rendering of a passive revolution as reflecting 'the success of the dominant groups in maximising the exclusion of the masses from defining political affairs and the reconstruction of the state' (1985: 25). None the less, Gramsci's notion of a passive revolution imposed from above has to be deployed with some care. It is, at least in one sense, inappropriate to regard this socially steered yet popular revolution as 'passive'. For it was the very conflicts (however suppressed and submerged at the time) of the 1920s and 1930s that provided the context within which this glimpse of the New Jerusalem was formulated and found resonance. Yet in another sense this 'revolution' was distinctly passive. For the aspirations of civil society were to become channelled through Beveridge's liberal philanthropism, thus both tempering the desire for and taming the ability of the working class to steer post-war social reform.

Accordingly, what limited struggle there was to define the new trajectory of the British state for the post-war period was effectively resolved by 1943 with the publication of the Beveridge Report. As a consequence, as Perry Anderson (1992a: 163) notes, Labour

> was initiated into power without having to mobilise for it; and it acquired a programme for government without having to originate the ideas behind it . . . Labour in 1945 inherited a popular radicalisation it had done little directly to stimulate, before which it could present itself as the responsible continuator of the social changes the War had put on the national agenda.

Much of this is extremely perceptive. Indeed, it is somewhat ironic that Labour was to become uniquely associated with the 'mood of change' at precisely the moment when it effectively abandoned any attempt to influence such perceptions and instead began to identify itself with the Beveridge proposals. Yet, as we have already seen, the extent of any 'popular radicalization' must be questioned. The effect of the Beveridge Report was in fact to *temper* the potential for any radicalization of wartime aspirations in the reconstruction debate. Its publication, the unprecedented popular reaction and Labour's accommodation to it were to conspire to prevent a more radical post-war rupture, for which there was now no popular mandate.

The growing influence of Keynesianism

A second crucial factor in the mobilization of the war effort and the framing of a promised 'New Jerusalem' was the growing prevalence of Keynesian influence (which had its origins in the inter-war years). If politics is the art of the politically possible, then the 'Keynesian revolution' (Booth 1983, 1984; Ingham 1984: 214; P. Clarke 1988; Pierson 1991: 26–8) was to redefine dramatically the boundaries of what was *perceived* to be politically possible.[12] Once again, however, we must proceed with caution. Keynesian influence, though prevalent, was certainly not un-contested. Moreover, the extent to which its precepts were put into practice in managing the economy in the post-war period is itself open to question (compare Booth 1983, 1984, 1989; with Tomlinson 1981, 1984, 1994; Rollings 1988; Newton 1991). Crucially, the 'City–Bank–Treasury nexus' – the core economic triumvirate of the City of London, the Bank of England and the Treasury (Ingham 1984: 131ff) – proved if not an entirely impregnable fortress then certainly a well-defended barricade to the nostrums of Keynesianism (Tomlinson 1984; Cronin 1991: 158–61). As Peter Hennessy (1993: 8) notes, 'it is quite plain that . . . Keynes's *General Theory* was not carrying all before it in late-1940s Whitehall' (cf. Marquand 1988).[13]

Important though this qualification is, however, the impact of elite resistance to Keynesianism should not be exaggerated. Far more significant was the general sense that aggregate demand management did offer the possibility of 'effective political control over economic life without the dreadful social, economic and political costs that social democrats feared "expropriation of the expropriators" would bring' (Pierson 1992: 27). It was the discursive dominance, then, of Keynesianism and of Keynesian assumptions (whether they would ever be put into practice or not) that made Beveridge's commitment to full employment appear realistic, attainable and hence a legitimate expectation of any post-war administration.

Churchill's reluctant conversion to social reform

The prevalence within the British wartime Establishment of the view that the promise of a New Jerusalem 'worth dying for' was the very condition of the successful prosecution of the war is well demonstrated by Churchill's reluctant conversion to social reform. Churchill, as is well documented, was no social democrat (Cronin 1991: 137–42; Addison 1993: 72–3; Morgan and Evans: 1993a: 50–1; 1993b: 121–3). Yet his initial ill-disguised hostility towards the Beveridge Report and social reform more generally was later tempered by the pleadings of civil servants and Conservative Party advisors. By late 1942 Churchill was prepared to pronounce that the aim of the war was indeed 'the forward march of the common people towards their just and true inheritance'. As David Morgan and Mary Evans (1993a: 50) note, 'he was less forthcoming about what this inheritance was to be', and not particularly well placed to judge. Indeed, the intensity with which Churchill concentrated upon immediate considerations of military strategy and defence allowed Labour members of the coalition to seize the agenda of post-war reconstruction (Cronin 1991: 137).

Accordingly, Churchill's tacit accommodation to a vision of a New Jerusalem, albeit one framed by others, was driven not so much by electoral opportunism in the wake of the Beveridge Report but more by the view that 'if that's what's necessary to win the war then we'll do it'. It is perhaps not surprising that the enduring perception of Churchill as not truly committed to Keynesianism, social welfare or full employment was to prove the single most important factor in Labour's surprise 1945 election landslide. None the less, as Eric Hobsbawm (1993: 22) rightly observes, 'even if Labour had *not* won we would have had a very marked advance towards a welfare state; if there had been a post-war Churchill government, I think this is a fairly safe counter-factual proposition.'

What this demonstrates once again is the extent to which promises with implications for post-war social reform were made with little regard to their subsequent consequences for the institutional structure of the post-war state regime (cf. Goodin and Dryzek 1995). Instead, under the dominance of the 'territorial moment of stateness', they were motivated by the overarching imperative to maintain the geo-political sovereignty and integrity of the state. To this end all else was subordinated.

Wartime surveillance and propaganda

A further crucial factor in the popular construction of visions of post-war reconstruction was the surveillance and propaganda role of the Ministry of Information, Home Intelligence, the Army Education Corps and the Army Bureau of Current Affairs. With the defeat of France and the birth of the cross-party Coalition in 1940, their activities were significantly stepped up. Their functions were: (a) to monitor levels of dissatisfaction, especially among the troops; (b) to disseminate propaganda legitimating the continuing war effort; and, above all, (c) to mobilize perceptions that the war was being fought to build a glorious 'New Jerusalem' to which Britain's victorious armies could expect to return.[14] In so doing this multiplicity of bodies sought to incorporate all sections of the population, but particularly the troops, into the very process of planning for reconstruction (Addison 1977: 145ff; Barnett 1986: 34ff, 44ff; Mason and Thompson 1991).

The incorporation of labour and Labour

Finally it is important to consider the incorporation of the Labour Party and the trade union movement within the war Coalition. This had the effect of further legitimating popular aspirations for a 'fairer' society and the long-term political incorporation of labour within a post-war settlement. Both Labour and labour, the party and the wider movement, became associated in the public imagination with the corridors of power. The Labour Party *could* be trusted to govern responsibly. Similarly, the trade unions *could* be granted the status of 'governing institutions' (Middlemas 1979) within a corporatist political settlement without threatening the very stability of capitalism in Britain. Thus, the Coalition was seen to embody many aspects of a social democratic ideology, which became not only politically acceptable but, more importantly, internalized within the redefined 'common sense' of this increasingly collectivist era (Middlemas 1979, 1986).

The above observations would suggest that the state's basis of legitimacy was extended *during the war* by the promise of realizing popular aspirations of wide-scale social reform in the post-war period. The legitimacy of the Attlee Government itself became dependent upon its ability to deliver what had now become popular aspirations for change (as encapsulated in the Beveridge Report).[15] This was without doubt the major domestic constraint upon its political autonomy, and indeed would have imposed the same constraints upon any post-war government regardless of its political complexion. The most obvious and striking evidence for this is provided by Churchill's election defeat in 1945, which arose out of a general lack of confidence in his enthusiasm for social reform. Yet Eric Hobsbawm (1993) is surely correct in suggesting that a Churchill Government would none the less have been obliged to deliver a commitment to full employment and a comprehensive welfare state initially free at the point of access to all.

This in turn suggests that rather than the Attlee Government being seen as a radical, pioneering agent of social reform, it should perhaps be re-interpreted as merely responding pragmatically, perhaps even conservatively, to constraints that any post-war government would inevitably have faced.

The argument so far can be summarized in five central claims:

1 The structures of the state were indeed fundamentally transformed in the initial post-war period.
2 This structural transformation of the state represented a response to the promises and concessions granted during the war by the coalition government relating to: (a) the incorporation of labour; (b) full employment; and (c) the creation of a comprehensive state-funded welfare system.
3 War was the crucial factor determining the need for and the subsequent trajectory (if not the extent) of this structural transformation.
4 The political autonomy of the Attlee Government (as of any initial post-war government) was thus heavily constrained. This is demonstrated by the fact that Churchill and the Conservatives were to lose the 1945 election largely because the promises of the New Jerusalem were adjudged unsafe in their hands.
5 Such constraints were to form the basis for the emergence of a new *state regime* in the initial post-war years. This in turn was to provide the structural foundations for a period of comparative political *consensus* lasting until the mid-1970s (see Chapter 3).

Assessing the impact of war

The above analysis would indeed suggest that the experience of war, or at least total war, is crucial to any understanding of the evolution of the British state in the post-war period. Yet the extent of lasting political, and especially social, change effected by the war can be overstated. It is thus important that we consider the substantial areas of political and economic continuity between the inter-war and post-war years, and the ways in which social changes brought about during the war were reversed in the initial post-war period.

Aspects of political and economic continuity

As has already been emphasized, the Attlee Government was no radical socialist or social democratic regime, and its mandate from the electorate scarcely provided it with the basis for a revolutionary upheaval in the institutions of state and society. Indeed, there is surely something in Ian Taylor's (1991: 26) suggestion that 'if there ever was a time when the opportunities to instigate radical change appeared to be greater than they actually were, it was probably 1945' (cf. Mason and Thompson 1991: 67). Furthermore, however counterintuitive it might seem, the Attlee Government was in many respects significantly more conservative than the Churchill Coalition. As

Hobsbawm (1993: 22) perceptively notes, the complex planning apparatus which had proved so successful during the war was comprehensively dismantled in the immediate post-war period. The Attlee Government was characterized as much by deregulation and the 'burning of controls' as it was by welfare reform. This, as Kenneth Morgan (1984) persuasively suggests, partly arose as a consequence of Labour's paranoia at being identified, however loosely, with the centralized economic planning of the state-socialist regimes. None the less, there is still a certain irony that a party that had used planning, as Peter Hennessy (1993: 8) notes, 'to distinguish itself from all other competitors in the political field, did so little to implement real planning of almost any kind . . . in the early post-war years, despite having a remarkable apparatus of control at its disposal under the wartime legislation' (see also Tomlinson 1992, 1995).

Moreover, even when Labour did seek to depart from the economic orthodoxy of the inter-war years and deploy more interventionist strategies, most notably with respect to industrial modernization, its initiatives were constantly thwarted by the civil service and the business community (see, for instance, Johnmann 1991: 30; Mercer 1991; Pollard 1992: 455; Cain and Hopkins 1993: 269–70; Tiratsoo and Tomlinson 1993; Tomlinson 1994: 157–9). Thus, as Helen Mercer (1991: 72–3) notes,

> Labour was unable to implement even [the] mildest of 'modernisation' strategies because it relied on co-operation from industry which was not forthcoming, and the main peak representatives of British businessmen at the time, the Federation of British Industries (FBI), adhered rigidly to its hostility to state intervention.

This has rightly led Lewis Johnmann (1991: 46) to challenge Addison's vision of a cosy consensus spawned within the war coalition, at least as regards industrial policy: 'Labour's victory in 1945 presented the party not with a "ripe plum" of consensus over industrial policy but a rather acidic bunch of sour grapes' (cf. Addison 1977).

A combination, then, of a less than revolutionary electoral mandate, a paranoid concern with being seen to be 'too radical' and resistance from the representatives of industrial capital to interventionist strategies, where they were contemplated, conspired to limit the extent of political transformation in the immediate post-war period. Neither the strategic context inhabited by the Attlee Government nor its appropriation of that context favoured radical outcomes.

War, gender and social change: from the home to the factory . . . and back again?

If the popular mythology which surrounds the Attlee Government presents it as a pioneering agent of radical reform, then the orthodox view of war and enduring *social* change is no less problematic. According to this account, the war led to a levelling of standards, promoting a heightened sense of egalitarianism which fostered a spirit of middle-class benevolence and philanthropy. The result, supposedly, was a flattening of the stratification pyramid.

This view is most clearly expressed by Arthur Marwick (1968, 1974, 1976, 1984), but relies crucially on the work of Stanislaus Andrzewski (1954) and Richard Titmuss (1958). Andrzewski famously developed the notion of the 'military participation ratio', arguing that the greater the level of war mobilization, the greater the level of resulting social equalization. Titmuss (1950, 1958) extends this analysis by suggesting that the experience of the war years, particularly the initial evacuation and the very real threat of invasion following the defeat of France, led to the development of an unprecedented spirit of social solidarity that was to become reflected in egalitarian proposals and legislation in the immediate post-war period. Marwick is rightly critical of the rather formulaic nature of both Andrzewski's and Titmuss's equation of war participation with the extent of social change, and their failure to identify the mechanisms through which such effects might be secured. None the less, this leads him to engage in a comprehensive attempt to recast the thesis that total war generates social equalization. In so doing he suggests that the Second World War contributed significantly to the growth of gender equality. The conscription of a large proportion of the male workforce necessitated the recruitment of women into the labour market, which, according to Marwick, was to have a significant and lasting impact in reducing gender segregation, raising the status of women employees and ending the marriage bar for women. The result was a 'social and economic revolution' (Marwick 1979: 1910). A similar argument is made by Alva Myrdal and Viola Klein (1968).

Enticing though this vision of social harmonization in war-torn Britain is, the evidence for a significant and enduring erosion of gender inequalities is, at best, ambiguous, as we shall see. Ultimately more convincing is the view that total war called on the opportunistic exploitation of the labour of women and that the armistice signified, as much as anything else, the time for women to return to the home and unpaid domestic labour. As Penny Summerfield (1993: 64) notes, 'if women had achieved higher status during the war it appeared that they had not retained it afterwards.' The post-war reconstruction was also a reconstruction of the traditional nuclear family unit and a reassertion of the centrality of women within this domestic setting as providers of unpaid labour. These gendered citizenship obligations were enshrined in the patriarchal structures of the welfare state proposed by Beveridge and starkly exposed by the withdrawal of central state funding for the war nurseries in the initial post-war years. As Denise Riley observes,

> Women's war work, even in presentations of their collective heroic capacities, was work done by women, marked through and through by the gender of its performers, and consequently by the especial temporariness of the work of women who were mothers . . . by 1945 the dominant rhetoric held out an opposition between the mother and the woman worker. *The post-war collapse of the war nurseries only underlined the 'special nature' of temporary concessions to working mothers.*
> (Riley 1983: 195, emphasis added; cf. Mitchell 1974: 226–8)

If the post-war period saw a return to women's inter-war status in the domestic sphere, then the story in the labour market was not less depressing, as Summerfield's calculations reveal. Between 1939 and 1943 there was an increase of 1.5 million women in the workforce; between 1943 and 1947 there was a corresponding decrease of 1.75 million. Similarly, the proportion of all adult women in paid employment dropped from 51 per cent in 1943 to 40 per cent in 1947, and 35 per cent in 1951, its level in 1931 (Summerfield 1988: 97–8). As Summerfield (1993: 69) notes, 'by 1948 there had been a return to the *status quo* in 1939' (cf. Smith 1986).

This in turn suggests the need to distinguish between those social and political changes which were seen as temporary expedients required by the exceptional circumstances of total war, and those which were to shape the emergent post-war state regime. In fact two factors can be identified that might suggest why it was that patriarchy was reasserted in the initial post-war period, while the old class alliances were to be decisively recast. First, the recruitment of women into the industrial workforce during the war years was necessitated by the conscription of men, and the essentially patriarchal construction of the 'male warrior' that underlay such a policy in the first place. Thus, women were incorporated into the war effort as temporary *substitutes* for male labour, required only in the exceptional circumstances of total war. Patriarchy was not retrenched during the war years only to return in the post-war period. Rather, the gendered division of labour was merely reinforced, deepened and adapted to the changing circumstances and requirements of total war. Patriarchy was rearticulated to production under the dominance of the territorial imperative of stateness. It should thus come as no surprise that the end of the war marked the return of women from the Home Front to the home, and of the male warrior from the front line to his 'natural' peacetime position as breadwinner.

Moreover, in the discussion of post-war reconstruction from the early 1940s onwards, difficult and divisive issues tended to be avoided. The 'road to 1945', despite the good intentions with which it was paved, was to be a consensual one. The question of patriarchy and the gendered division of labour was simply too contentious to contemplate.

Conclusions

In this chapter we have seen that by considering the impact of the war years upon the subsequent trajectory of the *state* in post-war Britain, we can identify the key processes of social and political change in this period. By contextualizing social and political transformations in terms of the evolving relationships between state, society and the economy we can begin to expose many of the superficially attractive myths, both popular and academic, which now surround the war years and the achievements of the Attlee Government in particular.

Such a theoretically informed analysis suggests that the structures of the state were indeed significantly transformed in the initial post-war period, though the blueprint for this reconstruction was in fact formulated between 1942 and 1944. The extent of this transformation, however, *can be*, and indeed *has been*, grossly exaggerated in much of the existing historiographic literature. Many of the economic practices which, as we shall see, were decisively to shape Britain's subsequent economic and political trajectory were in fact inherited largely intact from the inter-war years. Hence, we should be wary of comments like Kenneth Morgan's that the radical reforming zeal of the Attlee Government should be interpreted as 'the British variant of socialism in one country' (Morgan 1984: 89; cf. Marwick 1968; Addison 1977). A consideration of the structural transformation of the state would suggest that such an argument is the product of a somewhat selective nostalgia. Yet we should perhaps be equally sceptical about the claim that the war had no *lasting* social or political legacy (Miliband 1970; Thompson 1984; Blackwell and Seabrook 1988; Saville 1988). Angus Calder's account of the 'studied betrayal' of the working class who had sacrificed so much on the battlefields of Europe, Africa and Asia is certainly compelling. Yet it is no less problematic for that.

> The war was fought with the willing brains and hearts of the most vigorous elements in the country... Thanks to their energy, the forces of wealth, bureaucracy and privilege survived with little inconvenience, recovered from the shock, and began to proceed with the old business of manoeuvre, concession and studied betrayal.
>
> (Calder 1969: 18)

Though there was no miraculous socialist, or even social democratic, revolution in the immediate post-war period, the commitment to full employment and a comprehensive welfare state did represent significant social and political change.

The above analysis would further suggest that the experience of the war itself, and the need for total mobilization that it engendered, are crucial to any understanding of the process of post-war reconstruction. Yet here too we must proceed with caution. For as the previous section clearly demonstrates, it is imperative that we are capable of distinguishing between those *temporary* social and political changes necessitated by the exceptional conditions of total war, and those which were to become lasting features of an emergent post-war settlement. It is all too easy to extrapolate from the enforced harmonization which characterized the war years to imply an enduring social levelling and an emancipation of women that was to be enshrined in the post-war settlement. The evidence would instead support the view that Britain's post-war reconstruction embodied a reconstruction not only of the state, but also of the nuclear family, deeply inscribing patriarchal relations within the structures of the welfare state (see Chapter 4).

None the less, it is clear that the acknowledgement of the need for total mobilization led to an extension of the state's basis of legitimacy *during the war,* and significant structural change in the post-war period. The promise of a universal welfare state and a commitment to full employment was offered in return for the collective altruism of the British people. As a consequence, the very legitimacy of the government became dependent upon its ability to bring to fruition this vision of the New Jerusalem which it had in fact done little to shape. By the time it took office, the constraints facing Attlee and his Cabinet, though hopelessly neglected by much of the existing literature, were considerable (Cronin 1991: 161–71; Tiratsoo 1991: 1–5). Furthermore, these same constraints would have confronted any post-war administration regardless of its political creed. By 1945 the die was already cast. The origins of Britain's post-war reconstruction lie not in the ideological struggles which surrounded the election campaign. Instead they must be traced back further to the realization of the need for total mobilization in a time of total war, and the impact of the Beveridge Report. It was the war Coalition and not the Attlee Government that was the crucible in which Britain's post-war settlement was forged.

Notes

1 It should not, however, be forgotten that the Channel Islands were invaded on 30 June 1940 and were to remain occupied for almost the entire duration of the war (see P. King 1991).

2 To point to a degree of institutional continuity is not in any sense to imply that the structures of the state were not significantly transformed as the war effort was mobilized. Indeed, twelve new ministries and the Central Economic Information Service were established between 1939 and 1944 (Chester *et al.* 1968: 452–8) as the state took on vast strategic planning capacities. As Jim Cronin notes, 'The much-expanded administrative machine oversaw the mobilization of virtually the entire economy for war . . . The allocation of manpower, of scarce raw materials and even of financial assets was carefully rationed so as to minimize conflicts between domestic consumption and war production and competition between rival producers' (Cronin 1991: 145; see also Cronin 1988: 227; Newton and Porter 1988: 91). Though the initial post-war period was to be characterized by the ceremonial 'bonfire' of wartime controls, as Cronin again notes, 'The wartime changes in the state provided both the starting point for discussions of the future shape of the state and also a model of how it might be organized' (1991: 146; cf. Cronin 1988: 227).

3 By 'total war' I refer to war not fought on some distant land by a few mercenaries and professional troops, but involving the active participation of all sections of the population and a permanent and collective consciousness of war.

4 For a critique of the functionalist implications of Althusser's conception of 'ideological state apparatuses' (ISAs) and an attempt to overcome this tendency by supplementing the notion of 'ideological inculcation agencies' (IIAs) see Hay (1992a).

5 To borrow Arthur Marwick's (1968) telling phrase.

6 The Thatcherite motto might thus have read, 'you can only please all of the people some of the time, but you can please some of the people all of the time'. The challenge became that of ensuring that the 'pleased' continued to outnumber the 'displeased' and disaffected in the ballot box.

7 It is important to note that such altruism is unlikely to be equally distributed within the population. As well as extending the obligations and burdens of citizenship, total war provides opportunities for profiteering and is often associated with the proliferation of black markets (see Calder 1969: 254–5; Turner 1992: 171, 193, 359). Furthermore, despite the concerted efforts of the British state's propaganda apparatus during both world wars to mobilize an ethos of collective altruism and mutual self-sacrifice, total war does not temporarily suspend class conflict or industrial unrest, as is evidenced by the 1917 food riots violently quelled by the police (Turner 1992: 171) and the relatively high level of (illegal) strike action in 1914–18 and 1939–45 (Cronin 1991: 44–5, 68–9; Tomlinson 1994: 142–3).

8 Yet here too it is important not to accept uncritically the mythology of British wartime harmony and solidarity (Calder 1969). In fact no mobilization is ever 'total'. However, perhaps more significant than the actual extent of mobilization during the Second World War was the wide-scale *perception* of total mobilization – of a population (a re-imagined 'national community') fully and harmoniously integrated within a total war effort. Those conscientious objectors excluded from this symbolic reassertion of national unity and identity were thus cast as the 'enemy within', whose incarceration was thus to become an integral component in the forging of this totalizing national project.

9 This is an important point, for during wars in which the territorial integrity of a state is not seriously challenged (if, for instance, the conflict is between a global hegemon and a peripheral power) then it is extremely unlikely that the state will be re-unified under the dominance of the territorial imperative of stateness.

10 Though, as Philip Abrams (1963: 59) perceptively notes, despite the state's obvious need during the Great War for 'the active support of many social groups it had previously ignored', and the resulting promise of 'homes fit for heroes', this was not to result in significant social (as distinct from political) reform in the initial post-war period. This merely added to the pressure for more comprehensive social reform following the Second World War. Such aspirations could not be thwarted a second time without seriously compromising the continued legitimacy of the state regime.

11 In this respect the period of the inter-war years can be regarded as a 'catastrophic equilibrium', a fragile compromise brought to an abrupt end by war and the requirement for total mobilization that it engendered. The 1930s in particular can be interpreted as a decade of profound state and economic failure in which the costs were passed disproportionately on to a weakened labour movement (whose organizational strength had been radically curtailed by the legislation following the General Strike of 1926). This created a situation of 'catastrophic equilibrium' characterized by the paradoxical co-presence of a series of mature contradictions and a period of relative social and political stability. In such a conjuncture, as Gramsci (1971: 276) notes, 'the old is dying yet the new cannot be born; in this interregnum a whole variety of morbid symptoms appear'. This morbidity expressed itself in a series of generally submerged social tensions associated with the impact of persistent economic failure upon a proletariat already suffering the consequences of (markedly regional) mass unemployment. For although such tensions periodically gave rise to local forms of resistance and expressions of collective solidarity, overt national political protest was rare – the single notable exception being the Jarrow Hunger March of 1936 (Bagguley 1991). Accordingly, despite such generally subterranean and internalized unrest, the period was one of political stagnation and inertia. This was mirrored in a superficial and depoliticized elite consensus which continued to proffer the hollow rhetoric of corporatist conciliation and compromise up to the outbreak of war (Miliband 1970; cf. Middlemas 1979). The inter-war years, then, can be characterized, somewhat paradoxically, as an era of apparently constantly deferred crisis – a period of state and economic failure whose effect fell disproportionately upon the urban proletariat of the industrial north. Yet although inherently prone to external shock, this was also a period in which the stability of the state was not directly threatened by either institutional dislocation or social unrest. The shock was to come in the form of a *Blitzkrieg*.

12 As Scott Newton (1991: 75) notes, 'the debate about the extent and duration of the Keynesian revolution has generated enough contributions to create a sizeable clearing in the Amazonian rain forest.' Single-handedly responsible for much of this environmental devastation is Jim Tomlinson, who, in a myriad of articles, has suggested that the extent of the 'Keynesian revolution' has tended to be grossly

exaggerated by proponents of the thesis (Booth 1983, 1984; P. Clarke 1988; Addison 1991). The radical changes in economic policy in Britain between the 1930s and 1950s, he argues, owe their origins less to a revolution in economic thought than to continuity of policy in a dramatically changing domestic and global economic context (Tomlinson 1981, 1984, 1993, 1994, 1995). Moreover, in so far as budgetary policy was at no stage subordinated to the requirements of full employment, the Treasury cannot be considered to have undergone a 'Keynesian revolution' in the post-war period (Tomlinson 1984: 261). Neil Rollings (1988) tries to establish a conciliatory middle ground by arguing for the need to distinguish more clearly between the Treasury's conversion to the *rhetoric* of demand management (for which there is considerable evidence) and its consistent resistance to the *implementation* of demand management in practice. For our purposes, it is merely important to note that it was the rhetoric of Keynesianism (regardless of the extent to which it would later be operationalized) that made the commitment to full employment that was central to the Beveridge Report appear a realistic target.

13 Though this is undeniably the case, Hennessy seems to be constructing something of a straw man here. For Keynesianism, even to those most sceptical of a 'Keynesian revolution' like Tomlinson, is simply not reducible to Keynes' *General Theory*. To argue that few in Whitehall adopted Keynes' *magnum opus* as their bible is one thing; to suggest that Keynesianism was not prevalent is another thing altogether.

14 Until the publication of the Beveridge Report there was very little discussion as to what this promised 'New Jerusalem' might look like. From then on, however, the Army Education Corps and the Army Bureau of Current Affairs became powerful channels for the dissemination of a Beveridgean conception of post-war reconstruction (Barnett 1986: 34–5, 44–5).

15 A hypothetical alternative strategy would have been to seek to change such aspirations. The incoming government might have chosen to adopt a 'preference-shaping' as opposed to a 'preference-accommodating' strategy (Dunleavy and Ward 1991: 112–27). However, given Labour's considerable sympathy with the popular mood for change, this would have proved an unnecessary and risky tactic. It is highly unlikely that any post-war government would have lasted long had it attempted to convince potential voters that the 'New Jerusalem' could simply not be afforded, an impression apparently confirmed by the Conservative's electoral expediency in 1945. That Labour could have secured a popular mandate for a wholesale socialist transformation was, by 1943, perhaps equally unlikely. For although a truly leftist conception of the New Jerusalem might well have captured the public's imagination between 1940 and 1942, the reconstruction debate was effectively terminated by the decisive and hegemonic impact of the Beveridge Report. Following its publication, there could be no truly radical content to post-war reconstruction.

3 *The* sense *and* nonsense *of* consensus: *the* state regime *in* post-war Britain

In Chapter 2 we saw that although the consensus did not exactly fall 'like a branch of ripe plums into the lap of Mr Attlee', as Paul Addison (1977: 14) famously suggests, the experience of the war years did significantly shape the nature of Britain's post-war reconstruction. This was to result in a certain convergence between the parties as they were to accommodate themselves to widespread societal aspirations for significant social reform that had been mobilized during the war years.

In this chapter we will turn our attentions to the form of the state regime that was to emerge in the post-war period, considering the extent of the elite consensus widely held to characterize the years between the war and the mid-1970s. Once again we can usefully identify a number of questions which might frame our investigation.

- What was the nature of the state regime that was to emerge in Britain through the process of post-war reconstruction?
- Can this emergent state regime be usefully described as a post-war settlement? If so, what form did this settlement take?
- How would we identify consensus? Did Britain experience a period of post-war political consensus? What is implied by such a view?
- Did the period of post-war reconstruction usher in a new stage of consensual capitalism in Britain or did it pave the way for the much-vaunted 'democratic road to socialism'?

Settlement, consensus or Keynesian welfare state?

At the outset it is crucial to distinguish between the numerous terms that have been used, often interchangeably, to describe the British post-war experience (for a summary see Table 2). Once again much hinges on how we chose to define our concepts. Yet despite the enormous literature on this period, and despite the extensive use of the three terms post-war consensus, post-war settlement and Keynesian welfare state within this literature, these key concepts are seldom explicitly specified. The following definitions, as a

Table 2 Consensus, settlement or state regime?

Term	Object of analysis	Reference point	Duration	Term used by
Post-war settlement	State's mode of intervention within civil society; degree of state economic regulation	The state regime in post-war Britain	1948–1975	State theorists; some political historians
Post-war consensus	Political establishment: nature of party political competition; governing assumptions and expectations	The political system in post-war Britain	1942–1975 or 1945–1975	Political scientists; political historians
Keynesian welfare state	Capitalist state regime: responsibilities of the state; modes of state intervention within society and the economy	The state regime in post-war Western Europe	Late 1940s to late 1970s	Marxist historians and state theorists
Patriarchal welfare state	Patriarchal state regime: nature of the state's mode of intervention within the 'private' sphere	The state regime in post-war Western Europe	Late 1940s until the present, undergoing a change in form in the 1980s	Feminist political scientists and state theorists

consequence, are unlikely to be accepted by all protagonists in the debate, since different authors emphasize somewhat different aspects, adopt slightly different assumptions and refer to different time frames (cf. Seldon 1994: 504–8).

Post-war settlement

This is a term used predominantly by state theorists (Jessop 1980: 27–30; 1992: 16–18; see also Hay 1992a: 28–54; 1994a: 42–8) and, more sparingly, by political historians (Middlemas 1986: 1–2, 7–8, 74–92, 109–19; 1990, 1991: 447–8, 460–1, 478–9; Cronin 1991: 188–222). It generally refers to the relationship between the state, the economy, civil society and the public sphere that was to emerge and become institutionalized in post-war Britain. Yet two somewhat different, if co-existent, senses of 'settlement' can be identified: (a) 'settlement' as a stabilized and sedimented set of state structures, practices and modes of calculation – settlement as an *articulation of institutional relationships* and responsibilities (an institutional or systems-theoretical conception); and (b) 'settlement' as a *compromise* or accord with labour, laying the foundations for a period of relative social harmony (a class-theoretical conception). For the purpose of what is to follow, and to avoid potential confusion, we will restrict the usage of the term *post-war settlement* to the former conception, while referring to the form of the capital–labour relation as a *post-war compromise*.[1] None the less, it is important to recognize that any settlement in the institutional articulation of the political and the economy is necessarily dependent upon a capital–labour accord, settlement or *compromise*. Thus as Bob Jessop (1980: 28) suggests, 'the creation of the mixed economy and the welfare state during the post-war Labour administration laid the foundations for the economic and political settlement between capital and labour in the next two decades.' The concept as deployed here relates to the distinctive character of the *state regime* that emerged *in Britain* following the Second World War and which, it is argued, remained relatively unchallenged and untransformed at least until the mid-1970s.

Post-war consensus

This term is used predominantly by political scientists and historians (for reviews see Lowe 1990; Kavanagh 1992; Kavanagh and Morris 1994; Seldon 1994). The dispute which surrounds the appropriateness of this term has dominated the literature on post-war reconstruction and post-war British politics more generally. It is non-surprising then that for every reference to either the 'post-war settlement' or the 'Keynesian welfare state' there are perhaps one hundred to 'post-war consensus'.

    The term generally refers to an implicit accord *between the parties* as to the nature of political responsibility and the form and role of the state in the post-war period. Dennis Kavanagh and Peter Morris understand the term as implying 'a set of governing assumptions and expectations' (1994: 1), further defining it as 'a set of parameters which bounded the set of policy options regarded by senior politicians and civil servants as administratively practicable, economically affordable and politically acceptable' (p. 13). Similarly, in David Marquand's (1988: 18) terms, the Keynesian and social democratic consensus embodied a series of 'commitments, assumptions and expectations transcending party conflicts and shared by the great majority of the country's political and economic leaders, which provided the framework within which party decisions were made'.

According to this, the predominant account, this was an *elite* consensus and was not reflected in wide-scale social or 'popular' consensus within civil society (Seldon 1994: 505). Some commentators none the less resist this orthodoxy, preferring to use the term to refer to a (mythical) social consensus spanning all sections of society. In so doing they tend to present a grossly idealized and illusory vision of universal social harmony premised upon prosperity and a pervasive civic ethic (Bell 1960; Lipset 1960; Almond and Verba 1963; for a powerful critique see Pateman 1989a; and for a far less complacent view of consensus see Hall *et al.* 1978: 227–38). The dominant conception, however, is of a political and strategic convergence between the parties, whose origins can be traced to the experience of the war years (Beer 1965, 1982: 8–10; Miliband 1969: 46, 69; Gamble 1974; Addison 1975; Barnett 1986; Lowe 1990).

It is important to emphasize that the notions of post-war settlement and post-war consensus, despite their superficial similarity, cannot be conflated. They refer to fundamentally different objects of analysis. Thus while the former refers to the broad architecture of the state and its modes of intervention within the economy, the private sphere and civil society, the latter takes as its referent the ephemeralities of daily politics and hence the nature of the governmental process. As a consequence, consensus tends to be a far less tightly specified concept, and indeed has been understood in terms of a great variety of rather different things: policy goals; policy means; policy outcomes; political style; the presentation of policy to the electorate; and even the range of policies *excluded* from the political agenda (Kavanagh 1992: 176–7: Kavanagh and Morris 1994: 1–4; Seldon 1994: 504–7).

Much of the 'consensus debate' thus revolves around disputes over what would count as a refutation of the consensus thesis. Whether one agrees with his conclusions or not, Ben Pimlott (1988: 503) certainly gets to the heart of the problem when he suggests that 'the consensus is a mirage, an illusion that rapidly fades the closer one gets to it.' Indeed, this is something of a truism, for, since there will never be absolute agreement on all aspects of policy in a given political system over a given time frame, the nearer one gets to the policy-making process, the greater the extent of apparent dissensus and disagreement will be. The question, however, still remains: from what distance should we assess the consensus proposition? Unfortunately there is no consensus on the answer. As Anthony Seldon (1994: 503) perceptively notes, from the perspective of an archival historiographer,

> consensus might appear to have existed . . . when looked at from a very broad perspective. But when viewed from close to the ground, or the documents [the archives], the reality was very different. To an extent, the difference typifies the different approach of historians, who tend

to see the trees, and political scientists who prefer to see the whole wood.

This would appear to present an intractable problem, and one that rather undermines the significance of describing any political system at a particular moment of time as consensual. Yet, once we introduce into our considerations the nature of the state regime (which, after all, provides the very context within which governmental decisions are formulated), there are two potential solutions.

Missing the wood for the trees . . .

The first is to modify slightly Seldon's arboreal metaphor by suggesting that political historians in fact tend to focus on the branches, political scientists the trees and state theorists the forest. This in turn would imply that the deeply subjective concept of 'consensus' should be either abandoned altogether or tied by definition to the more significant question of the presence or absence of a consolidated state regime – the question of *settlement*. Such an approach would treat consensus as an *epiphenomenon of settlement*. An elite consensus could be said to exist in as much as the structures, practices, boundaries and responsibilities of the state regime are taken as circumscribing the politically possible, and as setting the context within which political projects must be conceived.[2] The important distinction can thus be drawn between:

1 *State-shaping governments* or *governments with state power* (such as the Attlee Government and the Thatcher Governments) whose strategy is to transform the very contours of the state itself, thereby imposing a new trajectory upon its evolution.
2 *Consensus* or *state-accommodating governments* (in the British context, perhaps all those elected between 1951 and 1979) which do not seek significantly to challenge the structures of the state inherited from the previous administration.

It might at this stage be protested that this respecification of the term 'consensus' in fact owes very little to any sense of the concept recognizable by the political scientists and contemporary historians who continue to use it. Once this might well have been the case. Yet what is interesting is that in recent attempts to salvage the concept from its increasing 'academic disrepute' (Seldon 1994: 503) it is very much this sense of consensus that has been appealed to (Kavanagh 1992; Kavanagh and Morris 1994; Seldon 1994; cf. Marquand 1988). Thus Seldon for one suggests that consensus can only usefully be understood as 'a broad parameter of agreement on many key areas of policy between the leadership of both main parties' (1994: 508). Those very same parameters might also be taken as defining the nature and extent of the settlement. Similarly, Kavanagh, in dismissing Charles Webster's rebuttal of the consensus thesis on the basis of a study of the origins of the National Health Service, makes the comment that, regardless of what one thinks of it, we have to distinguish between the claim that the creation of the NHS in 1948 was not a product of a inter-party agreement and the subsequent history of the NHS as part of the consensus. Even if Webster is right in his first thesis, he has not proved the case for the second. *A house once built becomes part of the landscape.*

(Kavanagh 1992: 185, emphasis added)

It would perhaps appear that state theorists and political scientists like Kavanagh are in fact engaged in the same enterprise: of mapping the contours of the state in order to distinguish between the glacial erosion which characterizes settlement and consensus, and the earthquakes of post-war reconstruction and Thatcherism that have reshaped it.

Relativizing consensus

A second, and not incommensurate, option is to recognize the essentially comparative nature of the term 'consensus'. There is no absolute measure of consensus, or for that matter settlement. Consensus and settlement are relative concepts. If, for instance, we were to live within a society in which political disputes were routinely resolved by ritual assassination, then even a fascist regime would begin to appear (at least superficially) consensual. From the perspective of such a social formation we would scarcely be able to contemplate the (academic) disputes which surround the 'post-war consensus' in Britain. Obvious though this might seem, however, the relative nature of the term consensus is scarcely ever acknowledged (though once again see Kavanagh 1992). The immediate question then becomes: 'In relation to what should we evaluate the post-war consensus thesis?' Five principal candidates present themselves (though no doubt there are others).

First, we could make *historical comparisons* with previous periods in the evolution of a particular political system: here we might contrast, say, the post-war era in Britain with the inter-war years (Lowe 1990: 156). Were we to do this we would, as Kavanagh suggests, probably be impressed by 'the amount of inter-party agreement on policy' in the post-war period (Kavanagh 1992: 178; cf. Seldon 1994: 504–5).

Second are *retrospective comparisons*, evaluating a historical political system with respect to its current form and characteristics: here we might contrast the post-war period with the Thatcher years. Indeed, one of the reasons for the partial rehabilitation of the term 'consensus' to characterize the post-war period has been the experience of Thatcherism, which, within the British context, might be seen as its very antithesis. Indeed, Thatcherism as a political project was in part defined through its own rejection of the 'proclivities of consensus'. As Mrs Thatcher herself declared in a widely reported interview in Australia in 1981, 'consensus seems to be the very process of abandoning all beliefs, principles, values and policies' (cited in Kavanagh 1992: 176). If Thatcherism was understood, or at least publicly presented, by its ideologues as marking the symbolic end to consensus (Joseph 1975, 1976), then it is perhaps not surprising that historians and political scientists have become increasingly less wary about describing 'life before Thatcher' as consensual. Yet some caution is still required. For there is a certain danger that vague and gestural uses of the term will merely be seen as tarring the post-war period with the same pejorative connotations conjured up by Bernard Ingham's (1991: 384) brusque comment, 'consensus is something you reach when you can't agree.' The term consensus is no neutral description, and the associations of such a term have changed significantly.

Third are *trans-national comparisons* between political systems with similar historical trajectories at the same stage in their development (Almond and Verba 1963). Here we might compare and contrast the form taken by post-war reconstruction and the more-or-less consensual characteristics of the resulting state regimes. The conclusions of such an enterprise would depend crucially on the choice of comparator political systems, and, it might be argued, would merely mask the generic drift towards a more consensual form of capitalism-patriarchy throughout the advanced economies in the post-war period (see option 5).

An altogether more interesting type of comparison would be to project *alternative feasible scenarios* for a particular political system as a particular stage in its development. Yet the value of such a project can perhaps be questioned. For, to paraphrase Eric Hobsbawm (1993), there is a sense in which alternative scenarios did not occur and thus were never feasible. None the less, counterfactual questions and the thought experiments they provoke can be useful in highlighting the principal processes at work. Indeed, despite the above comment, Hobsbawm is not averse to such comparisons himself. Much of the existing literature does at times seem to draw, albeit implicitly, upon a profound sense of historical surprise at the degree of social conciliation and political convergence in post-war Britain. Such reflections could be made more rigorous by considering the extent to which 'things could have been different'. Here we might think of the implications for consensus if: (a) the war had not occurred; (b) the Conservatives had won the 1945 election; (c) a more genuinely socialist programme had been pursued by the Attlee Government; (d) the post-war administration had been characterized by an authoritarian attempt to reimpose the status quo from the inter-war years. In comparison to each of these scenarios, some more feasible than others, the actual British post-war period emerges as genuinely consensual.

The final and perhaps the most rigorous option would be to consider the *type of* (advanced capitalist) *state regime* of which the British post-war settlement was a variant (and the British post-war 'consensus', if one can be said to exist, an epiphenomenon). Here we might ask whether this more generic state regime (linking the political economies of Western Europe in the post-war period) was a more consensual form than either previous or subsequent stages in capitalist-patriarchal state development. The answer, on both counts, would once again appear to be yes.

It would seem then as though there is certainly a case to be made for the existence of post-war consensus in Britain if by consensus we understand: the acceptance by the major parties of the parameters defined by a state regime; a degree of political convergence unusual in Britain by recent historical standards; or, more likely, a combination of the two.

The Keynesian welfare state and the patriarchal welfare state

In the previous section we saw that one of the ways of identifying consensus was by linking it to a particular type of state regime, a particular stage in the evolution of the (capitalist-patriarchal) state. Where such a state regime has been identified, it has tended to described as a Keynesian welfare state (Offe 1983, 1984; Pierson 1991: 26–8; Jessop 1992, 1993; Hay 1994a). This term is often used interchangeably with 'welfare capitalism', and refers to a particular capitalist state regime considered to have emerged in advanced Western capitalist societies in the post-war period. Such a regime is characterized, as the name would imply, by a universalist welfare state and the economic principles of Keynesian aggregate demand management.

This term is most frequently used by Marxist and post-Marxist authors in developing an analysis of the historical trajectory of capitalist state development in the post-war era (Offe 1983, 1984). However, the Keynesian welfare state is also a 'patriarchal welfare state' (Pateman 1989b; see Chapter 4) dependent upon the unpaid domestic labour of women. Thus, as suggested in Chapter 1, we can perhaps best characterize the British state regime in the post-war period as capitalist-patriarchal and, more specifically, as a patriarchal-Keynesian welfare state.

Claus Offe (1983: 62) identifies the Keynesian welfare state as 'the bundle of state institutions and practices . . . [which] developed in western capitalism after the Second World War'. He goes on to suggest that this particular state regime represents a politically instituted *class compromise* or accord with labour. The terms of this institutionalized social contract were: (a) the acceptance by labour of the logic of the market as the guiding principle of resource allocation, international exchange, technological innovation, product development and industrial location; and (b) the reciprocal acceptance by the state of responsibility for securing a minimum living standard preserved universally through state welfare provision, full employment, trade union rights and income increases approximately in line with labour productivity (Bowles 1981: 12; Offe 1983: 62–3; 1984: 193–5).

The effects of this, according to Offe, were to produce unprecedented and extended economic growth in the initial post-war period, and a profound transformation in the patterns of industrial and class conflict. The subject of class conflict in this phase of consensual capitalism is no longer the nature of the mode of production itself. Rather, such conflict has increasingly tended to take the form of disputes over the volume, form and regulation of production within a capitalist economy.

Similarly, in identifying the fundamentally *patriarchal* character of the contemporary welfare state, Carole Pateman (1989b: 180) is concerned to demonstrate the disproportionate 'importance of women in the welfare state and the importance of the welfare state for women'. She characterizes this current stage in the evolution of the patriarchal state as one in which: (a) the welfare agencies are a major source of paid employment for women, yet simultaneously a context within which female labour is systematically exploited in a rigid gender segregation of tasks (and salaries); (b) the welfare state relies for its very operation on the performance of unpaid domestic labour predominantly by women; and (c) 'there is one area . . . from which women have been largely excluded . . . The legislation, policy-making and higher-level administration of the welfare state' (p. 181). As Pateman concludes, 'welfare policies have reached across from public to private and helped uphold a patriarchal structure of familial life' (p. 183).

This sort of analysis, as will become clearer in later chapters, is highly applicable to Britain, as indeed it is to all advanced Western capitalist economies in the post-war period. It suggests that Britain's post-war reconstruction reasserted and more deeply entrenched the patriarchal character of the welfare state. Paradoxically, it institutionalized a reliance of the state upon the unpaid domestic labour of women while simultaneously reinforcing the dependence of women either upon a male 'breadwinner' or upon the state.

The edifice of consensus

We will return to Offe's work later in this chapter to see how it can be used to inform a more concrete analysis of Britain's post-war state regime, and to Pateman's extremely important account in Chapter 4. For the time being, however, we need to specify more precisely the form and structure of the emergent post-war settlement and the nature of the supposed consensus. We can usefully consider the following two hypotheses:

> *Hypothesis 3*: Britain's post-war reconstruction initiated an enduring post-war settlement and a period of political (if not social) consensus that lasted, generally unchallenged, until the mid-1970s.

> *Hypothesis 4*: This post-war settlement was premised upon the creation of the structures of a Keynesian welfare state and the political incorporation of labour.

To investigate these hypotheses we will consider the work of Dennis Kavanagh, who provides perhaps the clearest *descriptive* (as opposed to theoretical) account of the contours of post-war consensus (Kavanagh 1987: 26–62; 1992; Kavanagh and Morris 1994). It is important to emphasize at this stage that Kavanagh, as a political scientist, is primarily concerned with everyday political practice in the post-war period and not the nature and structural transformation of the state. As a consequence his work refers to 'consensus' as opposed to the more structural term 'settlement' and paints a series of independent tableaux as opposed to a panorama of the overall landscape. Moreover, the canvas of his work presents a series of static or synchronic images, offering little insight into the essentially dynamic nature of the state regime even in periods of apparent stability. None the less, the rich brushwork of such an analysis is extremely useful as the basis from which to develop some more general conceptions of the character of the state regime itself.

Kavanagh identifies six central pillars of the edifice of consensus, suggesting that it can be characterized in terms of the commitment of the major political parties to:

1 Full employment.
2 The 'mixed' economy.
3 Active government.
4 Social welfare provision.
5 The conciliation of the trade unions.
6 The cult of 'expertise'.

Full employment

Full employment is often presented, and with some justification, as the bulwark of an otherwise rather fragile consensus. The significance of this simple and unequivocal pledge can only be understood in the light of the experience of mass proletarian unemployment, particularly in Scotland and the North of England, during the 1920s and 1930s (Miliband 1970; Bagguley 1991). As Kavanagh and Morris (1994: 35) note, 'mass unemployment was the dominant economic and social feature of the inter-war years.' For large sections of the working class it was the condition and experience of mass unemployment that characterized this period, and that was to shape future aspirations. To this past there simply could be no return in the post-war period. Full employment became the New Jerusalem for which the war was fought. Indeed, this single policy commitment in-and-of-itself secured the overwhelming popularity of the Beveridge Report. That T. H. Marshall, very much the barometer of the times, should have suggested in 1950 that 'the basic civil right is the right to work' (Marshall 1950: 10–11) is clearly highly significant. That it should have escaped him that this right was to be denied to over half the population (those who did not conform to the image of the *male* breadwinner it implied) is scarcely less significant.

The principle of a job for men, for life, became enshrined at the heart of the emerging consensus by the 1944 Employment White Paper, which committed post-war governments to 'the maintenance of a high and stable level of employment after the war' (HMSO 1944). Once it was expressed as a commitment, the continued legitimacy of consecutive governments be-came dependent upon its realization. Yet, however paradoxically, debates as to how much *un*employment represented 'full employment' continued throughout the post-war period. The argument was increasingly made that low unemployment was a sign of a healthy economy, but no unemployment would merely produce an uncompetitive economy. None the less, the average official rate of unemployment for 1945–60 was less than 2 per cent, with a high of 3 per cent in 1947. The corresponding level throughout the 1930s was well in excess of 10 per cent (Godfrey 1986; Pierson 1991: 132).

Three principal factors can be identified which might account for the remarkable degree of consensus on full employment between the parties in the initial post-war period, and the more interventionist conception of the state that this implied.

First, and perhaps of most importance, a commitment to full employment was seen as a necessary, though not in itself sufficient, condition of any serious attempt to win an election after 1944. Certainly while the post-war economic boom lasted it would have been political suicide for either of the major parties even to contemplate abandoning the commitment to full employment expressed by the wartime coalition.

Second, if such a commitment was politically expedient, then it was also seen as essential for maintaining the insurance basis of the welfare state. For high levels of unemployment meant high levels of social security payments (as consecutive Conservative governments in the 1980s and 1990s were to find to their cost).

Moreover, in the initial post-war period full employment was not at all difficult to maintain, and imposed few constraints upon government autonomy (Tomlinson 1984; Newton and Porter 1988: 120–32; Newton 1991). In the 1940s and early 1950s the British economy was in fact characterized by labour shortages in certain sectors. The result was an active policy of promoting Commonwealth immigration in order to produce a 'reserve army of labour' to suppress the tendency towards wage increases while providing a cheap source of exploitable labour within both the private sector and the welfare state (Williams 1989a: 72; Pierson 1991: 80–1). The NHS, for instance, was actively to recruit migrant workers directly in the former colonies for low-paid, low-skill servicing occupations (Doyal *et al.* 1981; Ginsburg 1992: 159–61).

The commitment to full employment was to emerge as a central ideological pillar of the post-war consensus, reflecting a fundamental re-ordering of the priorities, responsibilities and boundaries of the state. As a consequence the role of the state and its mode of intervention within the economy was comprehensively redefined.

The state would now seek to secure the conditions for sustained economic growth through the techniques of Keynesian demand management.[3] The government would alter the volume of expenditure and borrowing, using adjustments in interest rates to affect the level of investment and consumer demand in order to create favourable conditions for industry and business and, above all, to *maintain full employment* (Thompson 1987; Coates 1991). This, at least, was the rhetoric. As David Coates notes, although the extent to which Keynesian techniques were put into practice is hotly contested, what is clear is that 'the politicians involved before 1979 invariably thought of themselves as Keynesians, and were prepared – as Keynes had suggested they should be – to stimulate private investment and spend public money to create employment and increase business confidence' (Coates 1994: 172).

Furthermore, the state was now expected to create conditions likely to stimulate industrial investment (in fixed capital formation) and research and development, and to offset regional imbalances in both employment and prosperity. Once again, although both parties might have been committed to the rhetoric, the reality was somewhat different (Ingham 1988; Tomlinson 1991; Coates 1994: 201–9).

The mixed economy

Between 1946 and 1949 the Bank of England, coal, rail, civil aviation, iron and steel, road passenger and freight transport, electricity and gas were all nationalized, creating the structural basis for the post-war 'mixed' economy.

These measures, pursued by the Attlee Government, represented a fundamental transformation of the boundaries and responsibilities of the state and a significant extension of the influence of the state within the economy. None the less, we should not allow ourselves to be entirely taken in by the labels 'publicly owned' and 'mixed economy'. Much in the politics of the post-war period is not what it seems. The newly nationalized industries are a case in point.

In many respects the nationalized industries were little more than *publicly regulated private monopolies* operating on modified market principles. Thus, although the nationalization programme of the Attlee Government represented a significant extension of the *scope* and *responsibilities* of the state, the internal structures, managerial hierarchies and operational culture institutionalized within these generally unproductive and inefficient monoliths remained largely intact (Middlemas 1986: 119–20; Chick 1991; Cronin 1991: 156). Bringing substantial areas of the private sector under 'public ownership' had the effect of merely imposing a set of extraneous political pressures and constraints without in any way enhancing the ability of such industries to satisfy increased expectations. As James Cronin (1991: 156; cf. Taylor 1991) notes, nationalization generally

> involved setting up a board to run the industry with little interference from the state and minimal input from the workers . . . The structures that came into being in the 1940s were thus recognisably similar to what had existed before, and the simple change in ownership did little to transform industrial relations.

The boards of directors of nationalized industries mirrored those of the private sector, and their composition certainly did not secure the representation of workers and consumers (a prominent theme of Labour proposals during the 1930s). Similarly, managers were recruited as in the private sector, with no element of industrial democracy (again a Labour Party electoral pledge before 1945). Furthermore, as the economies of the other European wartime protagonists began to rebuild and recover and the initial post-war British economic boom subsided, much stricter market criteria were imposed upon the nationalized industries under the weight of growing public pressure (Hall 1986; Newton and Porter 1988). As Ben Fine and Laurence Harris (1985: 154) note, 'the development of the nationalized industries has been a history of the reversal of the processes that created them. Capitalist mechanisms of control have been increasingly restored to the industries.' Thus Labour's chosen 'public corporation model' of nationalization did not significantly change the character of industrial relations:

> workers still worked in the old way, often for the same bosses and with roughly the same problems and grievances. Neither at the level of macro-economic policy nor at the mundane level of daily work did nationalisation bring about major changes. Not surprisingly, it therefore had not, by 1951, produced a wave of enthusiasm for further nationalisation or agreement on the virtues of the existing array of socialised industries.
>
> (Cronin 1991: 190)

So, as Colin Leys (1983: 378) perceptively notes, 'to the extent that the term "mixed economy" was used, to imply that the nationalised industries represented an alternative, non-capitalist or even "socialist" principle of organisation, or economic rationality, this was an illusion.'

The Tories, though never explicitly committed to nationalization and state ownership, generally accepted it pragmatically, introducing only minor privatization programmes. Indeed, the cross-party consensus on this area of policy is well demonstrated by Helen Mercer (1991: 71), who points to the fact that Labour's election manifesto in 1945 'argued for specific nationalisations on empirical grounds almost identical to those outlined in Harold Macmillan's *The Middle Way*' (see Macmillan 1938).

The Attlee Government's dramatic extension of the public sphere between 1946 and 1949 laid the foundations of the settlement in this arena. Although the Conservatives resisted the nationalization of iron and steel (a manufacturing industry which was to become something of a ping-pong ball, repeatedly batted over the public sector–private sector net) there was substantial agreement on the principal of 'state ownership' (however understood) and the principal constituents of this redefined sector (Dutton 1991: 45). Once again, a basic operational and pragmatic consensus can be said to have existed, reflecting a comprehensive redefinition of the role of the state and its mode of intervention within the economy.

Active government: the interventionist state

Both Keynesianism (with its assumption of state intervention through demand management to offset recessional tendencies) and the nationalization programme (with its extension of the responsibilities of the state within the economy) embodied a conception of a more active or interventionist role for the state (Kavanagh 1987: 43–5). This respecification of what the state could and should do was a central pillar of the post-war settlement. At the core of the vision of 'active' and 'responsive' government lay the commitment of both parties to the *management* (as opposed to *transformation*) of the structures of an 'extended state' (McEachern 1990). This was in turn reflected in the acceptance of: (a) the state's role in the regulation and management of the domestic economy, and of Britain's position within the global economy; and (b) the expanded responsibilities of the state in relation to the demands and aspirations of civil society, which were to be satisfied, primarily, through universal state welfare provision.

This active or interventionist role for the state clearly contrasts markedly to the liberal anti-statism of the inter-war period and the neo-liberal anti-statism of Thatcherism. Yet here too some caution is advisable. For, as the previous two sections have already demonstrated, there is a considerable danger in taking the political rhetoric of the post-war era at face value. Active government, though now synonymous with post-war British politics, was in fact something of a myth. The gap between rhetoric and political reality is well captured by Peter Hall (1986: 67) when he observes that 'the nation that most avidly advanced Keynesianism also adopted the most arms-length industrial policy in Europe.' Similarly, as Scott Newton and Dilwyn

Porter suggest, strategies of state-led industrial modernization were extremely rare and were resorted to only in desperation at times of perceived crisis. Such interventions were generally too little, too late and too infrequent (Newton and Porter 1988; see also Fine and Harris 1985: 153–64; Middlemas 1986: 108–9; Pollard 1992; Tomlinson 1993: 19; 1994: 170; Coates 1994: 63–4; 187–90).

Once again an elite political consensus and policy convergence can be detected. Its subject matter, however, was not so much *active government* as *fitful government*. It was characterized by periodic waves of misdirected and poorly coordinated activity, as opposed to the consistent, systematic and sustained intervention of a 'developmental state' (Marquand 1988, 1989).

The welfare settlement

Perhaps the most immediately obvious and politically significant component of the post-war consensus was the welfare settlement. Both parties accepted the necessity and legitimacy of state-funded welfare provision, committing themselves to:

1 A universal National Insurance scheme (including old age and invalidity pensions, benefits for unemployment, bereavement, industrial accidents and sickness financed through flat-rate contributions).
2 A comprehensive National Health Service initially free at the point of access to all (a wartime concession removed as early as 1951 with the effective introduction of means-tested charges for false teeth and spectacles).
3 Free and compulsory education to the age, initially of 14, and subsequently of 16, in a tripartite system of grammar, secondary modern and technical schools.
4 An extended state housing sector. By the early 1970s over a quarter of the population lived in state-subsidized council housing (Gough 1979: 2; Dunleavy 1981; Hay 1992a).

Although the structural basis of the welfare settlement was laid by the Attlee Government between 1945 and 1948 (following the blueprint of the Beveridge Report), these comprehensive reforms were, however grudgingly, accepted by the Tories. As Cronin (1991: 215) notes, 'the Conservatives largely acquiesced in the maintenance of the social programmes put in place during the late 1940s, but spent hardly a shilling more than was required by the exigencies of politics and the growing demand for services.' This is clearly demonstrated by the levels of expenditure on state welfare during the post-war period (see Table 3). These show a steady rise that appears relatively unaffected by changes in the political complexion of government.

The reforms of the Attlee Government were to become both the ideological linchpin of the consensus and the structural underpinning of the settlement. The resulting welfare regime, however, was once again not all that it appeared to be (Deacon 1982; Williams 1989a: 161–6, 178–203; Harris 1990: 183). For, as with so many aspects of post-war British politics, there was a certain gulf between the public legitimating rhetoric (of universality and equality) and the daily reality of life in 'welfare Britain' (of persistent

Table 3   The growth of state welfare expenditure in the UK

	Percentage of GNP at factor cost					
	1931	*1937*	*1951*	*1961*	*1971*	*1975*
All social services	12.7	10.9	16.1	17.6	23.8	28.8
Social security	6.7	5.2	5.3	6.7	8.9	9.5
Health	1.8	1.8	4.5	4.4	5.8	7.1
Education	2.8	2.6	3.2	4.2	6.5	7.6
Total state spending	28.8	25.7	44.9	42.1	50.3	57.9

Source: adapted from Gough (1979: 77).

mass poverty, of disciplinary means-testing, of the unpaid domestic labour of women and of deeply entrenched subjective, institutional and structural racism). Welfare rhetoric and reality may not have converged, but the parties certainly did – both rhetorically and in policy terms.

The conciliation of the trade unions

A further key constituent of the consensus thesis is the supposed conciliation and incorporation of labour within a wider political settlement. The British post-war consensus is generally described as 'corporatist', referring to the consultation and incorporation *on equal terms* of the representatives of capital and labour within the political decision-making process. In his numerous accounts of the post-war era Kavanagh repeatedly points to the conciliation of the trade unions as the weakest link in the consensus (1987, 1992; Kavanagh and Morris 1994). Certainly the Tories did not enjoy, or indeed try to cultivate, Labour's close 'fraternal' relations with the trade unions. Yet in many respects they were as committed to corporatism – or what in Britain was to pass for corporatism – as were Labour. Kavanagh is at times in danger of mistaking a lack of corporatism for a lack of consensus. For, although the extent of corporatism and the nature of the *tripartite* relationship between capital, labour and the state varied during the post-war period, this was owing mainly to changes in the economic context rather than the different attitudes of the parties towards the unions. Whether the post-war period can be described as corporatist is at least debatable. What is clearer is that it was broadly tripartite and consensual.

Corporatism–tripartism was a highly visible component of the settlement and represented something of a departure from the inter-war years (though for a counter-argument see Middlemas 1979). Far less visible, yet ultimately of much greater significance, were the structures of what might be termed *financial tripartism*: the private and informal channels linking the City of London, the Bank of England and the Treasury. This 'City–Bank–Treasury nexus' (Ingham 1984: 131ff; see also Leys 1986; Stones 1990; Cain and Hopkins 1993: 265–93) was inherited largely intact from the inter-war years and continued to exercise a far more fundamental influence upon economic and industrial policy than the more public and formal corporatist–tripartite structures (Wootton 1980; Newton and Porter 1988). The result was the ongoing subordination of industrial policy to the interests of financial capital, reinforcing a fundamental structural weakness at the heart of the state apparatus in the post-war period (Gamble 1990: 212; Anderson 1992a: 166).

Thus although it is important to emphasize the conciliation of the trade unions as a core constituent of the post-war consensus, it is crucial that we do not focus exclusively upon such highly visible phenomena – missing the roots for the branches. If we are adequately to categorize the state regime that emerged and was consolidated in post-war Britain then we must consider both the formal and informal channels of political influence.

'Expertise' and technocracy

The final component of the consensus identified by Kavanagh is somewhat cryptically referred to as 'expertise'. The sense that is being conveyed is perhaps better captured by the terms technocracy, managerialism and paternalism, which characterized the post-war elite 'mindset'. This dominant ethos, which infused politicians and bureaucrats alike, became encapsulated in the image of a scientifically managed virtuous circle of economic growth and a neutral bureaucratic rationality free from vested interest. Its development was tied to the spirit of post-war optimism, the technological revolution, the initial post-war economic boom and the emergence of the new 'science' of the economy – Keynesianism. The contradictions of this 'exaggerated assertion of the scientific ethos, a veritable ideology of technocracy' (Beer 1982: 121) are well illustrated in Daniel Bell's 'end of ideology thesis' (Bell 1960). This extremely influential account, and others like it, suggested that since science was now capable of managing the economy, and indeed society and the polity, there was no longer any need for political radicalism or confrontation, and that we were now entering the dawning of an idyllic epoch of consensus, harmony and affluence. The full naivety of such an argument, which became almost hegemonic within non-Marxist sociology in the 1960s and early 1970s, was clearly exposed by the economic, social and political crises of the late 1970s and the move towards authoritarian conservatism in Western Europe and North America in the years that followed (see Chapters 6 and 7).

Mapping the contours of the settlement

The shape of the post-war consensus outlined above is, within the existing literature, generally uncontentious if somewhat descriptive (though for a critique of the consensus thesis see Pimlott 1988). It does, none the less, support the suggestion: (a) that Britain's post-war reconstruction did bring into existence the structures of a Keynesian welfare state which was patriarchal in character; (b) that it institutionalized an accord with labour ushering in a new stage of (more) consensual capitalism; and (c) that it also defined the contours of an enduring post-war settlement, paving the way for a period of political consensus lasting, broadly unchallenged, until the mid-1970s.

The strength of such a descriptive account (which emphasizes the various constituents of the policy convergence and their structural underpinnings in the settlement) is that its historical detail gives flesh to the bones of the consensus thesis. Yet once again we must be wary of missing the wood for the trees. Having described selected aspects of the consensus it is imperative that we now consider the nature of the state regime itself, for the structure of the settlement is far greater than the sum of these component parts.

What the above discussion does demonstrate is the significant transformation of the relationship between the state, economy and civil society that occurred in the immediate post-war period. None the less, the extent of this transformation has tended to be somewhat exaggerated in existing accounts (though for more balanced surveys see Cronin 1991; Tiratsoo 1991a). For many of the structures of the post-war settlement were inherited largely intact from the inter-war years. This again raises the question of how to characterize the emergent state regime as a whole. In the final section of this chapter we will turn our attention to this important question, arguing that the state regime in post-war Britain can be best characterized as a contradictory settlement, but a settlement none the less. Aspects of this contradictory character have already been pointed to: the settlement was not so much Keynesian as a schizophrenic mixture of Keynesian techniques, strategies and rhetoric and distinctly pre-Keynesian practices in many areas of economic policy; the consensus was concerned not so much with state ownership as with the state's responsibility for 'public' sector industries whose internal structures remained fundamentally unreformed from the inter-war years; and while the welfare state proffered the rhetoric of universality and equality it in fact relied upon the unpaid domestic labour of women while failing to eliminate the persistent mass poverty of the 1920s and 1930s.

The twin settlements thesis

In seeking to contextualize these observations we might draw upon a number of different state theoretical perspectives. We will consider just two, both of which point to the existence of two domestic post-war settlements.

The contradictions of welfare capitalism

The first perspective is informed by Claus Offe's highly provocative and perceptive analysis, *The Contradictions of the Welfare State* (1984). Here he formulates a structural or systems-theoretical analysis of the form of the Keynesian welfare state – the form of 'welfare capitalism' (terms which he tends to use interchangeably). The state in welfare capitalism, he suggests, is composed of three subsystems: the economic, the politico-administrative (the administrative, institutional, democratic-representational, legal and bureaucratic structures of the state) and the politico-normative (the institutions of state welfare operating within civil society). These subsystems, however,

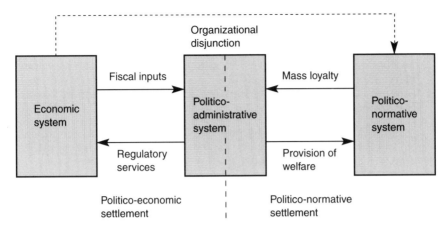

Figure 3 The twin settlements.
Source: Hay (1994a: 42), adapted from Offe (1984: 52).

do not exist independently of one another. Rather, it is their mutual inter-relationship which is characteristic of the stage of welfare capitalism (see Figure 3).

Thus, for Offe, the economy is dependent upon the politico-adminis-trative system (the 'state' narrowly defined) for the provision of regulatory services and economic management. The state must take decisions which though in the collective *general* interest of capital are not in the individual interests of *particular* capitals (cf. O'Connor 1987: 99–107). Accordingly, such decisions would remain untaken in the absence of the state acting as a more-or-less 'ideal collective capitalist' (Engels 1878).[4] In return, the economic system must provide the 'state' apparatus (the politico-administrative sys-tem) with fiscal inputs in the form of taxation to fund such regulatory activities. This is not, however, the end of the story. For the state, in an era of consensual capitalism, must also secure its continued legitimacy and that of the capitalist economic system in order to be able to carry out its regu-latory functions. To this end the state provides a range of (costly) welfare services which modify the inequalities of market outcomes.

This allows the state, through a series of welfare interventions: (a) to regulate civil society; (b) to contain and channel pressure for social reform; and (c) to secure and continue to re-secure the legitimacy of the state and the capitalist system by satisfying societal demands and expectations.[5] These functions impose a further financial burden upon the state and hence, through taxation, the economic system.[6] Ideally, then, a consensual civil society re-ciprocates by conferring and continuing to confer legitimacy upon the state, thereby allowing it to continue its primary function of economic regulation (Offe 1984: 51–7; cf. Habermas 1975: 5, 46–7; Pierson 1991: 58–61).

So to summarize, during the stage of welfare capitalism:

1 The state must intervene within the economy to secure the conditions for continued capitalist accumulation.

2 By so doing it incurs financial costs which must ultimately be born by capital in the form of taxation.
3 To preserve the stability of the social formation the state must act to secure the conditions for its continued legitimacy through forms of (welfare) intervention within civil society.
4 In return, the 'citizens' of the state provide it with a continuing basis of mass loyalty.

For Offe, the most serious problem facing the state within welfare capitalism is that the demands of (a) capitalist accumulation and (b) societal legitimation are, generally speaking, contradictory (Offe 1984: 57–61; cf. O'Connor 1973; Wolfe 1977; Keane 1978; Bowles and Gintis 1982, 1987). This tension, Offe argues, is temporarily ameliorated by the existence of an *organizational disjunction* or functional separation of tasks within the state apparatus (the politico-administrative system). This has the effect of achieving a 'relative insulation' of these twin 'problem complexes' (the avoidance of economic malfunctions associated with capitalist accumulation on the one hand, and political conflicts associated with democratic legitimacy on the other). Instead of each institutional or bureaucratic structure of the state being the focus of the conflicting pressures of capital and civil society – accumulation and legitimation – simultaneously, they are grouped and organized so as to direct themselves either primarily towards civil society or primarily towards the economy (Offe 1984: 53). In this way the symptoms of this fundamental tension are temporarily alleviated even if the basic contradiction remains unaltered. It now assumes a latent form.

Offe's identification of an organizational disjunction or functional division of tasks within the state apparatus would appear to have a certain resonance with the structures of the state that emerged in Britain through post-war reconstruction. This in turn suggests the existence of *two* domestic post-war settlements – effectively lying either side of the organizational disjunction:

- the *politico-economic settlement* specifying the relationship between the state and the economy;
- the *politico-normative* or *welfare settlement* specifying the relationship between the state and civil society (see Figure 3).

Moreover, if we follow the logic of Offe's argument then we might expect to find that these twin settlements are in fact mutually antagonistic. For, according to Offe, the very reason for the existence of the organizational disjunction is the separation (however partial, however temporary) of the conflicting demands of the economy and civil society, accumulation and legitimation. This observation suggests a potential source of structural contradiction within the British variant of the Keynesian welfare state, directing us towards an account of the origins of the crisis of the state during the 1970s (an argument to which we return in Chapter 6).

If we apply this sort of analysis to the state regime that emerged in Britain in the initial post-war years, then we can fairly readily identify two post-war settlements. The politico-economic settlement specifying the relationship between the state and the economy was characterized by a Keynesian, corporatist and interventionist *mode of calculation*. Yet this, as we have seen, was somewhat compromised in practice (the state's 'mode of economic intervention' was not particularly Keynesian, not particularly corporatist and not particularly interventionist). Similarly, the welfare settlement, specifying the relationship between the state and civil society, was characterized by the *rhetoric* of equality, conciliation and universality. This was once again systematically and routinely compromised in practice (see Table 4).

This theoretically informed means of specifying and characterizing the principal relationships within welfare capitalism sensitizes us to the deeply inscribed contradictions of Britain's post-war settlement(s). As we shall see in more detail in Chapter 6, this type of analysis can provide the basis for an account of the crisis tendencies of the state regime in post-war Britain and, hence, of the origins of Thatcherism in the Winter of Discontent.

Social democracy against itself: the politicians' and producers' settlements

A somewhat different, but no less useful, account of the contradictions of the Keynesian welfare state regime in Britain is provided by Bob Jessop (1992). If Offe's analysis focuses on 'settlement' as a *structural relationship* between various institutions and apparatuses within the state, then Jessop, by contrast, concentrates on 'settlement' as an *institutionalized accord* between different parties (politicians, producers, labour, the state), or on what we earlier termed the *post-war compromise*. Thus, although these two accounts draw on different senses of the term 'settlement' (see above), they do offer complementary analyses.

Jessop's account again stresses contradiction and can be usefully extended to highlight the crisis tendencies of the British state in the 1970s. It suggests the existence of: (a) a *productivist* or *producers' settlement* centrally concerned with securing the conditions for economic modernization through planning and enhanced productivity; and (b) a *redistributive* or *politicians' settlement* centrally concerned with the promotion of greater social justice through 'jobs for all and social democracy' (Jessop 1992: 16–17).

Unlike the more structural account developed above, Jessop tends to focus on the interests pursued by distinct groupings during the post-war period: the *producers' settlement* reflecting the understanding of producer interests and the state institutions directly involved in economic management; the *politicians' settlement* representing the view of the party leaders and the electorate towards the state. This produces a helpful account of two somewhat divergent and mutually contradictory settlements expressing different modes of calculation, images of social justice, goals and means of delivery. Yet it perhaps owes too much to appearances of the time: of a truly Keynesian redistributivism (cf. Tomlinson 1981: 84; 1984; Cronin 1988: 228; 1991: 153–87; Rollings 1988, 1994: 203–5; Newton 1991); of a coherent programme of interventionist planning and industrial modernization (cf. Strange 1971; Lereuz 1975: 179; Pollard 1982, 1992; Ingham 1984: 205–9; Tomlinson 1992: 173–4; 1994: 154–64; Porter 1993); and of a truly corporatist settlement (cf. Panitch 1976; Dorfman 1983; Coates 1989). Though Jessop is the first to

Table 4 The rhetoric and reality of Britain's twin post-war settlements

	Politico-economic settlement	Welfare settlement
Structural relationship	State – economy	State – civil society
Context	Settlement articulated within the structures of a capitalist mode of production and a patriarchal and racist social formation	Settlement articulated within the structures of a capitalist mode of production and a patriarchal and racist social formation
Mode of calculation	Keynesian demand management; corporatism (the conciliation of the trade unions); full employment; industrial modernization; nationalization and the 'mixed economy'	Social democratic legitimating rhetoric: elevating the principles of 'equality of opportunity', universality, cooperation, conciliation and consensus; comprehensive 'cradle to grave' welfare for all
Mode of operation	Export commitment to (shrinking) former imperial markets; hegemony of financial capital and the 'City–Bank–Treasury nexus'; industrial profile rooted in the first industrial revolution; limited government intervention within the economy; export of capital overseas in pursuit of short-term profits; satisfaction of consumer demand through import penetration; subordination of corporatist forms of interest representation to the exigencies of short-term crisis management; nationalized industries modelled on the private sector	'Socialism in one class' (Panitch 1976): redistribution within as opposed to between classes; systematic subordination and exploitation of immigrant labour; entrenched welfare inequalities of gender, ethnicity and class; retrenchment of women's position within the labour market; an institutionalized reliance of the welfare state upon the unpaid domestic labour of women

challenge the view that the post-war British state regime was simply and unequivocally corporatist or Keynesian, his analysis focuses almost exclusively upon producer interests, which, as he himself notes, were extremely weak, and a Keynesian welfarism which was more rhetoric than reality.

As our discussion of the importance of financial tripartism in economic policy-making would suggest, Jessop's analysis can be further extended to reveal a third, less public settlement: the *financiers' settlement*.[7] This was inherited largely intact from the inter-war years and was to continue to exercise an overdetermining influence on economic and industrial policy. Its principal protagonists were the City of London, the Bank of England and the Treasury (see Table 5).

Once this third settlement is identified, the tensions enshrined within Britain's Keynesian welfare state become even more starkly exposed. Given its deeply contradictory character, it is perhaps something of a miracle that the post-war consensus and its various settlements remained largely intact and unchallenged for so long. When the crisis eventually came, however, the disintegration of the state regime was rapid and comprehensive. We return to the moment of crisis in Part III.

Conclusions

In this chapter we have considered in some detail the nature of the state regime that emerged in Britain in the initial post-war period and that was to remain largely untransformed until the mid-1970s. We saw that although there was a significant transformation of the structures of the state, its modes of intervention within civil society, the private sphere and the economy, and its institutional boundaries and responsibilities, we should be somewhat sceptical of the manner in which this is often presented.

Consensus there may well have been. Yet this consensus was not particularly Keynesian, not particularly interventionist and not particularly social democratic. Many of the structures of the state regime (particularly those of the politico-economic settlement) were inherited largely intact from the inter-war years. The initial post-war period thus saw a partial and incomplete transformation of the state, redefining the contours of a deeply contradictory and tension-ridden regime. Britain's political frailty and lack of economic competitiveness, though temporarily hidden by the immediate post-war economic boom, were to be cruelly exposed by the slump into global recession in the early 1970s. We return to this pathology in Part III. For the time being, however, we must consider the promise of universal citizenship that the Keynesian welfare state was seen to embody.

Notes

1 I am indebted to Bob Jessop for suggesting this analytical distinction.
2 At this point it is important to note that it only makes sense to refer to consensus as an epiphenomenon of settlement, if the subject of consensus is in turn taken to

Table 5 Social democracy against itself

	Producers' settlement (productivist)	Politicians' settlement (redistributive)	Financiers' settlement
Interests involved	Industrial capital and the state	Government and electorate	Financial capital and the state
Economic goals	Economic and industrial modernization	Full employment, social democracy, mixed economy	Preservation of a stable value for Sterling
Political form	Tripartism–corporatism	Competitive party democracy	Private and informal networks
Leading actors	FBI/CBI, TUC, state institutions	Voters, parties, cabinet	City of London; Bank of England; Treasury
Means to full employment	Economic planning; productivity increases	Keynesian demand management	Full employment not a priority
Welfare state model	Activist: oriented to modernization	Liberal: responding to market failure	Minimalist

Source: adapted from Jessop (1992: 17).

be a political elite. Were we to reserve the term 'consensus' to refer to a convergence of social and political values within civil society more generally, then settlement might in fact emerge as a epiphenomenon of consensus. Thus, if we were to interpret the mobilization of popular perceptions of the New Jerusalem as giving rise to a consensus for social reform, then we would be forced to concede that the post-war settlement was, if anything, a product of an accommodation to this emergent consensus (though the question of how such a consensus emerged would then need to be addressed). For current purposes, and to avoid potential confusion, we will restrict usage of the term consensus to refer to the attitudes of a political elite to the state regime.

3 As indicated in the previous chapter we should be somewhat cautious about assuming that Keynesian techniques were in fact widely deployed in post-war Britain. Moreover, given the persistent structural weaknesses of the British economy, it is at least debatable that such techniques would have proved appropriate (S. Brooke 1989; Peden 1990; Johnmann 1991; Tomlinson 1991).

4 Examples include the policing of 'insider dealing', or the legal regulation of mergers and take-overs to prevent the emergence of monopolies and cartels. That cartelization, monopolization and 'insider dealing' continue to characterize capitalist accumulation would suggest that either such regulation is difficult to enforce and hence often ineffective, or that there are strong strategic motives and vested interests rendering it ineffective. Either way, the state is a 'less than ideal collective capitalist'. Herein lies many of its contradictions and crisis tendencies.

5 Expectations that it may have done much to influence in the first place (see Chapter 2).

6 This, in itself, is not a qualitatively new phenomenon. For in pre-consensual stages of capitalism, the state required similar fiscal inputs to finance its (less costly) repressive mode of intervention within civil society to secure the social conditions for capital accumulation. What is new, however, is the (quantitative) cost to the economic system of consensus.

7 Jessop does in fact consider the financiers in his treatment of the twin settlements: the Bank of England and the Treasury are treated as state economic institutions, the City as a business organization. All three are thus accorded a place within the producers' settlement. However, whether the City, Bank and Treasury can be considered active participants in a modernizing productivist settlement characterized by state intervention through planning is at best debatable (Thompson 1977; Pollard 1982, 1992; Ingham 1984; Cain and Hopkins 1993). Indeed, Jessop is forced to concede that the producers' settlement was progressively narrowed throughout the post-war period and that the City was the first group to split from it. Yet given (a) that Jessop accounts for the contradictions of the British variant of the Keynesian welfare state in terms of the gradual subordination of the producers' to the politicians' settlement, and (b) that he later describes as one of its main contradictions the simultaneous commitment to full employment and the welfare state on the one hand and an international role for sterling and the City on the other, a three settlement account might better capture the contradictory character of this state regime.

4 Citizenship: towards *a* patriarchal welfare state?

In the previous chapters we have considered the nature and major determinants of Britain's post-war reconstruction; the form that Britain's post-war settlement took and the origins of an elite political consensus lasting until the mid-1970s. We saw how the promises and concessions granted during the war years were to frame the context for Britain's subsequent post-war reconstruction.

In this chapter we will consider a somewhat different account of the resulting structural transformation of the state. This grand historical narrative interprets the development of the British state since the eighteenth century in terms of the progressive extension and universalization of the *rights of citizenship,* culminating in the granting of social rights in the post-war era. *Citizenship* is here understood as specifying the relationship between the state and civil society, as expressing the obligations and duties of the individual 'citizen' within civil society *to the state,* and of the state *to its 'subjects'.* The use of the term can be traced back to Aristotle, who understood by citizenship a status possessed by '*all* who share in the civic life of ruling or being ruled in turn' (1948: 1283b; cited in Oliver and Heater 1994: 11). Yet the contemporary renaissance of the concept within both academic and political debate owes its origins not to Aristotle but to the work of T. H. Marshall and his account of the evolution and extension of the rights of citizenship under capitalism (1950, 1981). Hence it is to Marshall's famous essay 'Citizenship and social class' that we will turn initially (1950). It represents perhaps the clearest expression of the relationship between citizenship and the welfare state and the central point of reference for much current debate. Before we do so, however, it will prove instructive to formulate a series of questions to guide our investigation.

- What is meant by citizenship and the rights of citizenship? Are they useful concepts?
- Should the development and extension of the rights of citizenship in Britain be seen as the progressive granting of civil, political and eventually social rights (T. H. Marshall)?
- Do the current bundle of rights conferred by the state upon its 'citizens',

and the obligations and duties they imply, together comprise a coherent whole that might usefully be understood in terms of 'citizenship'?
- What impact has the welfare state had upon patterns of class inequality, class conflict and social stratification?
- Are citizenship rights gendered? Is the welfare state patriarchal?

Citizenship, state and civil society

As we have suggested, the concept of citizenship can be seen as specifying the relationship between the state and individuals within civil society. This relationship, however, is not simply one in which a generous state concedes rights and status to its citizens. Citizenship is both *relational* and *reciprocal*. It comprises:

1 The obligations and duties of the individual within civil society *to the state*.
2 The individual's legitimate claims and expectations *of the state* (Marshall 1950: 41–2, 45–6; Roche 1992: 69–89; Pascall 1993: 121–4).

The state is often seen as *conferring* citizenship and the rights that this embodies collectively, even universally, upon individuals within civil society. Yet we should be wary of exaggerating the benevolent character of the contemporary state. States and the governments that give effect to state power are not, by nature, generous and philanthropic. Where they appear so, there is usually some underlying logic at work not immediately apparent from surface appearances. In the case of citizenship we do not have to delve very deeply to uncover it. By conferring the rights of citizenship upon its 'subjects', the state not only reasserts its authority over those thereby 'subjected' to it, and hence subjugated by it. It also effectively enters into a bargain with the individual members of civil society, a bargain constructed *on the state's own terms*. Thus, as well as considering the rights bestowed by the state upon its subjects (the right to a degree of freedom, to political representation, etc.), we should also emphasize the obligations and civic duties associated with citizenship. Here we can usefully distinguish between: (a) *formal duties* and *legally enforceable obligations* such as the duty to obey the law, to pay taxation and to perform jury service[1] and military service when called upon by the state; and (b) less obvious, *informal duties* such as the obligations of 'good citizenship'; the obligation to seek paid employment (Marshall 1950: 45–6; Pascall 1993: 121–2) and, perhaps most significantly, the duty of women to perform unpaid domestic labour within the home – as enshrined with the structure of the contemporary welfare state (Green 1985; Pateman 1989b; Gordon 1990a, b; B. Marshall 1994: 132–6).

Citizenship: inclusion and exclusion

If citizenship is a reciprocal relationship implying certain obligations and duties on the part of those on whom the status of citizen is conferred, then it is also a crucial mechanism of state boundary maintenance (Yuval-Davis

1990; Schlesinger 1991: 152–75; Anthias and Yuval-Davis 1992: 30–2, 48–50; Jenson 1993).

As Marshall claims, citizenship effectively defines those who are and those who are not members of a common culture. The term thus refers to participation in and membership of a *community*, an 'imagined' national community (Anderson 1983). Citizenship, he argues, echoing Aristotle, is a 'status bestowed upon those who are full members of a national community. All who possess the status are equal with respect to the rights and duties with which this status is endowed' (Marshall 1950: 18). Yet here again the reciprocal dimension of citizenship must be emphasized. For, as Marshall later suggests, 'citizenship . . . requires . . . a direct sense of community membership based upon loyalty to a civilisation which is a common possession' (p. 24).

As we saw in Chapter 1, the boundaries of the state, whether understood as a nation, an institution or a territory, are historically variable. So it should come as no surprise that citizenship as a status is also continuously contested, consistently renegotiated and constantly redefined (Turner 1986, 1990; Held 1989).

The evolution of the citizenship contract

The general expansion of citizenship over the past three hundred years, Marshall argues, has resulted in the extension of the rights of citizenship and the growth of the number of those entitled to its status. He divides this evolutionary account into three stages, which correspond respectively to the granting of civil, political and eventually universal social rights in the postwar period.

Civil rights

Civil rights, Marshall (1950: 8) suggests, are 'composed of the rights necessary for individual freedom – liberty of the person, freedom of speech, thought and faith, the right to own property and to conclude valid contracts, and the right to justice'. This bundle of rights effectively constitutes or 'interpellates' the freely contracting individual or the bourgeois subject, and can be identified with the rights necessary for the successful operation of a *capitalist* market economy (Macpherson 1962; Pierson 1991: 23; Scott 1994: 61–2).

The story of the development of civil rights, Marshall argues, is one of the gradual addition of new rights to a status that already existed and was held to apply to all adult members of the community – or at least to all *male* members, he adds as an afterthought. This latter point raises the important question of the *gendered* nature of these supposedly universal rights, to which we shall return.

Civil rights can be further broken down into a series of sub-categories, as follows:

- right to own property;
- right to conduct valid contracts;

- right to formal justice before the law;
- right to freedom of expression;
- right to freedom of association.

The formal universalization of these rights was essential to the generation and stimulation of mass demand within a capitalist market place, and indeed more generally to the commodification of labour (the *right* to sell labour power, and the *right* to starve if you didn't) and to the ownership of the means of production – the very defining traits of capitalism itself. Hence, the 'granting' or 'conceding' of formal civil rights to the adult male population represents little more than the universalization of capitalist principles of social organization – the 'right' to benefit from, or indeed suffer under, this system of structural inequality.

The institutions most closely associated with civil rights, Marshall observes, are the *courts of justice.*

At times Marshall is guilty of implying that civil rights, once granted, form some unassailable and uncontentious basis of liberty, autonomy and freedom. Yet as a moment's reflection reveals, civil rights are as contested and disaggregated a bundle of rights as any other. It is, for instance, somewhat ironic that Marshall's (1950: 10) first illustration of a civil right, that of *habeas corpus*[2] enshrined within the Magna Carta, should in fact have been removed in the United Kingdom by a combination of the 1939 Emergency Powers (Defence) Act and the 1974 Prevention of Terrorism Act. Similarly, as the operation of the 'sus' laws against young blacks (Reeves 1983: 144)[3] and the more recent Criminal Justice Act[4] both demonstrate, in a state in which there is no formal Bill of Rights and in which no distinction is drawn between the status of legislation concerning the rights, 'freedoms' and obligations of citizens and that relating to, say, parking offences, civil rights simply cannot be regarded as some historical invariant (cf. Oliver and Heater 1994: 75–6).

Political rights

Marshall (1950: 8) defines political rights as those which confer the power 'to participate in the exercise of political power as a member of a body invested with political authority or as an elector of the members of such a body'. The extension of citizenship to include these political rights (and the duties they in turn imply) is linked, he suggests, to the nineteenth century and is associated with the enfranchisement of the working class and the rise of mass political parties. That Marshall should situate this development in the nineteenth century is once again indicative of his deeply patriarchal assumption that citizenship is a public status and that women 'naturally' reside within the 'private' domestic sphere of home and family. For all women were denied the franchise in Britain until 1918, and it was not until 1928, after protracted political struggle, that women were granted the vote on equal terms with men.

Whereas the story of the development of civil rights, as we have already seen, relates to the gradual addition of new rights to a status that already existed, that of the development of political rights is one of the granting of an old status to new sections of the population. This occurred not only through the gradual extension of the franchise, but also through the concession of pay for MPs to enable all sections of the population to stand for (national) election.

The institutions most closely associated with the explicitly political dimension of citizenship are, not surprisingly, Parliament, local government and the ballot box.

In his account of the granting of political rights Marshall once again displays a certain tendency to treat a rather diverse bundle of rights and duties as a homogeneous status, which once conferred universally is set for all time in pillars of stone. Yet this is to invest too much in the formal status of 'citizen' at the expense of considering the mechanisms through which the rights this status implies might be realized. As Amy Bartholomew (1990: 257) notes, drawing on Marx, 'formal rights do not even out or even attend to unequal access to rights (such as unequal ability to take advantage of freedom of expression) and do produce unequal outcomes where they are applied in situations marked by substantive inequality in the first place.' The form of democratic representation is, in terms of political outcomes, *as* important as, if not *more* important than the abstract right to democratic representation itself. As contemporary calls for proportional representation, devolution and active participative democracy demonstrate, political rights do not so much provide the backcloth for struggles over social rights as constitute an arena of political contestation in their own right.

Social rights

Perhaps the most disparate category of rights identified by Marshall is that of social rights. This loose aggregation of rights comprises, according to Marshall (1950: 8), 'the whole range from the right to a modicum of economic welfare and security to the right to share to the full in the social heritage and to live the life of a civilised being according to the standards prevailing in the society'.

Such rights are realized and instantiated in the universal right to welfare. This view is shared by Bryan Turner, who suggests that citizenship, once inscribed in the institutions of the welfare state, is 'a buffer against the vagaries of the marketplace and the inequalities of the class system' (Turner 1993: xi). Yet, as the contemporary 'rolling back of the welfare state' in Britain and elsewhere clearly reveals, social rights form an arena of intense and continuing political contestation within the advanced capitalist economies. What emerges, then, is a far more complex, dynamic and contested story of the evolution, retrenchment and recasting of the rights of citizenship than Marshall's cosy evolutionism (born of post-war optimism) would imply (his view is summarized in Table 6).

Table 6 The rights of citizenship

	Civil rights	Political rights	Social rights
Period	Eighteenth century	Nineteenth century	Twentieth century
Defining principles	Individual freedom, liberty, autonomy	Political representation	Social welfare, community participation
Typical measures	*Habeas corpus;* freedom of speech, thought and faith; freedom to enter into legal contracts; freedom to acquire property	Right to vote; right to democratic political representation; payment for MPs; right to organize politically	Welfare state: free education and health care provision; comprehensive scheme of national insurance and pensions

Source: adapted from Pierson (1991: 22).

Citizenship and capitalism: enemies or sparring partners?

While citizenship is tied to the development of capitalism this raises a certain paradox. For citizenship is a system of equality, capitalism one of inequality.

This apparent tension leads Marshall (1950: 18) to the claim that 'citizenship and the capitalist class system have been at war' (cf. Turner 1986: 23; Hindess 1987: 33–42; Barbalet 1988: 76–80; van Steenbergen 1994: 148). An alternative explanation, however, is that the 'granting' of the rights of citizenship by a seemingly 'benevolent' state reflects the needs of the capitalist-patriarchal system to *legitimate* itself. This is achieved by masquerading its truly inegalitarian nature behind the rhetorical cloak of formal equality of status through the discourse of citizenship. Thus, as Turner perceptively notes, 'in acting as a buffer against the marketplace . . . social citizenship has contributed to the value consensus of late capitalist society' (Turner 1993: xi; cf. Dietz 1992: 66–7). This suggests an initial hypothesis:

> *Hypothesis 5*: The egalitarian language of citizenship and universal for-
> mal citizenship rights provides a legitimating ideology for the under-
> lying inegalitarian structures of capitalism, which remain unmodified.

Thus, citizenship and capitalist accumulation are not necessarily at war though they do embody different and contradictory principles of social justice. When they conflict – when, for instance, welfare expenditure threatens to precipitate an economic crisis of the state – the inegalitarian principles of capitalism are, within a capitalist system, necessarily asserted over the egalitarian rhetoric of citizenship. Indeed, as we shall see in Chapter 7, this is one interpretation of Thatcherism and the more general drift to the right in the advanced capitalist economies during the 1980s. This would in turn suggest that at any particular stage in the evolution of capitalism, citizenship effectively reflects those inequalities that the state can *afford* to treat as unacceptable. It is clearly in the interests of the state to be able to redefine the terms of the citizenship contract as the fortunes of the domestic economy fluctuate. The Thatcherite retrenchment of the social right to welfare and the economic crisis of the mid to late 1970s that it followed were clearly not unrelated. Indeed, much effort was directed by the ideologues of the new right at convincing the electorate that state welfare provision itself represented a threat to individual liberty and hence to fundamental civil rights. This challenge to the welfare settlement provided the basis for a recasting of the citizenship contract that had seemed unassailable throughout the postwar period.

The supposed war between citizenship and capitalism is now revealed as nothing more than a staged bout of shadow boxing. Its effect has been to detract attention from the continuing reality of capitalism's war with the proletariat and patriarchy's war with women. With the weapons of citizenship, continuous trench warfare can be replaced by a series of periodic skirmishes, the stakes of which are largely set by the state. This suggests a second hypothesis:

> *Hypothesis 6*: Capitalism and citizenship, far from being 'at war' with one another, are *in practice* complementary, since the concessions of citizenship are in fact subordinated to the needs of capitalist accumulation. Capitalism, armed with the legitimating rhetoric of citizenship, is thus better placed to divert its overt war against the proletariat into a series of minor skirmishes.

Altogether more perceptive, then, is Marshall's (1950: 7) claim that citizenship is 'the architect of legitimate social inequality' (see also Barbalet 1988: 48–50) or, rather, what is *perceived* to be legitimate social inequality. For the ongoing definition of what constitutes citizenship appears to set the bounds of what can be legitimately expected of the state in terms of its intervention within civil society to modify the worst excesses of market outcomes.

Marshall goes on to suggest that the development of citizenship, especially in the post-war period, was tied to the abatement or diffusion of class conflict. However, as he argues, 'class abatement . . . was not an attack on the class system . . . it aimed, often quite consciously, at making the class system less vulnerable to attack by alleviating its less defensible consequences' (Marshall 1950: 20). This is a perceptive point, especially given the time in which it was written, and it certainly demonstrates that selective readings of Marshall can sustain a great variety of mutually contradictory accounts (Barbalet 1988: 11; Pascall 1993: 114; Oliver and Heater 1994: 34–5). Yet despite this central ambivalence in his work, Marshall remains an apologist (however unwitting) for the role of citizenship in the reproduction and legitimation of the deeply entrenched structures of inequality within capitalist-patriarchal societies. Thus, for Marshall (1950: 38), the final outcome of the post-war extension of citizenship to include social rights is 'a structure of inequality *fairly* apportioned to unequal abilities'.

Here Marshall effectively offers a justification for patterns of inequality in post-war Britain in terms of the existence of a *meritocracy* ('to each according to their merit'). In so doing Marshall, writing from the ivory towers of Trinity College, Cambridge, would presumably see himself as looking down from somewhere near the pinnacle of this meritocratic hierarchy. The deeply conservative and somewhat patronizing tone of his comments owes its origins to his emphasis upon *formal* rather than substantive rights and on the *status* conferred by citizenship as opposed to real outcomes. He conveniently assumes a simple correspondence between equality of status and equality of opportunity, a proposition which does not stand critical scrutiny. Post-war British society was, for Marshall, characterized by *legitimate inequality*.

Welfare, citizenship and inequality: who benefits?

There is now a substantial body of evidence to suggest that far from generating an equality of opportunity, the welfare state *itself* (independent of the broader social context within which it is located) contributes to, and is a crucial factor in the reproduction of, the inequalities of class, gender and ethnicity (Titmuss 1964; Gough 1979; Williams 1989b; Gordon 1990a, b; Pierson 1991; Ginsburg 1992).

The clear danger in Marshall's account, therefore, is that it might be used to provide a conservative and complacent justification (in terms of a mythical meritocracy) for deeply entrenched structural inequalities that it in fact helps to hide (Turner 1986, 1990; Roche 1992). This complacency is further revealed in Marshall's (1950: 33) deeply condescending suggestion that 'equality of status is more important than equality of outcome.'

This remark, however well-intentioned, could perhaps only have been made by someone with both status and income. Equality of status does not buy many loaves of bread, or care for many children. Thus, as Wendy Brown (1992: 19) pointedly observes, 'it is as gratuitous to dwell upon an impoverished single mother's freedom to pursue her own individual interests in society as it is to carry on about the private property rights of the homeless.' In other words, Marshall should try telling a single mother that her impoverishment is acceptable and legitimate because at least she has a *formal* parity of status with, say, an employed male member of a nuclear family. Similarly, he is unlikely to be able to convince a prisoner of conscience being tortured at the hands of an authoritarian regime that this is somehow acceptable because at least he or she has a formal equality of status enshrined within international human rights legislation.

This discussion leads us to two further hypotheses, the first relating directly to Marshall's own claims, the second more general:

Hypothesis 7: The impact of the welfare state in advanced capitalist societies has not been, as Marshall suggests, 'progressively [to] abate class inequalities' but rather progressively to abate class consciousness while in fact legitimating deep-seated structures of class inequality.

Hypothesis 8: The impact of the welfare state in contemporary patriarchal societies has not been progressively to abate inequalities of gender, sexuality and ethnicity, but rather progressively to abate the forms of political consciousness to which they give rise.

In a defence of these twin theses it is useful to begin by examining Richard Titmuss's (1964) path-breaking work on the redistributive effects of the welfare state.

Diluting Beveridge: welfare access and welfare outcomes

Titmuss begins with an important observation which exposes one of the central assumptions underlying Marshall's account of citizenship. 'Equal opportunity of access by right of citizenship to education, medical care and social insurance is not the same thing as equality of outcome' (Titmuss 1964: 357). This provides the basis for a detailed investigation of the actual functioning of welfare services in Britain in the immediate post-war period. Titmuss uncovers their now widely acknowledged inegalitarian consequences (for more recent accounts see Williams 1989b; Bryson 1992):

National Health Service. Higher income groups and the white majority *tend* to make better use of the service by virtue of their greater knowledge of their formal rights and their relative social and cultural proximity to the service providers. As a consequence the affluent middle classes tend to receive more specialist attention, occupy more of the beds in better-equipped hospitals, receive more elective surgery and have better maternity care (Townsend and Davidson 1982; Goodin *et al.* 1987). Clearly these tendencies have only been exacerbated by the comprehensive restructuring of the National Health Service under consecutive Thatcher and Major Governments (Papadakis and Taylor-Gooby 1987).

Pensions. Throughout the post-war period the flat rate and, subsequently, earnings-related pensions scheme has consistently benefited the relatively affluent at the expense of the working class, a tendency merely compounded by a series of tax allowances on private pension schemes, subsidies to schemes sponsored by employers and the tax deductibility of life assurance policies. Thus, as John Scott (1994: 73) notes, even before the introduction of earnings-related state pensions, the effect of post-war pension reform was to the significant benefit of the middle classes (cf. Ginsburg 1992: 149–52). More glaring still is the gender redistributive effects of state pension schemes which have played an important role in the 'feminization of poverty' in Britain (Groves 1992; Lewis 1992: 98–9; Scott 1994: 70). Thus, as Gillian Pascall (1993: 121) observes,

> the core problem for Beveridge was the question of male employment and how to replace the security of men's wages in unemployment, sickness and retirement . . . Insurance is still the privileged form of social benefit, irretrievably tied to paid employment (despite family responsibility credits). Benefits arising out of parenthood or unpaid care have their lesser entitlement registered in their lesser value.

Housing. Even in 1964 many council tenants were effectively subsiding owner-occupiers owing to the differential effects of local rates, housing subsidies, interest rates and mortgage interest tax relief. In recent years the situation has become still worse for public or private tenants, leading Julian Le Grand (1982: 100) to conclude his own study by suggesting that when the total picture is considered, we find 'owner-occupiers receiving more than private or public tenants and the better off receiving more than the less well off' (cf. Hay 1992a).

Education. If education is heavily financed by the state (which it is), and if proportionately more children from better-off homes benefit in terms of passing more exams at higher grades (which invariably they do), then the system will be redistributive in favour of the affluent middle class. As Lois Bryson (1992: 128) points out, a 'virtually universal finding is that education is the public provision whose benefits are most systematically related to income'. Le Grand's research, for instance, indicates that in 1978 the wealthiest one-fifth of the population received approximately three times the state-funded educational resources of the poorest fifth (Le Grand 1982: 57).

This leads us to a further hypothesis:

> *Hypothesis 9*: The welfare state is not merely a mechanism by which the benevolent state intervenes to correct market generated structural inequality, but is a system of social stratification in its own right, 'an active force in the ordering of social relations' (Esping-Ånderson 1990).

Thus, however counterintuitive it might seem, it is difficult not to concur with Le Grand (1982: 3) when he suggests that 'almost all public expenditure on the social services in Britain benefits the better off to a greater extent than the poor.'

Towards a critique of Marshall

The above discussion suggests a series of fairly significant critiques of Marshall's evolutionary account of citizenship in the post-war period.

Marshall is all too keen and premature in his celebration of the redistributive effects of the welfare state. This leads him to view existing patterns of inequality in 1949–50 as a product of an increasingly meritocratic equality of opportunity facilitated by a benevolent welfare state.

Marshall is somewhat patronizing and superior in his assumption that a general shared civilization or universal status can be specified which would define an acceptable minimum suitable for the working class. The state is here held responsible for lifting an 'underclass' from its 'natural' condition of squalor. Provided 'they' too can participate in the white, middle-class and patriarchal culture which, we are told, is a 'common possession' (Marshall 1950: 18), then they no longer have a legitimate complaint against the state. It is important to note that Marshall is, in many respects, merely giving voice to the spirit of the times. His optimism is in fact characteristic of much Fabian literature which seeks to ameliorate inequality through incremental social reform within the confines of advanced capitalism. In this respect, the Fabians are rather like those environmentalists who seek solutions to global ecological crisis by collecting aluminium cans in plastic bin-liners for recycling – such strategies may temporarily alleviate the symptoms but the fundamental pathology remains.

Marshall's analysis, as numerous commentators have suggested, is

Anglocentric, evolutionary and historicist,[5] positing a fixed law of historical development (Giddens 1985; Turner 1986, 1990; Mann 1987; Pierson 1991; Roche 1992). Clearly the Thatcherite ideological crusade to reassert civil over social rights and the subsequent rolling back of the welfare state must lead us to challenge any simple evolutionary account of citizenship. As Tom Bottomore (1992) points out, Marshall's analysis of the progression from civil to political and ultimately social rights tends to obscure the fact that civil and political rights have not been established once and for all in some near-perfect form, as the basis from which social rights can develop, but are themselves also capable of further extension.

Marshall develops a highly idealized and abstract account of the structures of the welfare state, which he tends to reduce to the simple expression of the social rights of citizenship. As our discussion of the redistributive effects of the welfare state has demonstrated, the reality is far more complex. In painting a somewhat idyllic picture, Marshall conveniently overlooks what Pierson (1991: 202–3) usefully describes as the 'dark' side of welfare – the expansion of the state's interventionist power within civil society (cf. Rosenthal 1983). For, *welfare is the most significant structuring influence and mode of intervention of the state within civil society.* As an institution, the welfare state possesses an immense ideological, repressive and surveillance capacity – a capacity which has been consistently enhanced and extended since the war.

The functions of the contemporary welfare state are not as unambiguously benign as Marshall would lead us to believe, as a quick glance at some of the routine practices of the welfare state clearly reveals.

Structuring dependency. The welfare state exercises a profound and structuring influence over many aspects of the lived experience and reality of existence of broad sections of society – particularly women, dependent upon its interventions (McIntosh 1978; Balbo 1987; Hernes 1987; Fraser 1989; Pateman 1989b; Gordon 1990a).

Ideology and surveillance. Welfare agencies exercise a significant *surveillance* role in the supervision and monitoring of particular sub-populations of society 'in exchange' for welfare. This role is often tied inextricably to forms of ideological dissemination through welfare interventions directly within the home. Here we can think of schemes such as Home Start. This is a form of community-based social work in which volunteers who are generally white middle-class mothers visit (predominantly single) mothers 'in difficulty' with the aim of cultivating an increased sense of self-worth and confidence, yet without in any way altering the material circumstances of their existence. This might be interpreted as the harnessing of conventional middle-class mothers to draw 'deviant' women into line. Home Start thus attaches a form of individuated surveillance to what is primarily an ideological intervention. The effect is to reinforce within the home the patriarchal assumptions that: mothers 'naturally' care for children, their own needs being secondary; mothers must take responsibility for the material and social circumstances in which they find themselves; and even in conditions of intense poverty it is still mothers who are failing if their care does not measure up to the standards of their white, middle-class 'overseers'. A second and somewhat less specific example is social security. When people 'sign on' today, they enter into, and necessarily expose themselves to, a reciprocal relationship. This is characterized by surveillance on the part of the state, and an obligation to 'prove' an active pursuit of paid employment on the part of the claimant. Both of these examples (which are by no means unrepresentative of the experience of many 'consumers' of welfare) suggest a somewhat different conception of social citizenship from that elevated within Marshall's account.

Coercion. The relationship between the institutions of the welfare state and benefits claimants is very often a coercive and repressive one. Dependants must generally conform to certain norms defined by the state in demonstrating their continuing 'worthiness' and in 'proving' their need for benefit. Social workers, for instance, routinely control access to day-care and holiday schemes. In so doing they often make such 'extra' benefits conditional upon the modification of behaviour they consider 'deviant' or undesirable on the part of the potential beneficiary.

Marshall places virtually no emphasis at all on the *obligations* and *duties* of the citizen in relationship to citizenship. Citizenship is, as Roche (1992: 230) notes, a 'national social contract' and as such is a reciprocal relationship of mutual obligation, albeit one conducted on the state's own terms. It is a contract specifying the relationship of the state to individuals within civil society, *but also* the duties, often quite onerous, of the individual *to the state*. In any respecification of the citizenship contract, then, it is vital to consider the obligations implied by the bundle of rights conceded by a seemingly benevolent state. For, as Marx demonstrated, the 'freeing' of the mass of the population from ties of feudal 'obligation' through the granting of certain civil rights was in fact part of their very subordination to the power of capital. The new condition of 'freedom' is more dispassionately decoded by Marx (1867) as the 'freedom' to dispose of labour power as a commodity, the 'freedom' from any other means of subsistence and hence the freedom to starve otherwise (cf. Sayer 1987: 131–3).

Beyond citizenship? The Wollstonecraft dilemma

If the above discussion reveals a number of limitations and oversights within the dominant account of the development of citizenship rights in Britain, then there is nothing in this critique alone that would require a fundamental rejection of Marshall's basic framework. A reworked neo-Marshallian conception of citizenship might well prove itself capable of transcending the limitations detailed above. Such a framework would have to prove itself more sensitive to: (a) outcomes; (b) the distinction between formal and substantive rights; (c) the constantly contested and renegotiated nature of citizenship; and particularly (d) the obligations and duties of citizenship (see Turner 1986, 1990; Bottomore 1992; Roche 1992; Twine 1994). Yet this is not the end of the story. For two altogether more fundamental weaknesses can be identified within the dominant paradigm which threaten to gnaw away at the very foundations of the Marshallian conception of civil, political and social rights, if not that of citizenship altogether. The first concerns the apparent incommensurability of civil and social rights and the implications for the concept of citizenship. The second relates to the masculinism inherent in the Marshallian understanding of citizenship.

The incommensurability of social and civil rights

Marshall fails to consider the tensions between different forms of citizenship rights. There is an implicit assumption in his work that the bundle of (civil, political and social) rights which comprises citizenship is logically coherent, defining a hermetic and universal status conferred by their possession. This sits rather uneasily with Marshall's comments on the relationship between the rights of citizenship and the logic of capitalism itself. For, while *civil rights* (principally property rights) are required for the maintenance and legitimation of capitalist accumulation (Marshall 1950: 8–10), *political rights* are, for Marshall, 'full of potential danger to the capitalist system' (p. 25), and *social rights* represent a profound threat to the inequalities generated by the structures of capitalist accumulation.

Whether democratic political rights are seen as potentially threatening to the inegalitarian structures of capitalism or, in Lenin's (1917: 269) famous phrase, as providing the 'best possible political shell for capitalism' is certainly debatable, though most commentators would now probably concur with Lenin (see Alford and Friedland 1985: 47–54, 174–81, 279–87, 333–40; Przeworski 1985; Walzer 1985; Bowles and Gintis 1987). Yet what is clear is that civil rights and social rights are premised upon fundamentally opposed principles of social justice: individuality, liberty and freedom on the one hand; community, collectivity and redistributive social democracy on the other (cf. Fraser and Gordon 1994). Indeed, it is precisely this contradiction that has been exposed by the new right to provide a justification for the rolling back of the state in terms of a reassertion of civil over social rights.

Here we can usefully return to Claus Offe's analysis of the structural form of welfare capitalism, discussed in Chapter 3. As we saw, Offe identified an 'organizational disjunction' at the heart of the welfare state regime, which had the effect of separating the conflicting imperatives of capitalist accumulation and political legitimation.

The relevance of this observation becomes immediately apparent if we consider that civil rights can be considered as specifying the relationship between individuals (as workers or consumers) and the economic system; political rights that between individuals (as electors) and the politico-administrative system; and social rights that between individuals (as potential welfare recipients) and the welfare (or politico-normative) system (see Figure 4).

This would add further weight to the suggestion that while civil rights epitomize capitalist principles of social organization, social rights and the welfare expenditure they imply represent a potential drain on profits and are thus antithetical to the capitalist growth imperative itself.[6] When the two principles of social organization and social justice conflict – most obviously in times of economic crisis – the short-term interests of capitalist accumulation (and hence civil rights) will be asserted over those of public legitimation (and hence social rights). The retrenchment of social rights through the

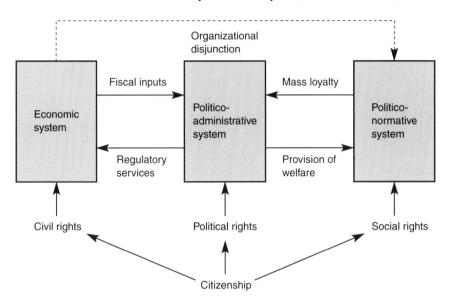

Figure 4   Contradictions of citizenship.

rolling back of the frontiers of the welfare state (and the supposed cutting of the 'burden of taxation') thus tends to be associated with periods of state fiscal crisis (O'Connor 1973; Habermas 1975). Any resulting legitimation deficit may be met by: (a) a more authoritarian role for the state to quell unrest; by (b) attempts to justify hardship (such as Mrs Thatcher's famous 'if it's not hurting, it's not working'); or more likely (c) a combination of the two.

So, to summarize, civil and social rights express fundamentally antithetical principles of social organization. During times of economic prosperity and growth the conflicting imperatives of accumulation and legitimation, civil and social rights, may be temporarily reconciled. Yet in periods of fiscal crisis something has to give. Within a capitalist social formation the short-term interests of the economic system will inevitably be asserted over those of the welfare system and hence the legitimating *luxury* of social rights will be subordinated to the economic *necessity* for capitalism of civil rights.

The patriarchal welfare state

Perhaps the most telling of all of the various criticisms of Marshall's work and 'the dominant citizenship paradigm' (Roche 1992) is that made by a number of feminists (Pateman 1989b; Dietz 1992; Pascall 1993; Fraser and Gordon 1994). Within this literature, Marshall stands charged of a failure to grasp the profoundly patriarchal nature of the welfare state and hence social rights. As Carole Pateman (1989b: 189) persuasively argues, Marshall's confidence in a status accorded to those who are full members of a community overlooks the fact that the formal status of citizenship can be held by categories of people (such as women and ethnic minorities) who, though they may possess the right to vote, do not thereby possess full and effective social membership.

Moreover, as Chantal Mouffe (1993: 80) suggests, 'who a "citizen" is, what a citizen does, and the arena within which *he* acts have been constructed in the masculine image' (emphasis added). Though women are 'theoretically' equal as citizens, the continuing sexual division of labour, the 'feminization of poverty' and the far greater involvement of women with care for children and the elderly contradicts this formal parity.

The broad architecture of the welfare state, to use Pateman's phrase, reflects a patriarchal division of labour in which full citizenship is associated with waged work and its benefit structure is predicated upon the superiority of this model. Caring, as unpaid domestic work, is seen as 'private' and is thus not recognized as a significant contribution to the *public* good.

In the face of a deeply patriarchal welfare state the feminist movement is confronted by the stark terms of the 'Wollstonecraft dilemma' (Pateman 1989: 195–204):

> to demand equality is to accept the patriarchal conception of citizenship that implies that women must become like men, while to insist that women's distinctive attributes, capacities and activities be given expression and valued as contributing to citizenship is to demand the impossible because such difference is precisely what patriarchal citizenship excludes.
>
> (Mouffe 1993: 80)

As such the Wollstonecraft dilemma is perhaps merely a particular expression of the central strategic dilemma of contemporary feminist political theory and praxis: if the state is indeed a core patriarchal institution, then to lobby the state is to confer authority upon it, thus subordinating one's demands to its inherent masculinism; yet not to lobby the state is to limit feminist struggle to a series of disjointed skirmishes around the peripheral edge of patriarchal power within advanced societies (cf. Brown 1992).

There is no obvious route out of this paradox. With respect to citizenship, its effect is to leave a series of unresolved questions:

> Should we try to achieve citizenship for women, in the knowledge of how inadequately it has served women in the past, and how fundamental are the problems? Should we reject it, as a state of grace reserved for men? Should we try to transform the notion of citizenship to acknowledge the way that the public/domestic divide has undermined women's participation in citizenship as usually understood?
>
> (Pascall 1993: 124–5)

Given this unenviable choice Pascall understandably prefers the last option. Yet there is perhaps an alternative: to conceive of citizenship as itself a contradictory and paradoxical status – seemingly universal and egalitarian in its conception, yet marginalizing and hierarchical in the relations of domination that it sustains (cf. Marx 1843: 219). Citizenship is here understood as a legitimating rhetorical device, a mirage, an illusion. Citizenship is a myth 'which helps to make present reality appear to be what it too rarely is in reality, namely potentially just, rational and bearable' (Roche 1992: 224).

Notes

1 An obligation until 1974 restricted in Britain to those with property (Oliver and Heater 1994: 94).
2 *Habeas corpus* is the right not to be unlawfully detained, the right to demand to be brought before a court to determine the legality of the arrest.
3 The 'sus' laws refer to Section 4 of the 1824 Vagrancy Act, under which the police retain the power to arrest anyone they consider to be 'loitering with the intent to commit a felonous offence'.
4 Removing, among other things, the right to peaceful protest and the right to remain silent without incrimination.
5 *Anglocentric*: assuming a common 'national' culture by virtue of which citizenship of the British state might be understood. The existence of a homogeneous and inclusive national culture coextensive with the administrative boundaries of a state is, as we saw in Chapter 1, at best extremely rare. As a description of the contemporary British experience it is scarcely credible, as a moment's reflection on Scotland – a 'stateless nation' within an alien state – would suggest (McCrone 1992; cf. Nairn 1981). Marshall is thus guilty of: (a) presenting an unduly homogeneous and idealized image of 'Englishness'; and (b) extrapolating from this mythical experience to imply the existence of a common British culture and identity (Turner 1986: 46). It is surely telling that there is no reference to Scotland, Wales or Northern Ireland in Marshall's entire discussion of 'UK' citizenship.

   Evolutionist and *historicist*: assuming a single unfolding historical dynamic relating to the inexorable development of citizenship through the progressive (in both senses) granting of civil, political and ultimately social rights. As Maurice Roche (1992: 227) notes, 'whatever the pleasing evolutionary logic of this story, it takes on . . . the character of a myth when compared to the details of group and class struggles over citizens' rights and when compared with the variety of alternative sequences which, equally plausibly, could be read into the record of British history' (cf. Giddens 1982, 1985; Mann 1987).
6 It is important to note that this does not necessarily imply that they are antithetical to capitalism itself. For capitalism is more than a growth imperative. As a social formation it requires a degree of legitimation which may in part be secured through seemingly non-productive welfare expenditure. In this way, the structures of a welfare state, rather like those of liberal democracy, may provide a social and political shell for capitalist relations. None the less, for the purpose of legitimation, capitalist states do draw upon the discourse of social rights, which is fundamentally anathema to the conception of social justice implied by a liberal notion of civil rights.

Part **III**
RE-STATING CRISIS

5 Theories *of* state crisis: legitimation crisis *or* political overload?

In Part II we began to develop a theoretically informed analysis of the state in post-war Britain, charting the emergence and consolidation of a Keynesian welfare state and the associated elite post-war consensus. We saw how these developments have been related to the extension of citizenship to include the social right to welfare, and to the development of corporatist forms of interest intermediation to supplement purely democratic forms of representation. Yet we also saw that, despite appearances, many of the economic structures of the post-war period were inherited largely intact from the inter-war years. The result was a deeply contradictory settlement whose tensions were temporarily hidden by the post-war economic boom but were to be cruelly exposed by the slump into global recession during the mid-1970s.

In Part III we move on to consider the disintegration not only of the consensus but, more fundamentally, of the state regime of which it was an expression. Before we can consider the specific nature of this crisis, however, we must devote some attention to the concept of *state crisis* itself. In this chapter, then, we will pursue what might at first appear to be something of a theoretical detour, by considering the internal contradictions, crisis tendencies and crisis management techniques of capitalist state forms. Such a generic theory of state crisis, as I hope to demonstrate, puts us in a much better position to analyse and interpret the uniqueness and specificity of the crisis of the British state that was to surface in the mid-1970s. In the next chapter we will move on to consider how such a theoretical framework might sensitize our analysis of the crisis of the British Keynesian welfare state in the 1970s, helping us to identify the structural and ideological discontinuities enshrined within Britain's post-war reconstruction and shedding some light on the moment of crisis itself.

However, for the time being we will concern ourselves with the major theoretical perspectives that have sought to account for the crisis tendencies and crisis management techniques of advanced capitalist state regimes during the 1970s. Once again we can usefully begin by identifying a number of key questions.

- What is a crisis of the state and how might we identify one? How would we recognize one if we saw one or, indeed, experienced one?

- What is meant by a 'legitimation crisis' (Habermas 1975)? Can this concept help us to understand the crisis tendencies of advanced capitalist state regimes in the post-war period?
- Was the crisis of the advanced capitalist state form in the 1970s a fundamental crisis *of* capitalism or merely a crisis *within* capitalism? How widespread was such a crisis?
- What is meant by 'political overload' (King 1975; Douglas 1976) and 'ungovernibility' (Crozier *et al.* 1975; Rose 1979)? Are such concepts useful in helping us to identify a 'crisis of democracy' (Brittan 1975; Crozier *et al.* 1975) in the 1970s?

In this chapter we will concentrate on the two most prominent interpretations of the crisis of the advanced capitalist state in the mid to late 1970s. Though these accounts come from opposite ends of the political spectrum (the neo-Marxist left and the new right respectively), their basic diagnoses of the crisis afflicting the British state in the 1970s are remarkably similar (see especially Offe 1979; Birch 1984). Needless to say, their prescriptions diverge considerably.

1 The theory of 'legitimation crisis' principally associated with the critical theorists, Jürgen Habermas and Claus Offe. This body of neo-Marxist theory aims to explain the origins of the crisis of 'late capitalism' in the 1970s (see especially Habermas 1975, 1992; Offe 1984, 1985).
2 The theory of 'overload' and political 'ungovernibility' initially formulated in the mid-1970s by, among others, Anthony King, Michel Crozier, Samuel Huntingdon, Joji Watanuki and Samuel Brittan. This body of theory has proved highly influential in shaping the neo-liberal critique of the welfare state and informing the state projects of the Thatcherite and Reaganite new right (see especially Crozier *et al.* 1975; King 1975; Douglas 1976; Rose 1979).

Towards a critical theory of crisis

Before we begin to review the existing literature on state crisis it will prove instructive to develop a few crucial concepts and analytical distinctions.

Crisis as discursive unification

If we are to adjudicate between conflicting theories of crisis we should at least decide what it is that we wish them to explain: *what exactly is a crisis?* Crucial as such a question might seem, we have to search long and hard to find an answer within either of the contending theoretical perspectives. Indeed, theorists of both camps seem united in subscribing to the view that although it is very difficult to define tightly the condition of crisis, when one comes along we'll definitely know about it. The exception is Habermas (1975: 1), who returns to the term's usage within medical discourse, where it refers to 'the phase of an illness in which it is decided whether or not the organism's self-healing powers are sufficient for recovery' (cf. Koselleck 1988:

103–4). This is immediately significant, for it suggests, as Habermas himself notes, that 'the crisis cannot be separated from the viewpoint of the one who is undergoing it.' This in turn implies that crisis is as much a *lived* experience as it is an objective property of a system – an important point to which we shall return.

If we trace the etymology of the term, we find that this fusion of subjective perceptions and objective conditions is in fact crucial to the origins of the term. 'Crisis', from the Greek κρισις, κριηειυ – literally 'to decide' – is a moment of decisive intervention, a moment of rupture and a moment of transformation (Keane 1984: 10–13; Hay 1994b). Crisis, then, is not merely a moment of impending breakdown, but a moment of transition, a moment of transformation – a moment in which a new trajectory is imposed upon the system *in* and *through* crisis. Contradiction and crisis are not synonymous. Crisis is a *lived* (and hence subjective) *experience* and a moment of action and intervention in the shaping of institutions and the reshaping of the state. For a crisis to provide the opportunity for decisive intervention it must be perceived as so doing – it must be seen as a moment in which a decisive intervention *can* (and perhaps *must*) be made. As John Keane (1984: 11–12) notes, crisis is a process of destruction and construction, crisis is *Dämmerung* – dusk and dawn.

The temporality of crisis

[T]ime is to politics what space is to geometry.

(Debray 1973: 90)

Crisis, as Régis Debray notes, is an intense and contested moment of political time. Furthermore, 'time is clearly not a homogeneous continuum; each period of social development, each social grouping has its ups and downs in time . . . political time moves faster in periods of crisis, and stagnates in times of regression' (Debray 1973: 90). Hence it is crucial that we consider the temporality of crisis. In so doing it is important that we distinguish between two moments of crisis: the *synchronic* and the *diachronic* (see Figure 5).

A *synchronic* analysis focuses upon the contradictions and crisis tendencies existing within a particular system at a particular moment. Thus, a synchronic analysis of (state) crisis is one that effectively takes a snapshot of the (state) structures existing at a specific point in time, using this as the basis from which to *read off* the internal contradictions and crisis tendencies of the system (the state form). Such an analysis of crisis is most clearly developed by Offe (1984, 1985) as we shall see in more detail in the next chapter.

A *diachronic* analysis, on the other hand, focuses upon the historical development of a system (for our purposes, the state) with time. A diachronic analysis of crisis looks at the actual way in which a crisis *develops and unfolds historically* within a system or set of structures; the moment of crisis itself; and the structural transformation or disintegration of the state in response to crisis. Such a dynamic conception of crisis is pioneered by Habermas in his analysis of the *'logic of crisis displacement'*, to which we turn in the next section.

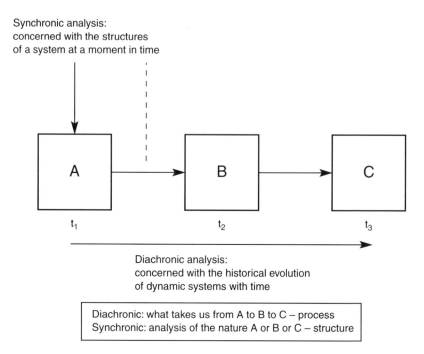

Figure 5   The temporality of crisis: synchronic and diachronic.

Legitimation crisis and the 'logic of crisis displacement'

In *Legitimation Crisis* (1975), reputed to be one of the most dense and difficult works of social theory ever written,[1] Habermas develops an extremely
perceptive and path-breaking account of the crisis tendencies of late capitalism. At the core of his theory of state crisis is the distinction that he draws
between 'system crises' and 'identity crises'. By 'system crisis' Habermas refers to a breakdown of *system integration*. A system crisis is thus a structural
and *objective* property of the system in question, and is associated with the
accumulation of unresolved 'steering problems'. As he argues, 'steering problems can have crisis effects if (and only if) they cannot be resolved within
the range of possibility that is circumscribed by the original principles of the
society, [system or state]' (Habermas 1975: 7).

System crises, then, are characterized by the exhaustion of techniques
for coping with the internal contradictions and steering difficulties of the
system as they arise. A hypothetical state regime dependent for its continuing stability upon the achievement of goal A (say, capitalist accumulation)
and goal B (say, legitimation) can be said to be in crisis if A can no longer
be achieved without compromising B, or vice versa.

The classic Marxian example of system crises would be the crises of
overproduction to which capitalist economies are prone owing to their in-
adequate coordination of production and consumption (Kautsky 1892; Baran

and Sweezy 1966; Clarke 1994: 24–36, 97–112, 176–207). Rather more spe-cifically, we might identify the Winter of Discontent of late 1978 and early 1979[2] as a crisis of the system of corporatist intermediation – the point at which corporatist conciliation could no longer secure the degree of wage restraint necessary to stave off impending 'fiscal crisis'.

An 'identity crisis', by contrast, is defined as a breakdown of *social integration* arising when members of society become aware of the existence of a system crisis and, in Habermas's (1975: 3) terms 'feel their identity threatened'. An identity crisis is thus tied to *subjective perceptions* as opposed to objective conditions. In identifying identity crises, Habermas is referring to situations in which a subjective or perceptual link is made by individuals (or groups of individuals) between their own direct experiences and a generic condition of crisis. Individuals in such a context interpret and make sense of changes in their routine modes of existence in terms of a failure of the system (in this case the state), treating their experiences as confirmation of the crisis diagnosis.

Identity crises thus refer to the wide-scale *perception* within civil society (or the 'socio-cultural system') of system crisis. Now, at this stage it should be noted that perceptions do not necessarily mirror objective conditions terribly accurately. Indeed, we might go as far as to suggest that perceptions of crisis are necessarily partial and thus distort 'reality' in some way (Hay 1995b). When we also consider the lengths that governments, parties and social movements go to in influencing, constructing and even deconstructing perceptions of crisis we should be rather wary of implying some simple one-to-one correspondence between 'unresolved steering problems' on the one hand and societal perceptions of crisis on the other. For, as Paul t'Hart (1993: 41) perceptively notes, 'the most important instrument of crisis management is language. Those who are able to define what the crisis is all about also hold the key to defining the strategies appropriate for [its] resolution' (cf. Hay 1994b, c). Once this is acknowledged, it is possible to conceive of the mobilization (by the tabloid media, for instance) of perceptions of crisis which bear little or no relationship whatsoever to underlying structural con-tradictions. Yet although the distinction between system and lived crisis might provide a means to recognize the politically contested and discur-sively mediated nature of crisis, this is something Habermas himself seems rather oblivious to.

Habermas subdivides system crises into 'economic crises' arising within the economic system and 'rationality crises' which relate to the political system. Rationality crises refer to the incapacity of the state to cope with the conflicting demands placed upon it. They are characterized by the exhaus-tion of the repertoire of steering mechanisms and crisis management tech-niques available to reconcile competing political objectives. The result is the accumulation of political steering problems, growing irrationality, contradic-tion and eventually crisis.

Habermas also subdivides identity crises – into 'legitimation crises' arising within the political system, and 'motivation crises' which relate to the socio-cultural system. Legitimation crises refer to the subjective perception of crisis within the political system, resulting in the withdrawal of the legitimacy

Table 7   Systems crises and identity crises

Subsystem	System crisis	Identity crisis
Economic	Economic crisis	–
Political	Rationality crisis	Legitimation crisis
Socio-cultural	–	Motivation crisis

Source: Habermas (1975: 45).

that society confers upon the state. As Habermas (1975: 69) argues more generally, 'if governmental crisis management fails, it lags behind the programmatic demands that *it has placed upon itself.* The penalty of this failure is the withdrawal of legitimacy.' By motivation crisis, Habermas refers not only to a withdrawal of societal legitimation for a state regime, but also to a more fundamental breakdown in the social and cultural practices upon which the state regime relies. Motivation crises thus imply 'a discrepancy between the need for motives declared by the state, the educational and occupational systems on the one hand, and the motivation supplied by the socio-cultural system on the other' (Habermas 1979: 74–5). These, then, are the key terms Habermas deploys in developing his account of the crisis tendencies of capitalist state forms (see Table 7).

The originality of Habermas's contribution lies in three key factors:

1 The emphasis that he places upon the *lived* (or at least perceived) nature of moments of crisis.
2 His examination of the relationship *between* system and lived crisis, between structural contradictions and the experiences and perceptions to which they give rise.
3 His development of a *diachronic* analysis of the crisis tendencies within state systems and their political consequences.

It is to his model of the evolution of state crises that we now turn.

Habermas invites us to picture a hypothetical capitalist economy unregulated by the state (the archetypal free market) and comprised inevitably of a multitude of competing capitals. Such an economy, he argues, like all capitalist economies is prone to crisis. For no individual capital competing for its very survival will sacrifice its own interest in the general interest. Contradictions or 'steering problems' which inevitably arise within such a free market economy can never be resolved and accumulate until they eventually pose a terminal threat to capitalism itself. So a capitalist economy without regulation is inherently unstable (cf. Offe 1975; Aglietta 1979; Jänicke 1990: 8).

Enter the state as a more-or-less ideal collective capitalist:

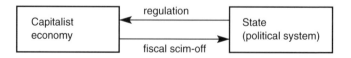

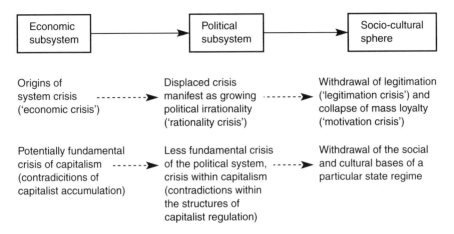

Figure 6 The 'logic of crisis displacement'.
Source: adapted from Habermas (1975, 1979, 1992: 278–81).

Habermas argues that the state must necessarily intervene within the capitalist economy to secure the conditions necessary for ongoing and stable
capitalist accumulation. Such intervention and regulation, however, is constrained by the continual need of the state to secure its own legitimacy
within civil society (the socio-cultural sphere).

The intervention of the state within the economy establishes what
Habermas terms the *'logic of crisis displacement'* (see Figure 6). By this he
means that fundamental (systems) crises originating within the economy
(and which previously would have rung the death-knell of capitalism *per se*)
now become the responsibility of the political system (the state) as supreme
regulator of the economy. The crisis is thus displaced from the economy
(which does not have the internal capacity to resolve it) to the political
system (which might have). Here it becomes manifest as a 'rationality crisis'
– a breakdown of politico-economic rationality and a failure in the state's
regulation of the capitalist economy. To summarize, if an economic crisis
does arise it is deemed to be the responsibility of the state, and thus becomes
a crisis of political rationality.

The result of this logic of crisis displacement is that a potentially profound crisis of capitalism deriving from its inherent economic contradictions
and the inability of individual capitals to respond to collective need through
collective altruism becomes, through displacement, merely a crisis of a *particular regime* of the capitalist state. A potentially terminal crisis of capitalism
may thus become, through displacement, a crisis of a more transient state
regime, such as the Keynesian-patriarchal welfare state. A crisis that might
potentially have threatened to ring the death-knell of capitalism altogether
now becomes translated into a crisis that merely exhausts a particular regime
of the capitalist state at a particular stage in its historical evolution.

This deals with the displacement of crises from the economic to the
political. Once a political or rationality crisis arises, Habermas argues, it is

likely to become the subject of a 'legitimation crisis' of the state. For the state's legitimacy has become dependent upon its ability to regulate 'success-fully' the economy (where 'success' is here measured in terms of capitalist economic growth). The societal consent upon which the state regime relies is thus threatened by its failure to deliver fiscal responsibility and sustained economic growth (two of the 'programmatic demands that it has placed upon itself'). The very legitimacy of the state regime evaporates as individu-als, whether mobilized by the media or not, begin to equate changes in their lived experiences (price increases, food and petrol shortages, wide-scale strike activity and so forth) as symptomatic of a generic condition of political and economic crisis.

Habermas certainly formulates an original, perceptive and provocative (if somewhat abstract and overgeneralized) analysis of the development of political crises and the threat to the state's very legitimacy that they pose. Yet his account is not unproblematic. For in the somewhat heady climate of the late 1960s and early 1970s in which these ideas were conceived, Habermas became perhaps just a little carried away with the 'spirit of 1968' (see Held 1982: 189–93; Kellner 1989: 200). His scarcely constrained optimism led him to the enthusiastic suggestion that once a legitimation crisis exists there is a real possibility of a slow, revolutionary yet democratic transformation of the state and society from below. Comforting though such a diagnosis must have been, subsequent experience exposes Habermas's wishful thinking for what it was. He conveniently overlooked the potential inherent in the crisis of the 1970s for the expression of a new 'state project', such as Thatcherism, able to secure all the legitimacy that it required for a regressive and author-itarian project to restructure the state in response to crisis.

Habermas's theory of crisis displacement can be summarized as follows (see also Figure 7):

- the capitalist economy is inherently unstable and prone to crisis;
- the state engages in attempts to regulate the economy while seeking to maintain its societal legitimation;
- rationality crises develop as the state fails to reconcile these conflicting demands;
- legitimation crises emerge as confidence in the political system is under-mined by such rationality deficits;
- in the context of crisis still greater pressures are brought to bear upon the political system that it continually fails to satisfy;
- a vicious circle is thereby initiated;
- the vicious circle is broken by state failure and slow revolution from below.

Snakes and ladders and state crisis

If we are going to take Habermas's model seriously, and I would suggest that we should, then it is first essential that we do something to resurrect it from his own, rather utopian, illusions (such as the inevitability of a slow demo-cratic revolution from below). Thus we have to consider the structural trans-formation of the state in *response* to crisis, something, as we have seen, that Habermas simply ignores.

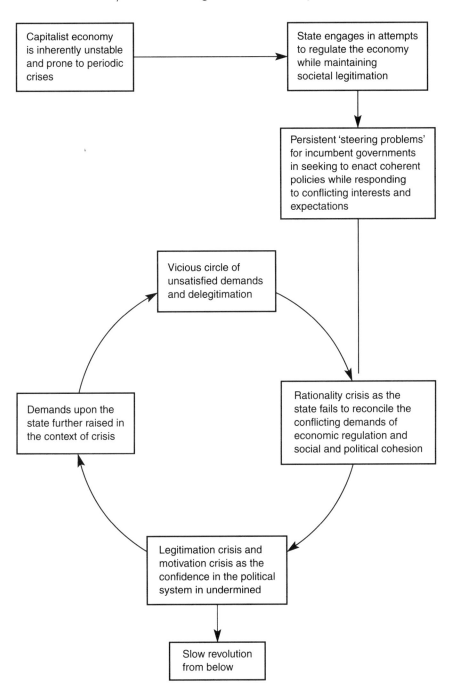

Figure 7 Legitimation crisis.
Source: adapted from Held (1984: 326).

In so doing, we need to make two major qualifications to Habermas's analysis. These can be expressed in terms of two related hypotheses.

Hypothesis 10: Capitalist states may undergo structural transformation in response to periodic (legitimation) crises without compromising their capitalist nature. A crisis of a particular capitalist state regime need not necessarily imply a crisis of capitalism itself.

Hypothesis 11: States may also be capable of responding to legitimation crises without in fact undergoing significant structural transformation at all. Sometimes very minor modifications may re-secure legitimacy without changing the organizational principles of the state in any way.

These twin hypotheses suggest the need to differentiate between types of response to crises. Here we can usefully draw upon Offe's (1985: 223–6) important distinction between *structural* and *conjunctural* responses, or as he prefers to term them, structural and conjunctural 'modes of political rationality' (cf. Altvater 1984: 9–10). However ungainly the terminology, the distinction is in fact quite simple and intuitive.

A *structural mode of political rationality* is a response to an economic or political crisis in which the structures of the state or other system are fundamentally transformed. The Attlee and Thatcher Governments both adopted *structural* modes of political rationality. Structural responses to crisis are those in which 'the physical and economic parameters of production and the institutional parameters of interest representation [i.e. the form of the state and its relationship to the economy] . . . become subject to redesign' (Offe 1985: 226). A structural mode of political rationality thus involves a restructuring of the system itself – its mode(s) of operation, the subsystems that comprise it, its relationships to other systems, etc. are all transformed.

A *conjunctural mode of political rationality*, on the other hand, is a response to crisis in which a solution is sought *within the existing and unchanged structures of the state*. A conjunctural mode of political rationality is thus associated with minor *tinkering* as opposed to structural transformation. As Offe himself notes, a conjunctural response to crisis is one that seeks 'to maximise the adequacy of policy responses to problems as they appear on the agenda; the concomitant expectation is that such problems and demands will remain within a range of manageability defined by existing capacities of state action and their continuing improvement' (Offe 1975: 225–6). The response of the post-war British governments between 1950 and 1975 to periodic fiscal crises was *conjunctural* by this definition. Similarly, it might be argued, the Major Government has seen the return to what might be termed *conjunctural politics* – politics conducted within the limiting parameters of an accepted set of state structures (see Chapter 8).

If we must be careful about differentiating between structural and conjunctural responses to crisis, then we must also be sensitive to the different levels at which we might identify crises. It is one thing to identify a crisis within a particular historical regime of the capitalist state; it is another thing altogether to identify a crisis of capitalism itself. Yet much of the literature referring to a crisis of the state in the 1970s is guilty of precisely this conflation, assuming a simple correspondence between the crisis of the Keynesian welfare state regime and a generic crisis of capitalism (O'Connor 1973; Habermas 1975; Wolfe 1977; Hall *et al.* 1978).

For our purposes it is particularly important that we are able to differentiate between those crises which threaten the capitalist nature of the social formation, those which threaten the specific form taken by the capitalist state at a particular stage in its historical development and those which can be accommodated within the crisis management techniques of the existing state regime. This requires quite a significant departure from Habermas's somewhat one-dimensional conception of crisis. It is elaborated in the 'snakes and ladders' model of state crisis, as outlined schematically in Figure 8. This model classifies crises in terms of two criteria: the level at which a crisis can be identified; and the depth of the crisis at a particular level. For our purposes three levels of crisis can usefully be identified (though the model could be extended).

1 Crises of the *mode of production*, which refer to crises of capitalism, crises of the very dominance of the bourgeoisie.
2 Crises of the *state regime*, which refer to crises of the specific regime of the capitalist state (the Keynesian welfare state, for instance).
3 Crises of the *mode of policy-making* within a particular policy arena, which refer to crises occurring within a particular capitalist state regime that can be dealt with without threatening its structural form.

Second, we might classify crises in terms of their *depth* at a particular level. Here we can distinguish, as above, between crises (at whatever level) that require a *structural* response and those that merely require a *conjunctural* response. Thus, at the level of the state regime we might distinguish between crises *of* the state regime (which cannot be alleviated through the deployment of existing crisis management techniques) and crises *within* the state regime (which can be). This allows us to draw up a typology of crises within contemporary capitalist social formations (see Figure 8).

Within such a framework, the crisis of the British state in the mid to late 1970s can be interpreted, as we shall see in more detail in the next chapter, as follows.

1 A contradictory post-war settlement gave rise to periodic crises *within* modes of policy-making in particular policy fields (manifest as balance of payments crises, housing shortages, waves of industrial unrest and so forth).
2 Initially such crises proved manageable within the parameters of the existing modes of policy-making (industrial unrest would be responded to by a new round of corporatist conciliation, for instance).
3 The repertoire of such crisis management techniques, however, was gradually exhausted, generating a series of *structural* crises *of* the modes of policy-making within a number of policy arenas (corporatist conciliation could no longer secure both industrial harmony and wage restraint, for instance).
4 While a single structural crisis of a particular mode of policy-making might have proved manageable *within* the existing structures of the state regime (representing merely a *conjunctural* crisis at this level), the accumulation of

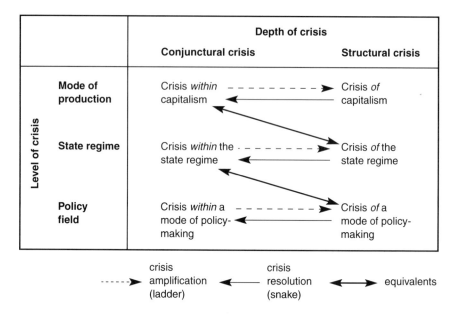

Figure 8   The 'snakes and ladders' model of crisis.

such unresolved crises posed a more generic, *structural* crisis *of* the state regime itself.

5 A series of unresolved crises within particular policy arenas had eventually condensed to precipitate a crisis of the state regime itself – a crisis which could no longer be managed within the structures of the settlement.

6 This in turn represented a *conjunctural* crisis *within* the capitalist mode of production in post-war Britain – a crisis *within* but not *of* capitalism.

The crisis of the British state in the 1970s was not, then, a crisis *of* capitalism. Though the regime of the state was threatened, its capitalist form was never seriously challenged. This would perhaps suggest, as indeed does the history of the last century, that advanced capitalist states are just as successful at breeding snakes as they are at building ladders. In this respect they are somewhat more slippery than much Marxist theory has previously given them credit for. It will take rather more than a crisis of the state regime to dislodge capitalism.

Recycling the state regime: crisis and structural transformation

We can now begin to formulate a model of the structural transformation of the capitalist state in response to crisis, building on the distinction between conjunctural and structural crises at the level of the state regime. This allows us to demonstrate how capitalist social and system reproduction is secured through the periodic redefinition of forms of state intervention within the economy and civil society in response to structural crises of the state regime (see Figure 9).

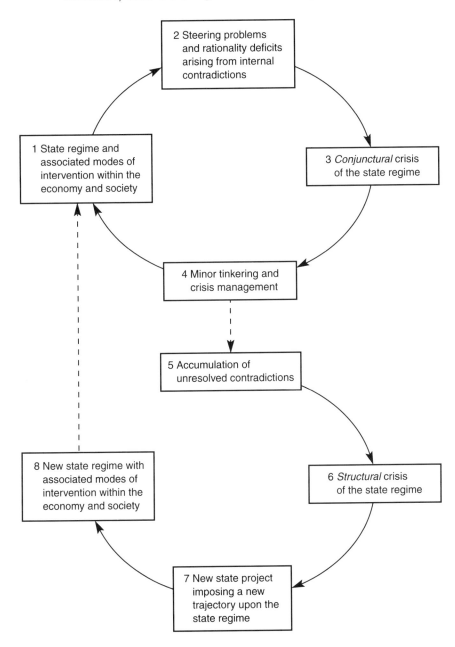

Figure 9 The structural transformation of the state.

This model demonstrates how the depth of crisis conditions different responses by the state. The deployment of 'conjunctural' crisis management techniques may, at least temporarily, re-secure the legitimacy of the state with minimal structural change to the institutions, apparatuses and modes of operation of the state regime (4–1 in Figure 9). However, if the steering problems that initially precipitated this crisis derived from inherent structural contradictions within the state regime, then the available crisis management techniques will fail fully to re-secure social and system stability. The result is the gradual accumulation of unresolved contradictions and steering problems and the eventual precipitation of a fully fledged structural crisis of the state regime (4–5–6 in Figure 9). Within such a scenario, a structural transformation of the state (expressed in a new state project) is a necessary, though not in itself sufficient, condition for the restoration of social and system stability. The form that this restructuring will take is the subject of ideological and political contestation as competing parties vie for state power (as distinct from merely governmental power) by offering alternative visions of the future trajectory of the state to the electorate. The resulting structural transformation of the state, though ushering in a new state regime, still takes place within the constraints imposed by the state's defining capitalist nature.

This diachronic model of the evolution of the state in and through crises, as we shall see in the next chapter, can be readily applied to the transformation of the state in post-war Britain.

Political overload and ungovernability

> Once upon a time man looked to God to order the world. Then he looked to the market. Now he looks to government.
>
> (King 1975: 288)

The 'overload' thesis in interesting ways parallels that of Habermas and Offe but from an antithetically opposed political position (Birch 1984; Held 1984). The aim of its protagonists is to establish the inherent tendency of the advanced Western democracies to become 'ungovernable'. In so doing, they provide a highly influential though somewhat simplistic account of the social democratic impasse and economic malaise of the 1970s (Brittan 1975, 1979; Crozier *et al.* 1975; King 1975; Douglas 1976; Rose and Peters 1978; Parsons 1982).

The increasing intervention of the state into the spheres of the economy and civil society, they argue, results in a politicization of new areas of social and economic life, sanctioning ever spiralling societal expectations (Brittan 1975; King 1975; Douglas 1976). This is in turn reflected in a seemingly inexorable increase in the number of interest and pressure groups actively lobbying the state (Brittan 1979). The result is to create a political *market place* for votes, yet one lacking the disciplining constraints of a formal market. As a consequence, electoral barter and fiscal irresponsibility predominate as competing parties seek to 'buy off' a sufficient share of the electorate by promising to satisfy the demands of more and more pressure groups. This degenerates into a vicious circle in which the 'price' of a vote spirals, precipitating political overload, ungovernability and fiscal crisis (see Figure 10).

The unanimous diagnosis is of a condition of 'political bankruptcy' (Rose and Peters 1978) afflicting an 'overloaded crown' (Douglas 1976) and threatening to precipitate a fundamental 'crisis of democracy' (Crozier *et al.* 1975; Usher 1981). Democracy, according to Peter Jay, 'has itself by the tail and is eating itself up fast' (Jay 1977: 181). Governments have assumed vastly increased responsibilities which they simply lack the resources (both organizational and fiscal) to satisfy. The result is a condition of overload in which 'the national product grows more slowly than the costs of public policy and the claims of take-home pay and there is not enough money in hand to meet both public and private claims' (Rose and Peters 1978: 29–30). If the diagnosis of the overload theorists is unanimous, then their prescription is certainly no less so. The clear solution to these crisis tendencies, such theorists argue, lies in fiscal austerity, tight monetary control and a rolling back of the frontiers of the state from the economy, the private sphere and civil society.

This, they argue, will not be pleasant. For, as Richard Rose and Guy Peters (1978: 40) suggest, 'the future is open but not unconstrained. Past events have future consequences. The greater the weight of past commitments, the more restricted and less palatable are the choices of an overloaded government.' This sentiment is clearly echoed in Mrs Thatcher's clarion cry, 'if it's not hurting it's not working'. We must all 'tighten our belts' if we are to rescue advanced liberal democracy from its otherwise terminal crisis.

It is perhaps telling that Anthony King's widely cited aphorism with which we opened this section should begin 'Once upon a time . . .'. For like most good fairy-tales, the 'overload thesis' contains a grain of common sense, a number of distorting overgeneralizations, simplifications and clever plot devices, and a convenient moral: *the state is overextended and must be rolled back*; Thatcherism or bust (on the link between the overload thesis and the new right see Parsons 1982: 424; D. S. King 1987: 63–4).

Attractive and convincing as this framework certainly appeared at the time, as an account of the crisis of the British state in the 1970s it is irretrievably flawed. Its simplistic and deterministic description of the crisis of the 1970s is, at best, politically opportunistic; at worst wilfully cynical. It provides a convenient justification for the policies subsequently pursued by consecutive Thatcher Governments but little else (see Chapter 7). Indeed, it is never entirely clear whether the overload thesis is being offered as a political manifesto for Thatcherism and the new right (in which case some of its obvious distortions and simplifications might be excused as mere rhetorical posturing), or whether it is seriously being put forward as a contending theory of state crisis. Whatever the answer to this question, its impact has been immense. Its advocates certainly warrant the dubious accolade of being regarded as chief among the 'organic intellectuals' of Thatcherism.

Moreover, there is little historical evidence to substantiate the thesis. The major factor determining electoral outcomes since the 1950s seems to have been the perceived economic success of governments. This rather puts

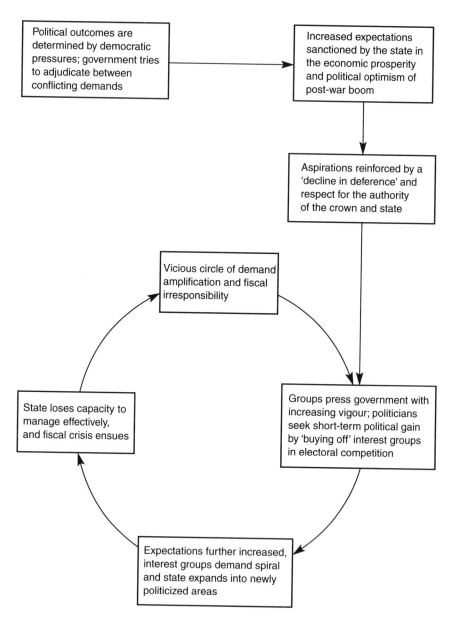

Figure 10   Political overload and ungovernability.
Source: adapted from Held (1984: 324).

paid to the image of growing fiscal irresponsibility and the 'buying off' of the electorate by Machiavellian social democrats. For if electoral competition revolved around perceived economic propriety then it is difficult to see the political mileage to be gained by offering ever greater concessions to ever greater constituencies. Once this central assumption of the overload–ungovernability thesis is dismantled, the rest crumbles with it.

Such an analysis clearly embodies an immensely patronizing, condescending and superior attitude to the electorate, who are conceptualized as greedy, unthinking, unprincipled, self-serving opportunists who are simply too stupid to realize the cost of their demands. They presumably need to be awakened from their deep trance of post-war optimism by a large injection of the down-to-earth 'common sense' of the political scientists of the new right who 'know better'.

Finally, and perhaps most worryingly of all, the thesis suggests that the greater democratization and pluralization of political discourse since the war is ultimately responsible for the fiscal crisis of the 1970s. This now represents the necessary price to be paid for political stability. As Michel Crozier (1975: 8), for instance, argues, 'the operation of the democratic process . . . appears to have generated a breakdown of traditional [i.e. undemocratic] means of social control, a delegitimation of political and other forms of authority, and an overload of demands on government, exceeding its capacity to respond.' Later in the same text, Crozier and his co-authors Samuel Huntingdon and Joji Watanuki join together in suggesting that it is 'the democratic idea that government should be responsive to the people that creates the expectation that government should meet the needs and correct the evils affecting particular groups in society' (Crozier *et al.* 1975: 164). It is precisely this sort of argument that has been used to justify the authoritarian and profoundly anti-democratic reassertion of 'traditional means of social control' to replace democratic representation that has characterized the right-wing backlash of the 1980s.

Conclusions

In this chapter we have reviewed the two prominent accounts of the crisis of the British state in the 1970s. As the above analysis would suggest, neither account is unproblematic. Yet, while that of Habermas and Offe is at least salvageable in some form, that of the overload theorists is deeply and irretrievably compromised by its scarcely concealed intention to provide a theoretical justification for Thatcherism. Much as we might wish to reject the overload thesis as a theory of state crisis, however, we cannot afford to dismiss it out of hand. For, as a popular account of the social democratic impasse of the 1970s, its impact has been considerable, something that certainly cannot be said of the theory of legitimation crisis.

The triumph of the new right theory of overload and ungovernability lies in two principal factors: (a) its ability to offer a narrative *sufficiently flexible* to account for a whole variety of disparate events, experiences and conditions while unambiguously recruiting them all to a single 'crisis' diagnosis; and (b) its ability to provide an account *sufficiently simple* to appeal to all sections of society, providing an instant diagnosis of the 'symptoms' and a *lived* sense of crisis.

Here it is instructive to recall t'Hart's (1993: 41) perceptive suggestion that 'the most important instrument of crisis management is language. Those who are able to define what the crisis is all about also hold the key to defining the appropriate strategies for [its] resolution.' In the theory of overload, ungovernability and the 'crisis of democracy', the new right held precisely that key.

It is to the specific nature of the moment of crisis and to the victory of Thatcherism and the new right in the events of the Winter of Discontent that we now turn.

Notes

1 With the publication of Habermas's more recent 1400 pages and two volumes of *The Theory of Communicative Action* there is not much doubt that this dubious honour still rests with Habermas. The only question is which is the more difficult: *Legitimation Crisis, Theory and Practice,* or *The Theory of Communicative Action.* My money's on the latter.
2 The moment in which the trade union movement effectively withdrew its support from the Social Contract between the TUC and the Labour government. Four years of wage restraint evaporated in a wave of industrial stoppages during the worst winter in living memory. The media portrayed events as a 'Winter of Discontent' in which the country was being 'held to ransom' by militant trade unionists. The reality was somewhat more complicated (Dorfman 1983; Gourevitch *et al.* 1984; Marsh 1992; Hay 1994c).

6 *From* contradiction *to* crisis: *the* structural transformation *of the* British state

Thus far we have developed a rather abstract and generic account of the contradictions and crisis tendencies of the state regimes that emerged in the advanced capitalist economies following the war. In Chapter 3 we began to characterize this state regime as it evolved and was eventually consolidated in post-war Britain. We saw how the initial phase of the post-war reconstruction was to usher in a period of consensus lasting relatively unchallenged and uncontested (at least in elite political discourse) until the mid-1970s, and how such a consensus was in fact an epiphenomenon of a structural and institutional settlement. In examining the contours of this emergent state regime we identified twin domestic settlements. These, we tentatively suggested, might be seen as internally contradictory and mutually antagonistic. It is to the concrete reality of such tensions, internal contradictions and steering problems that we turn in this chapter.

In Chapter 5 we focused our attention on the various theories that have been offered to account for the widely observed – indeed, widely *experienced* – crisis of this state regime in the mid to late 1970s. We noted the considerable impact of the 'overload' and 'ungovernability' theses in moulding both popular conceptions of crisis and appropriate responses, and in providing a convenient theoretical justification for the Thatcherite retrenchment of the state. Yet we saw that in a number of crucial respects this thesis was irretrievably flawed, while, somewhat ironically, the far less influential critical theory of Habermas and Offe could provide the basis for a more sophisticated account of the transformation of the state in and through crisis.

In this chapter it is time to attempt a synthesis of this *diachronic* account of the transformation of the state (as formulated in the previous chapter) with a *synchronic* account of the tensions, internal contradictions, steering problems and crisis tendencies of the state regime in post-war Britain (such as that outlined in Chapter 3). Our analysis will proceed in two stages. In the first we consider the tensions, contradictions and transformation of the state since the war. In the second we concentrate more specifically upon the events of the 'Winter of Discontent' and the moment of crisis itself. In so doing we will address the following questions.

- What was the nature of the crisis of the British state in the 1970s?
- How deep-seated was the crisis in the structures of the state that emerged in the post-war period?
- How far back can we trace the origins of the crisis?
- What were the specific crisis tendencies, structural and ideological contradictions and discontinuities that condensed to precipitate the crisis of the 1970s? Were these primarily endogenous (internal) or exogenous (external) to the British state?
- What was it about the specific conjuncture of the 1970s that brought this array of crisis tendencies to condensation?
- What was the nature of the resulting moment of crisis?

Once more on the synchronic and the diachronic

As we suggested in Chapter 5, it is useful to distinguish between a diachronic and a synchronic conception of crisis. A synchronic analysis focuses upon the specific crisis tendencies existing within a particular system at a particular moment, and relies upon the structural analysis of a historical snapshot or freeze-frame of an evolving system. By contrast, a diachronic analysis focuses upon the historical development of the system with time, looking at: (a) the mechanisms and processes involved in the fusion of contradictions to precipitate a crisis; (b) the moment of crisis itself; and (c) the structural transformation or disintegration of the system in response to crisis. A diachronic conception of crisis focuses on crisis as a *process*.

In Chapter 5 we looked primarily at the diachronic, considering the general mechanisms and processes through which crisis tendencies develop and condense to produce moments of crisis, and the impact of such crises on the system itself. And this is very important, for as Régis Debray (1973: 152) observes, 'the crisis moment is the strategic moment in the "*evolution of things*" ' (emphasis added). Crisis, then, is an inherently dynamic process. As such, it demands a diachronic analysis.

Crisis, for Debray, is a critical moment of fusion and explosion, 'an indeterminate moment of determination' (p. 99). It is 'indeterminate' in the sense that its outcome cannot be predicted in advance – it is contingent on the complex interplay of a multitude of disparate processes and political struggles. The outcome of crisis is thus *under-determined* by the contradictions which together comprise it, yet the moment of crisis is none the less *determining* historically. Crisis, for Debray, 'brings to the surface – to the level of open, political and public struggle – a break that spreads outwards, a split that soon extends to all the levels of the social totality it touches' (p. 103).

Crisis is a strategic point in historical time and as such we cannot afford to dispense with a diachronic or dynamic analysis. However, such a perspective, though necessary, cannot in-and-of-itself provide an adequate account. We must give due weight to the internal crisis tendencies (contradictions, discontinuities, internal ruptures, tensions and steering problems) of the system in order to see how these fuse to create the ruptural moment of crisis itself. This requires a synchronic analysis reflecting the specificity and uniqueness of a particular system (in this case a particular state regime) at a particular moment, and its relation to other systems. We cannot generalize from an abstract analysis of the capitalist state form or of the mode of production to the concrete reality of a crisis of the British variant of the Keynesian welfare state. For the latter is a unique and specific system, generating a unique and specific moment of crisis.[1] As Andrew Gamble (1988: 11) notes, though global economic recession and the exhaustion of the post-war 'Fordist' mode of growth 'made a new politics possible and necessary', the specific content of this new politics was 'provided by local concerns, specific to the institutions and circumstances of particular countries'.

Thus, although we can produce a theoretically *informed* analysis of the crisis of the British state, we cannot theoretically *derive* that crisis. This is an important point and one worth bearing in mind when assessing much of the literature on the crisis tendencies of 'late capitalism' (O'Connor 1973; Habermas 1975; Offe 1984) and indeed liberal democracy (Brittan 1975; Crozier *et al.* 1975) in the 1970s.

The structural transformation of the state in post-war Britain

If we are to contextualize a detailed analysis of the specificities of the crisis of the *British* state in the 1970s within a more generic account of the evolution of *capitalist state regimes* in and through crisis, then we can usefully begin by applying the model developed in Chapter 5 (see Figure 9). The result is a theoretically informed and provisional account of the transformation of the state in post-war Britain. Such an account identifies two strategic moments in the evolution of the state in this period: (a) the initial post-war reconstruction; and (b) the somewhat more gradual though no less significant Thatcherite restructuring. It interprets the emergence of the crisis of the Keynesian welfare state in terms of the exhaustion of the repertoire of crisis management techniques available to governments operating within the confines of the settlement (for a similar, though more generalized, interpretation see Gamble 1988: 3; Jessop *et al.* 1988: 77). This highly suggestive analysis is schematically outlined in Figure 11.

Such a framework allows us to differentiate between periods in which the structure of the state regime remains relatively static and untransformed (periods of settlement), and those in which the very institutions, structures and boundaries of the state are themselves exposed to contestation and transformation. The initial post-war period emerges as a moment of decisive intervention in which the contours of the state were re-landscaped, setting the context within which governmental power would be exercised until the late 1970s (1–2, Figure 11). The effect of this bout of *structural* transformation (as opposed to *conjunctural* tinkering) was: (a) to redefine the nature of the 'political' by extending the bounds of the state's responsibility within both civil society and the economy; (b) to transform the expectations of civil society sanctioned by the state by renegotiating the terms of the 'citizenship contract'; and (c) to set the very parameters within which responses to both

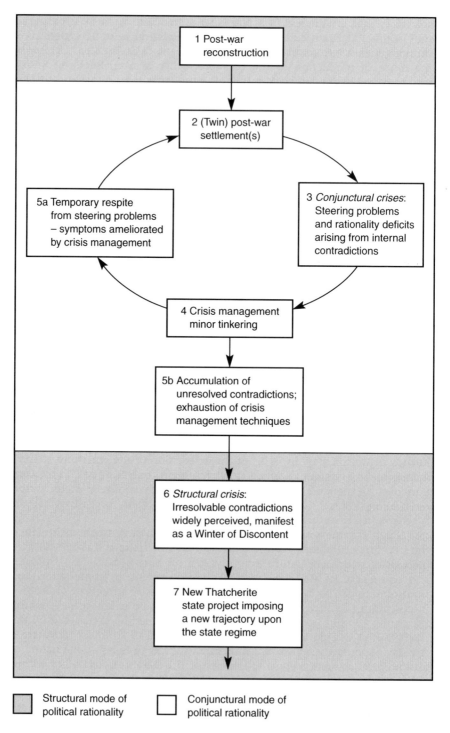

Figure 11 The structural transformation of the state in post-war Britain.

interest and pressure groups, and internal contradictions and steering problems would have to be met. In short, its effect was to set in place the structures, institutions and practices of a new state regime.

This state regime was in many respects deeply contradictory. Indeed, as we suggested in Chapter 3, its structural form is perhaps best characterized in terms of twin domestic settlements reflecting contradictory conceptions of social justice and conflicting institutional compromises. The result, inevitably, was a series of steering problems or *conjunctural crises* (2–3, Figure 11). These surfaced periodically throughout the post-war era as: (a) government policy oscillated between deflation and reflation as both Labour and Tory administrations sought to juggle the conflicting imperatives of full employment, the welfare state and the 'productive economy' on the one hand, and the maintenance of an international role for Sterling and the City on the other, resulting in Britain's distinctive 'stop–go' cycle[2] (Jessop 1980: 31; 1992: 21–2; Ingham 1984: 201, 214–16; Pollard 1992: esp. 368–9; Coates 1994: 185–6; Gamble 1994a: 111–13); (b) the export of capital overseas and import penetration[3] from the advanced capitalist economies of the USA, Japan and Western Europe conspired to produce balance of payments crises (Aaronovitch *et al.* 1981: 193–215; Fine and Harris 1985: 44–6; Cain and Hopkins 1993: 283; Gamble 1994a: 109–12); and (c) the breakdown of successive rounds of wage restraint resulted in waves of industrial unrest (Minkin 1974, 1991; Dorfman 1983; Coates 1989). Though expressive of more fundamental underlying contradictions, these symptoms proved, at least in the short to medium term, manageable within the contours of the settlement (4–5a–2, Figure 11). However, crisis *management* and crisis *resolution* are by no means synonymous. Indeed, the increasing preoccupation of government with short-term crisis management and symptom amelioration[4] was at the expense of any longer-term strategy which might have addressed the underlying structural weakness of the British economy (Thain 1984: 582).

Such attempts to manage conjunctural crises and steering problems as they arose became increasingly ineffective, and the respite they secured ever more temporary, as the weight of basic and unresolved contradictions grew. In the worsening global economic conditions of the mid to late 1970s, these contradictions were cruelly exposed. The repertoire of crisis management techniques available within the Keynesian welfare regime was eventually exhausted (4–5b, Figure 11) in the events of the Winter of Discontent (5b–6, Figure 11). In this moment of crisis (a crisis *of* the state regime itself) the social basis of the Thatcherite 'project'[5] was mobilized. In the following years consecutive Conservative Governments were to impose a new trajectory upon the structures of the state (6–7, Figure 11).

Though still tentative and provisional at this stage, this theoretically informed account of the evolution of the British state since the war is highly instructive. It sensitizes us to strategic moments of transition, highlighting periods of decisive intervention by administrations wielding *state* power (as distinct from merely *governmental* power). As such it provides a means to order and periodize the social and political history of post-war Britain in terms of the transformation of the state, demonstrating the crucial mediating role of state crises in the recasting of social and political relationships.

Above all, it allows us to *re-state* social and political change in post-war Britain, suggesting that:

1 Despite its internal contradictions, the post-war settlement lasted substantially unchallenged until the mid-1970s. It was reflected in a period of consensual and *conjunctural* politics characterized by the *management* of a set of state structures which was thereby consolidated.
2 In the changed global economic circumstances of the 1970s the repertoire of crisis management techniques was eventually exhausted. This gave rise to a more fundamental *structural* crisis of the state which could not be resolved within the parameters of the existing state regime.
3 During the Winter of Discontent the social basis of Thatcherism was forged. In the ensuing period of ideological contestation, the legitimation basis of the state was redefined in terms of a Thatcherite project to impose a new trajectory upon the state. An era of gradual structural transformation was initiated.

From contradiction to crisis

Suggestive as the above account is, however, it still tells us very little about: the concrete and specific steering problems, internal contradictions, tensions and hence crisis tendencies of the state regime itself; or the processes and mechanisms through which a series of specific contradictions were to coalesce, condense and fuse to precipitate a ruptural moment of crisis. If we are to address these issues we must return to the account of the structure and form of the British variant of the Keynesian welfare state that we began to develop in Chapter 3.

At the time we suggested that Britain's post-war reconstruction might usefully be conceived of in terms of the emergence of twin domestic post-war settlements (and, perhaps, triple post-war compromises).[6] The value of such a claim might not, then, have been terribly clear – after all, what extra mileage do we get for the theoretical trouble of identifying two settlements when most commentators are content with one?

Yet if these twin settlements do indeed reflect different conceptions of social justice and embody different institutional compromises, then such an observation might sensitize us to the inherent structural weaknesses and crisis tendencies of the British variant of the Keynesian welfare state. For, as I hope to demonstrate, these twin settlements were both mutually antagonistic and internally contradictory. Accordingly, the origins of the crisis of the British state in the 1970s can be traced to the very structures of the settlement that emerged in the initial post-war period. If this is indeed so, then the twin settlements thesis is vindicated. For such an argument could not have been formulated if we had merely assumed, along with much of the existing literature, the existence of a coherent, unified and homogeneous settlement. The widespread assumption within the dominant paradigm of a hermetic, functioning and functional settlement has had unfortunate consequences. It has tended to result in a polarization of accounts between: (a) those which seek 'external shocks' (such as the 1973 Oil Crisis) to explain the crisis of the British state in the 1970s (see, for instance, Atkins 1986; S. Clarke 1987, 1988; Murray 1989; Taylor 1989, 1992; McEachern 1990; Bonefeld 1993); and (b) those which conveniently pin the blame for the crisis on the government that presided over the eventual demise of the settlement (see, for example, Holmes 1985a). Thus, where internal contradictions are considered they are interpreted in terms of departures from the 'true spirit' of the settlement by governments in the 1970s introducing distortions into an otherwise functional state regime. The exceptions are the accounts of the (new) right and the (neo-)Marxist left, both of which seek to identify the internal contradictions and structural weaknesses of the settlement. While the new right concentrate their fire upon the liberal philanthropists of the 'enlightened' English Establishment and their attempts to foist their vision of the 'New Jerusalem' upon a malleable post-war electorate (Barnett 1986; cf. Weiner 1981), the neo-Marxists focus upon the contradictory imperatives of capitalist accumulation and legitimation (O'Connor 1973; Habermas 1975; Himmelstrand and Lundberg 1981; Offe 1984; Hay 1994a; cf. Jessop 1980, 1990: 216–7;[7] 1992).

In turning to the structures of the state regime in post-war Britain, we observe a series of tensions, contradictions and steering problems. These are expressive of a functional separation of tasks, referred to by Offe as an 'organizational disjunction'. Its effect is to isolate the conflicting imperatives of accumulation and legitimation. It marks the boundary of the twin settlements. A Keynesian welfare state regime such as that in post-war Britain thus faces a perpetual dilemma: *its continued legitimacy is dependent upon the satisfaction of expectations that it has itself sanctioned but which threaten to undermine economic competitiveness.*

Though something of a tension within all welfare state regimes, this central dilemma was particularly acute in the British context, which was characterized by a popular desire for comprehensive welfare provision and a structurally weak, arcane and declining economy (Pollard 1982; Fine and Harris 1985; Newton and Porter 1988; Cairncross 1992; Coates 1994; Gamble 1994a).

When we further consider that: (a) there is no single general interest of capital and hence no simple means of satisfying the conflicting imperatives of capitalist accumulation (Burnham 1990: 170–88); (b) the competition between individual capitals and between different sections of capital is peculiarly intense in Britain because of the 'distinctive dislocation' between financial and industrial capital (Jessop 1980: 30; cf. Ingham 1984);[8] and (c) there is no common societal interest that if appeased would necessarily secure legitimacy; then we might expect to find not only a series of tensions *between* Britain's twin settlements but also a series of internal contradictions *within* each settlement taken on its own.

What we in fact discover is the inherently contradictory yet simultaneously *expressed* commitment to: (a) industrial modernization (and the intensive capital investment which that entailed); (b) the maintenance of Sterling as an international currency; (c) the preservation of an empire and a global military role effectively inherited from the inter-war years; and (d) comprehensive, universal welfare provision free at the point of access. Put simply, although the continued legitimacy of the state was dependent upon the realization of the promise of a Keynesian welfare state (as expressed in the welfare settlement), this was simply incompatible with a domestic accumulation strategy premised upon the maintenance of Sterling as an international trading currency (as expressed in the politico-economic settlement). For the latter undermined the very basis for Keynesian economic intervention through demand management, insisting as it did upon the suppression of demand at precisely the point at which 'the restocking of industry made real growth a possibility' (Ingham 1984: 281n; see also Jessop 1980: 30–3; Held 1984: 311–13; Gamble 1994: 109–18). Similarly, the articulated aim of industrial modernization (itself a condition of sustained economic growth in an ever more competitive global economy) did not sit comfortably with: (a) the renegotiation of the 'citizenship contract' and the immediate extension of the welfare state in the post-war period; (b) the balance of payments crisis that was the direct legacy of wartime conditions (Newton and Porter 1988: 100–1; Tomlinson 1994: 164ff); (c) the (largely successful) attempt of the Bank and Treasury to re-establish their political power of the inter-war years (Ingham 1984: 202); and (d) the 'pathological fear' on the part of many industrialists of any form of state interference (Tiratsoo and Tomlinson 1993: 170).[9] For the capital investment that would have been necessary for industrial modernization (and which might conceivably have generated the sort of economic growth required to sustain a universal welfare state) had already been committed to welfare expenditure. The die had been cast during the war: economic modernization would have to follow social welfare reform. Yet, and herein lies the central paradox of the post-war reconstruction, *once welfare reform was initiated, industrial modernization* (to the extent necessary to underpin a comprehensive welfare state) *could no longer be afforded.* The forging of an advanced, high technology, manufacturing economy was the very condition of being able to pay for (or continue to pay for) the welfare state.

What this demonstrates very clearly is that the forging of the post-war settlement in the initial post-war period was driven primarily and necessarily by *political* imperatives. The maintenance of societal legitimation and the building of a New Jerusalem were pursued at the ultimate cost of sacrificing the economic basis for the emergent settlement. Thus, although the primary contradiction was perhaps economic, there was a distinctive *political* logic to this *economic* contradiction (grounded in the limited strategic capacities of the state in the initial post-war period). Yet if this is the central crisis tendency of Britain's peculiarly flawed Keynesian welfare state then it is certainly not the only one. For, as the above discussion suggests, we should be looking not only for a lack of complementarity *between* the twin settlements but also for a series of *internal* contradictions. This is precisely what we do observe.

Taking the *politico-economic settlement* first, the dominant mode of calculation characterizing the settlement (and expressing the supposed economic responsibilities of the state) was one of: Keynesian demand management; corporatism; 'Fordist' accumulation, production and consumption; and comprehensive industrial modernization. However, the structural contradictions within this settlement become readily apparent if we consider the

Table 8   The contradictions of the politico-economic settlement

Mode of calculation	Mode of operation
Keynesian demand management	• Limited state intervention within the economy. • Hegemony of financial over industrial capital and the influence of the City–Bank–Treasury nexus. • Maintenance of Sterling as an international trading currency.
Corporatist conciliation	*Quasi-corporatism*: the subordination of corporatist forms of interest representation to the exigencies of short-term crisis management.
Industrial modernization	• Industrial profile rooted in the first industrial revolution. • Conditions favouring the export of capital overseas.
Fordist accumulation, consumption and production	• Export commitment to (shrinking) former imperial markets. • Satisfaction of consumer demand through import penetration.
Mixed economy	Inefficient nationalized industries modelled on the private sector – 'state-regulated private monopolies'.

actual practices enshrined within the settlement itself – the actual relation-ship between the state and the economy in post-war Britain. The state's mode of regulation and intervention within the economy in fact system-atically compromised its articulated principles of organization (this is sum-marized in Table 8). The structures and, indeed, crisis tendencies of the politico-economic settlement were in fact largely inherited from the inter-war years and were merely exacerbated by the parallel commitment to a universal welfare state free at the point of access to all (a similar point is made by Mercer 1991: 84; cf. Booth 1989; Anderson 1992b).

The structural contradictions of the politico-economic settlement

The *commitment to shrinking imperial markets*. Such markets were increasingly threatened by the penetration of rapidly developing new capitalist econo-mies with much greater rates of labour exploitation in inherently labour-intensive industries. Britain's export profile was thus focused away from the rapidly expanding and dynamic economies of North America and Western Europe[10] towards the traditional and declining markets of its former colo-nies. Such markets were also subject to increasing import penetration from Japan and the USA under the conditions of an international post-war settle-ment. The result was industrial inertia and stagnation (as opposed to mod-ernization and regeneration). As Peter Burnham (1990: 11) perceptively observes, 'while the major nations of Western Europe engaged in vigorous intra-European trade, Britain concentrated on renewing its traditional trading links with the Commonwealth.' This inevitably exacerbated Britain's structural economic weakness and her inability to carve a stable niche within global economic dynamics in the immediate post-war period (Jessop 1980: 37; Burnham 1990: 11–13, 176–9).

The *hegemony of financial over industrial capital, the role of the City in the global economic order and the resulting economic primacy given to a stable value of Sterling*. As Andrew Gamble and Geoffrey Ingham both argue, Britain's seemingly inexorable decline within the international economic hierarchy in the post-war period can be traced in part to the attempt to re-establish the international financial role of the City on the one hand, and the predominance of the 'City–Bank–Treasury nexus' (through which this was effected) on the other (Ingham 1984: 131ff; Gamble 1994; cf. Leys 1986; see also Chapter 3). The willingness of foreign capital to hold Sterling[11] relied upon confidence in its stable value. It was this, rather than the maintenance of full employment, the promotion of domestic demand or the attempt to establish conditions favourable for capital investment, that became the principal goal of government economic policy. As Perry Anderson (1992b: 166) has argued, the result of the continued hegemony of finance capital 'was to penalise British manufacturing as the exigencies of Sterling – a high and stable exchange-rate – were translated into the vagaries of a credit control erratically expanding and contracting domestic demand in response to pressures on the external account'.

The *limited degree of state intervention in the economy to create the conditions to encourage capital investment, research and development, and thus the industrial modernization necessary to restore Britain to a 'Fordist' growth trajectory* (Overbeek 1990; see also Tomlinson 1994: 170–84). Such intervention remained restricted to the restraint of public spending, the defence of Sterling and short-term economic crisis management (increasingly through the imposition of 'corporatist' solutions). All of these can be seen to compromise the grand ideological pillars and defining motifs of the settlement (Pollard 1982; Hall 1986; Marquand 1988).

The regular and consistent *export of capital overseas* in search of short-term profits. This was a further consequence of the dominance of financial capital. Its effect was to debilitate further the domestic economy and exacerbate Britain's periodic and increasingly frequent balance of payments crises (Aaronovitch *et al.* 1981: 193–215; Fine and Harris 1985: 44–6; Overbeek 1990: 105–6; Gamble 1994: 110).

Quasi-corporatism: the subordination of corporatist forms of interest intermediation to the requirements of capital, and the adoption of tripartite mechanisms only as a last resort – as a crisis sharing, crisis displacement or crisis management strategy. Though corporatist structures blossomed, the actual range of policy issues on which trade union influence was maintained was gradually eroded as inflation rose, and balance of payments crises loomed. It was not advice but acquiescence or approval that was studiously courted through the façade of corporatism, usually after policy decisions had already been made (Allen 1960; Panitch 1976; Coates 1989; Leys 1989).

The contradictions of the welfare settlement

Although there is much less historiographic work on the contradictions within the welfare (or politico-normative) settlement, a similar discontinuity between the legitimating ideology and mode of operation of this settlement can be observed.

Here, however, we must proceed with some caution. For to identify these as (logical) contradictions[12] is neither: (a) to suggest that they were necessarily to shape the form of the subsequent crisis; nor (b) to suggest that they were to be dealt with or even addressed in response to that crisis. Once again it is imperative to stress that *the moment of crisis is radically underdetermined by the contradictions of the system itself.* As we shall see, although the contradictions of the politico-normative or welfare settlement may have contributed significantly to undermining the social basis of the post-war settlement, they were not decisively to shape the form of the crisis itself, and were in fact merely further exacerbated in the ensuing period of structural transformation.

The mode of calculation and dominant legitimating ideology within this settlement was one of egalitarianism, welfarism and social democracy. This elevated the principle of 'equality' (whether of opportunity or outcome) as the criterion by which state policy should be judged. Yet in practice the structures of the Keynesian welfare state in fact enshrined and entrenched deep-seated inequalities of gender, ethnicity and class within the settlement. The result was a form of redistribution *within* as opposed to *between* classes and a welfare settlement with an institutionally inscribed reliance upon the unpaid domestic labour of women and the poorly paid labour of immigrant workers granted only partial citizenship (Doyal *et al.* 1981; Pateman 1989b; Gordon 1990a, b; Yuval-Davis 1990; Anthias and Yuval-Davis 1992; Ginsburg 1992).[13]

The egalitarian ideology of welfarism was simply incompatible with the capitalist growth imperative and the structures of a deeply entrenched patriarchal and racist society to which it was inevitably subordinated. This can be illustrated by a brief consideration of the consequences of structurally inscribed racism within the architecture of the welfare state. The link between racism and the crisis tendencies of the post-war years might not at first seem an obvious or direct one. For although the exploitation and subordination of ethnic minorities within the welfare state unquestionably compromised its articulated principles of equality and universality, this was enshrined within its very institutional contours, practices and procedures from its inception.[14] It can scarcely be regarded as posing a direct or significant threat to the legitimacy of the state in the post-war period. None the less, the experience of systematic racism within the welfare state by ethnic minorities – whether as a 'reserve army of cheap labour' (Doyal *et al.* 1981), as objects of social control (Williams 1989a: 187–93) or as recipients of (limited) welfare services (Jacobs 1985)[15] – certainly contributed to a justifiable sense of exclusion and alienation. This was increasingly to find expression in a variety of forms of cultural resistance and symbolic displays of black identity, such as Rastafarianism (Cashmore 1979; Gilroy 1987: 187–92,

241–4; Keith 1993a), that were to bring black working class youth into con-flict with the police on the streets of the inner cities. This would in turn contribute to, and reaffirm, the tabloid media's construction of the black urban proletarian youth as 'drug addict', 'street fighter' and 'mugger' – pro-viding the convenient 'folk devils' that were to animate popular narratives of what increasingly came to be perceived as a condition of social dislocation and crisis (Hall *et al.* 1978; Gilroy 1982, 1987; Solomos 1985, 1988).

As the above illustration would suggest, the 'logical contradictions' within the architecture of the welfare state were thus increasingly to give rise to 'social antagonism' and political protest (Colletti 1972, 1975; and note 12 above) as the symptoms of economic failure began to impinge directly upon the lived experience of individuals. Though this did not pose an immediate threat to the Keynesian welfare state itself, it was reflected in: (a) increasing social unrest on the streets of the inner cities from the early 1960s; (b) a series of 'moral panics' as the media whipped up popular fervour against certain 'deviant' sub-populations of society (principally the black urban pro-letariat);[16] and (c) growing industrial unrest as 'corporatist conciliation' was increasingly used as a means to discipline labour and secure wage restraint. These various responses to the gradual disintegration of the settlement and the growing economic hardship to which it gave rise provoked their own reaction. An authoritarian counter-cultural backlash from the (new) right developed. It became closely associated, if not entirely synonymous, with the emergence of 'Thatcherism as a social movement' between 1975 and 1979 (Jessop *et al.* 1988: 61–2). Its principal target was the 'deviance and greed' supposedly spawned by a 'dependency culture' and an overextended state. The right was already mobilized and positioning itself for the now seemingly inevitable moment of crisis.

What this in turn suggests is that if we wish to trace the origins of Thatcherism in the pre-history of the crisis of the 1970s, then it is not so much to the contradictions of the welfare settlement that we should be looking, as to the response to such contradictions (by those defined vari-ously as the 'undeserving poor', 'welfare scroungers', 'state dependants' and the 'enemy within') and the backlash that this generated. The contradictions of the welfare settlement merely reinforced the impression that the Keynesian welfare state regime was not working, and that a decisive alternative was called for. Yet there seemed little desire for the social harmonization prom-ised in the initial post-war years. This was now regarded as a fanciful illusion that Britain could no longer afford to entertain. The compromised promises and shattered illusions of the welfare settlement certainly contributed to the delegitimation of the extant state regime. They did not dictate that any successor would need to prove itself more successful at realizing what now seemed remote and distant aspirations.

Putting off the inevitable

As the above discussion clearly reveals, the state regime that emerged in Britain in the post-war period was characterized by internal tensions and contradictions. Indeed, the onset of crisis was only postponed until the 1970s by virtue of two factors.

First, it is important to note the comparative strength of the British economy in the initial post-war period at a time of wide-scale continental European reconstruction and regeneration. Thus although the British economy was to fail to modernize to the same extent as its European competitors, it was, in 1945, well placed (having suffered only comparatively minor physical destruction) to benefit from the initial upturn in the global economy that immediately followed the war (Burnham 1990: 176, 188). Buoyancy, however, bred complacency. This was further to militate against the structural modernization of the economy (Burnham 1990: 59; Anderson 1992; Gamble 1994a: 113–17). For the duration of the long post-war boom, then, the internal contradictions of the settlement were temporarily hidden.

Yet by the mid-1960s the structural frailty of the British economy was once again starkly exposed. The inevitable onset of a fully fledged crisis of the state regime was now only postponed by the use of voluntary and subsequently compulsory incomes policies under the façade of consensual corporatism. It is to the eventual exhaustion of this last and most desperate attempt at crisis management in the events of the Winter of Discontent that we must now turn.

The crisis of crisis management and the disintegration of the settlement

In December 1978 an NOP opinion poll gave Labour a 1 per cent advantage. By January 1979 the same pollsters were giving the Conservatives a lead of 18 per cent. In the intervening months Britain had experienced a protracted wave of industrial conflict. This was accompanied by an intense media barrage, which fostered a sense of profound political crisis without precedent since the General Strike of 1926. It was to become immortalized by the then editor of *The Sun*, Larry Lamb, as the 'Winter of Discontent'.

Remarkable as this political turnaround was, something far more remarkable and unprecedented (at least in the post-war British context) was occurring during this period. For while such a swing in the electoral pendulum might well account for a change in *governmental* power, it cannot in-and-of-itself provide an adequate explanation for the more significant shift in *state* power that was to originate in the winter of 1978–9. Thatcherism as a state project, though conceived long before, was born in the context of crisis during the Winter of Discontent.

From the social contract to the winter of discontent

If we are to move beyond the simplistic media narratives which abounded during the winter of 1978–9 then it is important that we attempt to reconstruct the context within which the government and trade unions were to formulate strategy in the run up to the Winter of Discontent. Two contextual factors are particularly important.

First, it is important to note that the Wilson Government was elected, and indeed re-elected, in 1974 largely because it was perceived that the Tories were incapable of handling the unions (Warde 1982; Dorfman 1983: 93–100; Marquand 1988: 51; Middlemas 1991; Marsh 1992: 47–9; Taylor 1993: 214–20). The Wilson Government thus inherited something of a poison chalice. This noxious cocktail comprised: an economy characterized by a massive public sector borrowing requirement, high rates of inflation and rising levels of unemployment, and in a condition of shock following the 1973 Oil Crisis (S. Clarke 1988; Overbeek 1990; Gamble 1994a); a highly politicized trade union movement which was widely perceived as having 'brought down' the previous Government (Dorfman 1983; Holmes 1985a; Marsh 1992);[17] and a widespread public desire for some miraculous mollification of the trades unions at the same time as radical wage restraint (Middlemas 1991).

Furthermore, since the 1960s the trade union movement had become increasingly characterized by the decentralization and diffusion of power,[18] as shopfloor bargaining tended to replace national agreements (Dorfman 1983: 3; Gourevitch et al. 1984: 62, 71; Coates 1989; Marsh 1992: 29). The immediate consequence of this was to weaken further the already fragile authority of the TUC leadership and its control over a rank-and-file membership which was itself to become increasingly militant as the effects of consecutive rounds of wage restraint were to manifest themselves in reductions in real wages. The TUC's predicament is neatly summarized by Gerald Dorfman (1983: 12): 'the overall record was that the TUC, with a few exceptions, either would not or could not deliver its co-operation even though the consequences of their refusal reverberated against important union interests.' This, as we shall see, was to prove crucial during the events of the Winter of Discontent.

Once these contextual factors are considered it becomes impossible to attribute responsibility for the Winter of Discontent so simply and unequivocally to the immediate participants. The signing of the Social Contract in 1974 emerges as a 'tipping point' (Block 1987b: 89–91). Initiated as a means of temporarily postponing the then almost inevitable onset of state and economic crisis, it had the unintended effect of channelling the failures of the state in such a way that the crisis, when it came, would involve the withdrawal of rank-and-file union support for corporatist conciliation (cf. Gourevitch et al. 1984). This was to set the context in which the crisis became narrated as that of an 'overextended' state 'held to ransom' by the trade unions. From 1974 onwards, then, the trade union leaders, their rank-and-file members and the government were on a collision course.

Far from a concession to the trade unions, the Social Contract was initially a means of ameliorating labour and of attempting to reincorporate it within a rapidly disintegrating post-war settlement. Alan Warde's (1982: 143) suggestion that 'the Social Contract was turned into a formula for securing the collaboration of the trade union interest' would seem to be justified. The only doubt that perhaps remains is whether the Social Contract was ever intended as anything other than a means of incorporating and disciplining labour (compare Coates 1980: 53–85, 202–26; 1989: 68–112;

Marsh 1992: 49–53; with Middlemas 1991: 149–92). Whatever the situation in 1974, however, it is clear that from 1975 things were to get far worse. The 'cycle of union influence' which had come to characterize successive waves of corporatist conciliation (Minkin 1991: 639) was now to run its course. The Social Contract was to become little more than a euphemism for voluntary and subsequently statutory wage restraint (Warde 1982: 160). As David Marquand (1988: 47) persuasively argues, 'after a year of accelerating infla-tion [the government] . . . launched a quasi-statutory incomes policy, the unstated objective of which was to restore private-sector profitability and to cut real wages' (see also Flanagan *et al.* 1983: 429–30). It failed to offset the onset of economic and political crisis for long, and was to shape profoundly the form that crisis was eventually to take.

Corporatism, or what in Britain had passed for corporatism, effectively expired in 1975. As David Marsh (1992: 52) notes, 'the government from June 1975 onwards took little notice of the TUC's advice or interests. In so far as the Labour Government had adopted a corporatist strategy . . . by late 1975 that strategy was abandoned.' Yet during the initial phase of the Social Contract the government in fact made certain quite substantial concessions to the unions. With hindsight this is perhaps best understood as a down-payment on continued cooperation. It repealed the infamous Industrial Relations Act, ended the constraints on collective bargaining imposed by the Heath Government, extended the existing system of price controls, increased pensions, raised top rates of taxation and created the independent Advisory Conciliation and Arbitration Service (Warde 1982: 150; Marsh 1992: 49). Similarly, after its re-election in October 1974, the government once again studiously courted the acquiescence of the trade unions by passing a series of employment protection and health and safety measures. In terms of material concessions to labour this was perhaps the high point of corporatist concili-ation in post-war Britain (with the possible exception of the period 1945–8). However, the cynicism of these measures was almost immediately revealed as a 'voluntary' incomes policy was introduced in 1975 (Marquand 1988: 47; Coates 1994: 118–21). The quotation marks are important. For 'voluntary' wage restraint was effectively secured by a series of buttressing measures which rendered it 'quasi-statutory' in Marquand's (1988) terms (see also Jessop 1980: 41–2; Gourevitch *et al.* 1984: 53). As Dorfman (1983: 120–1) observes,

> the Labour Party had broken through the taboo against incomes policy which had stood as a cornerstone of union–Labour relations ever since the defeat of *In Place of Strife* . . . Events sapped union strength and the government took advantage, however much its buffering measures 'sweetened' the bitter medicine.

Thus, 'incomes policy – the "unmentionable" of the original Social Contract – now became its central motif' (Gourevitch *et al.* 1984: 53). From here until the Winter of Discontent itself, the Social Contract was revealed as a tech-nique of short-term crisis management. The incorporation of the unions, as Marsh (1992: 32) persuasively argues, 'reflected the failure of successive British governments to solve basic economic problems'. The Social Contract, then, should not be understood as an attempt to *cure* Britain's now perennial economic frailty so much as a means of temporarily postponing the inevitable onset of a fully fledged crisis by managing the symptoms. It had the effect of displacing the cost of systematic state and economic failure as much as possible away from capital and on to labour.

As such its shelf-life was clearly limited. None the less, as the last and increasingly desperate technique of crisis management of an exhausted state regime, its success should not be understated. By the time Wilson was elected in February 1974, Britain's post-war settlement was already beginning to unravel, its structural weaknesses and inherent contradictions merely exacerbated by the worsening global economic climate in the wake of the 1973 energy crisis (Warde 1982: 153; S. Clarke 1988).

Held to ransom: the state or the trade unions?

With hindsight, the Social Contract proved almost unbelievably *successful* considering the sacrifices that it inflicted upon union members. For, as Simon Clarke (1988: 301) observes, 'in the absence of an effective interventionist mechanism for ensuring that productive capital increased investment and raised productivity sufficiently to validate raising wages and public expenditure, incomes policies could only relieve inflationary pressure by forcing down real wages' (cf. Warde 1982: 151–2). During consecutive rounds of the Social Contract the government further extended the strictures of wage restraint. Yet it continually failed to provide the unions with any concessions that might be offered as evidence to rank-and-file members of the merits of such collective altruism (Dorfman 1983: 91). What should be considered remarkable, then, is not that the Social Contract eventually evaporated in the Winter of *Dis*content, but that the long summer of comparative *content* was effectively to last for four years (Coates 1980: 260). During that period, the number of days lost through industrial stoppages fell to its lowest for ten years. Even more significant was that real wages fell by an average annual rate of 13 per cent between 1975 and 1978 (Gourevitch *et al.* 1984: 56). As Robert Taylor's (1982: 207) calculations reveal, 'the weekly take-home pay for a worker on average industrial earnings at February 1979 prices was £63.00 in 1974–5, £59.10 in 1975–6, £58.10 in 1976–7, £58.40 in 1977–8, and £61.60 in 1978–9.'

By the time the government imposed the conditions of Phase IV of the Social Contract,

> the TUC found itself brought face to face with the irreconcilable contradictions of its position in Britain's political economy. Three years of exemplary wage restraint involving cuts in real wages and requiring the marshalling of vast organisational resources for its enforcement had not sufficed to restore stability and growth to the country's feeble economy.
>
> (Gourevitch *et al.* 1984: 63)

Far from it. It was not since 1931–2 that workers had suffered such a reduction in real wages (Middlemas 1979: 156). The situation was one in which *the trade unions were effectively being held to ransom by the government*. The only certainty for the leaders of the TUC during this period was that conditions could only get much worse under a Thatcher Government. In this conviction they were certainly right, as events were subsequently to prove. The consequence, as the 'phoney election' episode at the TUC annual congress of 1978 illustrates only too well, was that despite their obvious discontent, 'the mere whiff of an election still produced spasms of loyalty by trade unionists which well exceeded the rewards of self-interest which another Labour victory might produce' (Dorfman 1983: 61). Indeed, trade union political strategy was increasingly to turn from a concern with 'the rewards of self-interest' to mere damage limitation. No gains were anticipated.

The political and economic terrain inhabited by trade union members and leaders alike was deeply rutted and heavily contoured. It presented a narrow range of unenviable strategic choices. The options were basically wage restraint – a devil well known – or Thatcherism – an incalculable monster dreaded more than anything else. Callaghan and the Cabinet were well aware of this and were fully to exploit the political mileage to be gained by backing the unions into a corner. As Callaghan basically admits in his memoirs, the 5 per cent ceiling imposed on wage increases during Phase IV of the Social Contract was a conscious strategic attempt to pin the blame for further inflation upon the unions (Callaghan 1985: 518–19; Middlemas 1991: 159). What Callaghan had not bargained for, however, was that the government's bluff would be called not by the TUC, but by the resistance of rank-and-file union members themselves.

The moment of crisis

The Winter of Discontent was not, as is often popularly imagined, precipitated by changes in the attitudes of TUC leaders. Rather, it was a rank-and-file rejection of the strictures of wage restraint imposed by the TUC in line with the terms of Phase IV. The Social Contract became progressively more fragile as the TUC found itself trapped in a 'hostage situation' (Gourevitch *et al.* 1984: 374–7). It was forced to act as an unwitting intermediary between a trade union movement resentful of an accelerating erosion of its real standard of living, and a supposedly 'fraternal' government set on passing the costs of impending economic crisis directly on to labour. Increasingly the legitimacy of the TUC leadership was itself threatened as its actions were interpreted as 'collaboration' with a government which had betrayed its fraternal allies in the labour movement. Further exacerbated by the diffusion and decentralization of trade union power and the rise of the shop steward movement, local rebellions against nationally imposed bargaining structures were to multiply inexorably during 1978 (Hitchens 1979). As Gourevitch *et al.* (1984: 57) point out,

> even those unions such as the NUR and the GMWU, that continued to support incomes policy in principle grew steadily less confident of their ability to discipline their restless local organisations. What made the position of moderate union leaders especially difficult was that they were able to show their members very few trade offs from government in return for the acceptance of incomes policy.

Ironically, then, the Winter of Discontent was symptomatic not of union *strength* but in fact a profound union *weakness* (Dorfman 1983: 59–60; Marsh 1992: 62).

Conclusions: the end of an era

The Social Contract, as Marsh (1992: 49) notes, was first and foremost an incomes policy. Its eventual demise in a flurry of industrial unrest intermingled with snow represented the final exhaustion of a last ditch attempt to manage the contradictions, tensions and failures of a post-war settlement that had been visibly disintegrating throughout the 1970s. The period of conciliation, compromise, coercion and ultimately studied betrayal of the unions that was to end in 1979 marks a strategic moment in the transformation of the British state. In the construction of the Winter of Discontent as a crisis of an 'overloaded' state 'held to ransom' by the unions, the post-war settlement was symbolically shattered. The assumptions, compromises and practices which had sustained it were torn apart. In this strangely liminal moment of transition, Thatcherism as a state project secured state power.

The moment of crisis, as Régis Debray (1973: 148) notes, 'is part of the new process that is growing out of it'. It is to this new process, to Thatcherism and to the Thatcherite project, that we turn in Part IV.

Notes

1 It should be pointed out at this stage that crises of particular national variants of more generic state regimes may well be unique, but that they are rarely exceptional (Poulantzas 1970: 57–9, 314–18; 1976: 92–3; 1978: 87–92; Hall *et al.* 1978: 273–323). For, although the specific outcome is different for each particular state regime, similar (and hence *un-exceptional*) processes combine, albeit in complex and different ways, to produce this outcome, which is thus 'different but not exceptional' (Jenson 1989; cf. Jessop 1990: 64–8).
2 As Geoffrey Ingham (1984: 281n) notes, 'all other advanced capitalist economies experienced economic fluctuations – the effects of the so called "business cycle". But due to the unique world role of maintaining a major trading and reserve currency with a structurally inappropriate economy, Britain's responses were particularly disruptive. When the reflationary "go" phase increased imports and threatened the balance of payments (and thus sterling), deflationary "stops" were imposed just at the moment . . . that the restocking of industry made accelerated growth a real possibility.'
3 Though a persistent structural weakness of the British economy, in the post-war period this tendency was associated particularly with periodic attempts by consecutive governments to inject demand into the domestic economy. Unfortunately, this was satisfied not by domestic production, but largely and increasingly by an influx of foreign consumer goods, worsening the balance of payments position.
4 A discipline imposed by the temporal constraints of electoral cycles.
5 The notion of a Thatcherite 'project' (be it a state project or a hegemonic project) is highly contentious. It is often seen as giving a spurious coherence to what was in fact a heady cocktail of disparate and often conflicting ideas (compare Riddell 1989, 1991 with Hall and Jacques 1983; Gamble 1988); and as implying an adherence to

ideology at all cost, which fails to give sufficient attention to the pragmatic 'statecraft' of the Thatcher administrations (Keegan 1984; Bulpitt 1986; Ranelagh 1991). There is even more controversy over the extent to which any 'project' was implemented (on the 'implementation gap' see Savage and Robins 1990; Marsh and Rhodes 1992; Savage *et al.* 1994). Yet to identify Thatcherism as a project is, as Andrew Gamble (1988: 222–3) rightly observes, neither to ascribe any coherence to that project nor to imply its simple translation into policy. However, there can be little doubt that, from the vantage point of an electorate reeling from the media barrage during the Winter of Discontent, Thatcherism did *appear* as a coherent project.

6 For current purposes, our attempt to map the fault-lines of the post-war settlement will be couched primarily in terms of the twin settlements thesis informed by Offe (see Table 4). It is important to note, however, that a similar mapping of the contradictions, steering problems and internal tensions of the state regime that emerged in post-war Britain could equally well be constructed in terms of Jessop's 'twin compromise thesis' – provided, that is, that a third *financiers'* settlement (or compromise) is added to those of the politicians and the producers. By extending Jessop's formulation in this way, we might replace his own argument that the 'growing crisis' of the post-war settlement be accounted for in terms of the progressive subordination of the politicians' to the producers' settlement (Jessop 1992: 16–26) with a more complex picture. In this alternative account, the initial post-war reconstruction might be seen as an attempt first to construct and then to reconcile the producers' and politicians' settlements under the dominance of the former. The subsequent evolution of the state regime might then be understood in terms of: (a) the gradual (re-)emergence of a financiers' settlement (inherited largely intact from the inter-war years); (b) its divergence from the producers' settlement; (c) the subordination of the latter to the former; and (d) the subordination of the politicians' settlement to both. This might be summarized as follows:

Phase	Dates	Objectives	Priorities
Post-war reconstruction	1944–7	Legitimation and the creation of the welfare state as principal objectives; accumulation and legitimation seen as compatible	Dominance of politicians' over producers' settlement
Divergence of settlements	1947–51	Balance of payments crises exposing the conflicting imperatives of the settlements; divergence of politicians' and producers' settlements; re-emergence and divergence of financiers' settlement	Politicians' v. producers' v. financiers' settlement
Consolidation of contradictory post-war settlement	1951–75	Maintenance of Sterling as international trading currency v. industrial modernization v. universal welfarism; primacy of Sterling	Dominance of financiers' over producers' over politicians' settlement

7 Jessop prefers the language of 'accumulation strategies' and 'hegemonic projects' to that of 'accumulation' and 'legitimation', as the latter tends to imply a rigid separation of the economic (accumulation) from the political and ideological (legitimation). As he rightly observes, the two are inextricably interwoven (Jessop 1990: 216). Similar observations are, however, made by Offe (1984, 1985) and Hay (1994a).

8 As Ingham notes, this dislocation was increasingly to be reflected in the state apparatus. Thus, 'by the early 1960s, postwar developments had... produced a situation in which conflicts based upon the potential contradictions between cosmopolitan commercial/wholesale banking capital and national productive capital were beginning to be openly expressed within the state... The separation of the City (commercial and banking capital) and industry (productive capital and labour) was now almost perfectly reproduced within the state itself' (Ingham 1984: 211, 214).

9 Thus, as Jim Tomlinson notes, despite the Attlee Government's often neglected concern with improving both the long-term efficiency and short-term output of British industry, 'primary, perhaps, was the necessity for an increase in present output rather than future competitiveness, which postwar macroeconomic and political circumstances made unavoidable. Also important was the difficulty of dealing with a suspicious and largely hostile private sector which at the same time lacked the incentives for radical change in a world of easy markets and high profits' (Tomlinson 1993: 20; cf. 1994: 161–3).

10 Still engaged in post-war physical reconstruction, and a simultaneous industrial modernization.

11 Upon which the international financial, shipping and insurance services provided by the City, and essential in counteracting the tendency towards balance of trade deficits, depended.

12 Here it is useful to follow Lucio Colletti in distinguishing between logical contradictions (taking the form of A, not A) and real oppositions or antagonisms (taking the form of A versus B). In identifying a lack of correspondence between welfare contract and welfare reality we are identifying a logical contradiction which may or may not have given rise to class or other antagonisms (Colletti 1972, 1975; Laclau and Mouffe 1985: 122–7). As we shall see, it is likely that such a logical contradiction (and the experiences to which it gave rise) did indeed promote antagonisms of class and ethnicity, and that these would in turn be recruited to narratives of the disintegration of the post-war settlement mobilized within the media in the late 1970s.

13 Thus, as Fiona Williams (1989a: 179) pointedly observes, 'The post-war expansion of the welfare state drew its workforce, skilled and unskilled, from the "reserve army of cheap labour" – Black and white women and Black men. As well as constituting the low paid workers in the welfare services, women, Black and white, have been the unpaid welfare workers in the home and the unpaid voluntary workers in the community.'

14 As Williams (1989a: 162) again notes, 'When Beveridge announced his attack on the five giants – Want, Squalor, Idleness, Ignorance and Disease – he hid the giants of Racism and Sexism, and the fights against them, behind statues to the Nation and the White family.'

15 As Jacobs (1985: 13) argues, 'black workers were acceptable as cleaners, porters, kitchen staff, even nurses and doctors, but never wholeheartedly, as patients. They could build council houses but were not expected to live in them.'

16 Stan Cohen (1972: 28) usefully describes a *moral panic* as a situation in which 'a condition, episode, person, or group of persons emerges to become defined as a threat to society's values and interests; its nature is presented in a stylized and

stereotypical fashion by the mass media' (see also Hall *et al.* 1978; Goode and Ben-Yahuda 1994; Hay 1995a).

17 In fact, as David Marsh (1992: 47) rightly observes, 'few things are simple, and the glib assertion that the miners brought the Heath Government down is just that: glib and simplistic.'

18 As Dorfman (1983: 3) notes, the TUC had 'long suffered from its construction as a loose federation . . . once government took command of the economy the TUC sorely needed sufficient authority to negotiate with national leaders about the terms of economic policy.'

Part **IV**
RE-STATING SOCIAL
and POLITICAL CHANGE

7 Thatcherism: authoritarian populism, hegemony *and the* state

It is finally time to consider that somewhat shadowy phenomenon that has loomed ominously on the horizon throughout our discussion of the post-war settlement and its crisis – *Thatcherism*. Thatcherism, however, is a peculiarly difficult object of analysis. If the dynamic and constantly evolving nature of modern political systems means that state theory is about keeping pace with a rapidly moving target, then the Thatcherite state project poses particular problems. Its interpretation is highly contested; it continues to exercise a decisive effect upon the structures, responsibilities and boundaries of the state; and there is no distinctively *post*-Thatcherite hindsight from which we might evaluate its impact. Accordingly, we must still be somewhat tentative in our attempts to assess and account for what is essentially an on-going process which is continuing to recast the very nature of the political.

What is clear, however, is that Thatcherism does represent a profound social, political, economic and indeed cultural break with the discourses and practices of post-war settlement. If we are to evaluate the extent of its structural transformation of the state and its lasting impact upon British society then we can usefully begin by identifying a series of questions.

- What is Thatcherism?
- Should Thatcherism be seen as a genuine response to the crisis of the British state of the 1970s, or merely as a new way of managing such a crisis?
- To what extent can it be said that consecutive Thatcher Governments really sought to achieve hegemony on the basis of either 'authoritarian populism' or a 'two nation strategy'?
- Were the Thatcher Governments characterized by strategic calculation, ideological zeal or pragmatic opportunism?
- What impact has Thatcherism had upon the structures of the state, the economy and civil society? How lasting is its impact likely to be?

What is Thatcherism?

There are dangers in consensus: it could be an attempt to satisfy people holding no particular views about anything. It seems more important to have a philosophy and policy which, because they are good, appeal to sufficient people to secure a majority... No great party can survive except on the basis of firm beliefs about what it wants to do. It is not enough to have reluctant support. We want people's enthusiasm as well.

(Margaret Thatcher, address to Conservative Political Centre,
10 October 1968, cited in Riddell 1991: 1)

Thatcherism has come to mean a multiplicity of different things to different people. It is thus essential that we begin our investigation of this distinctive, even unique, phenomenon by clearing up a number of widespread, yet perhaps understandable, misperceptions.

'Thatcherism' as a term was initially coined within the pages of *Marxism Today* (see especially Hall 1979a; Jacques 1979). There is not a little irony in the fact that the 'theoretical discussion journal' of the then Communist Party of Great Britain should have introduced this frequently used phrase into contemporary political debate. Equally ironic, and certainly no less telling, was that this term was not alienation, exploitation, hegemony or even class struggle, but rather 'Thatcherism'. Not deterred by this rather dubious honour, its principal authors (Stuart Hall and Martin Jacques) went on to develop one of the most perceptive, insightful and, at the time, highly prophetic accounts of the significance of the Thatcher administration's accession to power in 1979 (see especially Hall *et al.* 1978; Jacques 1979; Hall 1983, 1988a; Hall and Jacques 1983). Their conception of Thatcherism is as good a place as any to begin.

Thatcherism as a hegemonic project

Like most 'essentially contested' concepts (Gallie 1956; Connolly 1993), it is perhaps easiest to begin with what Thatcherism is not. Thus, for Hall and Jacques, Thatcherism cannot be simply reduced to: (a) Thatcher's *personal* qualities as a leader, figurehead or intransigent battle-axe; (b) the *cult of personality* which surrounded her style of political leadership; (c) the *policies pursued* by the Conservative Party under Thatcher; or even (d) some combination of the above (cf. O'Shea 1984; Gamble 1988: 20–6; Jessop *et al.* 1988: 40–4). The sense which comes closest to that which Hall and Jacques are trying to convey is captured in Bob Jessop's conception of a 'hegemonic project': 'a national-popular programme of political, intellectual and moral leadership which advances the long-term interests of the leading sectors in the accumulation strategy[1] while granting economic concessions to the masses of the social base' (Jessop *et al.* 1988: 162; see also Jessop 1990: 207–9).

As a hegemonic project, Thatcherism, in Andrew Gamble's terms, sought

to rebuild the political dominance of the Conservatives, firstly by assembling a large enough coalition of voters and interest groups;

secondly by projecting a new conception of the public interest and a vision of the ideal social and political order; and thirdly by defining policy priorities, developing a credible programme of policies, in part tailored to the specific fears and demands of voters and organised interests but also addressed to the main problems of government, particularly economic policy and external relations.

(Gamble 1988: 23–4)

In this sense, Thatcherism was an inherently *strategic project*, which sought to construct a new set of dominant ideologies and 'common sense' assumptions through which individuals within civil society might appropriate and interpret their various lived experiences. The values of compromise, consensus, equality and welfarism were to be replaced by a combination of those of consumer capitalism, enterprise culture and initiative, tradition, moral fortitude and decency. In Thatcher's own words, 'economics are the method: the object is to change the heart and soul' (cited in Holmes 1985b: 209).

To say that Thatcherism is a 'hegemonic project' is one thing; to argue that it is a successful hegemonic project is quite another. Did the Thatcher Governments succeed in transforming the 'hearts and minds' of the populace?

Here we must proceed with considerable caution, for there is a certain tendency within the existing literature to dismiss the suggestion that Thatcherism has had any kind of 'hegemonic' impact on the basis of the electorate's less than ardent enthusiasm for Thatcherite policies (as displayed in opinion polls). Thus, Ivor Crewe concludes his analysis of attitudinal change since 1979 by suggesting that 'House- and share-owners do not become Conservatives; rather Conservatives become house- and share-owners' (Crewe 1989: 31). This, and evidence like it, is often (mis)taken as a rebuttal of the thesis that Thatcherism has had any effect in recasting the 'common sense' assumptions of civil society (Jessop *et al.* 1988: 78–9, 137–8; Heath *et al.* 1991: 125–6; cf. Leys 1990; Hay 1994d: 42–3). Yet this is profoundly to miss the point. In a first-past-the-post electoral system in which both major parties are committed to defending both the 'right to buy' and the right, having bought, 'to carry on owning', a lack of converts to the Conservatives is no indication that the Thatcher Governments failed to transform the material interests and susceptibilities of large sections of the electorate. Indeed, if new home- and share-owners were asked whether they would rather vote for a party committed to preserving '*their* property rights', or one which would return privatized industries to the public sector and buy back *their* homes, the evidence might look somewhat different.[2] In the selling off of council housing, the Thatcher Governments certainly succeeded in transforming the material interests of broad sections of the population. It is to the susceptibilities and sensibilities of this recomposed electorate that the parties have increasingly come to accommodate themselves (Hay 1992a). Thus, as Colin Leys (1990: 127) notes, the electorate during the 1980s 'seem[s] to have drifted back towards Labour more or less in step with the Party's gradual acceptance of the Thatcherite "settlement"'. The question of Thatcherism, then, is still fundamentally 'a question of hegemony'. The success or failure of a hegemonic project cannot be evaluated in terms of electoral dominance. A hegemonic project, as Anna Marie Smith (1994: 37) argues,

> does not dominate political subjects: it does not reduce political sub-
> jects to pure obedience and it does not even require their unequivocal
> support for its specific demands. It pursues, instead, a far more subtle
> goal, namely the naturalisation of its specific vision of the social order
> itself. To describe a political project as hegemonic, then, is not to say
> that a majority of the electorate explicitly supports its policies, but to
> say that there appears to be no other alternative to this project's vision
> of society.

The success of the Thatcherite project lies not in the emergence of a 'one-party state' (Nairn 1994: 46–7), which now looks increasingly fragile, but in: (a) the extent to which we are witnessing the consolidation of a 'one-vision democracy' (Hay 1994e); (b) the degree of convergence between the parties around a distinctly Thatcherite agenda; and (c) the extent to which this represents a departure from the politics of consensus which characterized the post-war settlement.

Seen this way the question as to whether Thatcherism has existed and/ or continues to exist is of central importance and is not merely a matter of which labels we affix to a transient swing of the electoral pendulum.

Thatcherism and the new right

Useful though such a term is, 'Thatcherism' is something of a misnomer. For to understand Thatcher is certainly not to understand Thatcherism, and to understand Thatcherism is not necessarily to understand Thatcher. Thus although Mrs Thatcher was to come to epitomize, even personify, the state and hegemonic project of the new right, this strategic project was formulated prior to its interpellation of Thatcher as the very essence of Thatcherism. It is thus essential that we consider 'Thatcherism before Thatcher' and particularly the growing ascendancy of the ideologues of the new right since the 1960s (Levitas 1986a; Kaye 1987; King 1987; Whitaker 1987; A. M. Smith 1994).

Yet the new right, despite its decisive impact upon the political agendas of the advanced capitalist economies from the mid-1970s, is not some homogeneous school of thought. It is in fact characterized by an extremely broad spectrum of deeply contradictory intellectual factions, from the 'anarcho-capitalist' libertarians (Rand 1957, 1964; Rothbart 1978) to the authoritarian guardians of Christian 'virtue' of the 'moral minority' (such as the National Viewers and Listeners Association and the anti-abortion lobby). What they share is a common identification with the label 'right' (in both senses), and a revulsion for the cloying welfarism and consensual conciliation of the post-war settlement. The central axis along which they are divided is that of liberalism–conservatism: the neo-liberals advocating a minimal state to maximize the condition of liberty and freedom, the neo-conservatives calling for an interventionist and authoritarian state which will centrally impose a rigid morality upon society.

Neo-liberalism

From the late 1950s onwards a number of neo-liberal think-tanks were established on the peripheral edge of the Tory Party, an enclave of resurgent free-market liberalism in a time of 'statism' and welfarism. The key figure behind this political rehabilitation of classical liberalism in Britain was Keith Joseph, later Sir and ultimately Baron Keith Joseph. In many respects he was the Thatcherite puppet-master general (Stephenson 1980: 12; Gamble 1988: 80–3; Thatcher 1993: 14, 562; Desai 1994).

The oldest, most prominent and still perhaps the most influential of these reactionary hotbeds of economic insurgency was the Institute of Economic Affairs (better known by its acronym, IEA). It was established in 1957 by Anthony Fisher, who had earlier been encouraged by Friedrich von Hayek, his adopted free-market guru, to found a 'scholarly research organization'.[3] This he duly did, but only once he had accumulated sufficient funds from his chicken business, Buxted Chickens. Despite this enterprising start, it was to remain a somewhat paltry concern until 1959 when Fisher was asked to organize the bi-annual conference of the Mont Pelerin Society in Oxford (Desai 1994: 46).[4] Its influence steadily grew, as did that of its principal ideologues, Arthur Seldon (a journalist and former member of the Communist Party) and Ralph Harris (now Lord Harris of High Cross, a lecturer at St Andrews University).[5] The IEA still remains the most important 'external' influence upon government policy publishing a constant stream of reports and policy reviews which have often, and increasingly, provided blueprints for Government White Papers (on the continuing link between the IEA and the Major Government see Pirie 1993; Atkinson and Savage 1994).

It was not until the 1970s, however, that new right institutes, think-tanks and journals began to 'sprout like mushrooms' (Gamble 1988: 147) in the damp, dark corners of the disintegrating consensus. And spread they did. In 1974 Keith Joseph and Margaret Thatcher established the Centre for Policy Studies (CPS), which has, perhaps not surprisingly, remained the closest of the think-tanks to Thatcherite strategy and policy. Indeed, between 1975 and 1979 it began to take over the strategic role of the Conservative Research Department.[6] Its self-appointed task was to prepare the groundwork for the Thatcherite crusade, its goal to change the 'climate of opinion':

> The Centre's research and publication policy will be strategic in the sense that the studies and research projects will be designed to prepare public opinion for specific policy decisions sometimes in the present but often in the future rather than simply extend the boundaries of knowledge.
>
> (Internal CPS memo from Simon Webley, cited in Desai 1994: 55)

The Adam Smith Institute (ASI) was established in 1977, and is run by two more graduates of St Andrews University, Madsen Pirie and Eamonn Butler. The institute is distinguished by a concern with policy implementation and has been particularly closely associated with the formulation of policy proposals for privatization, denationalization and compulsory competitive tendering (Kavanagh 1987: 87–8). Its influence has waned to some extent over recent years, largely as a consequence of its principled and consistent objection to un-elected quangos (bringing it into conflict with the Major Government).

Together these constitute the big three, a triangulation point in neo-liberal intellectual thought. It is here that the origins of what was to become Thatcherism should be sought. For, from the mid-1960s onwards, the IEA, and later the CPS, began drawing upon the neo-liberal free-market economics of Friedman and Hayek in developing a powerful intellectual assault on the institutions, practices and underlying assumptions of the Keynesian welfare state. The full force of this ideological barrage was only to be unleashed within the public domain with the downturn of the global economy and Britain's slide towards crisis in the mid-1970s.

The central precepts of neo-liberalism are:

1 The reassertion of the free market, the principles of *laissez-faire* economics and a quasi-religious belief in the sanctity and supremacy of market mechanisms as a means to deliver equitable outcomes ('the morality of the market').

2 The maximization of individual liberty and freedom through the 'rolling back' of the institutions of the state from the economy, the private sphere and civil society.

3 *Monetarism*: a belief that inflation and not unemployment was the major problem facing the British economy and that it could be controlled through the regulation of the money supply[7] (the monetarist thesis was particularly associated with the work of Milton Friedman, whose key lecture was published by the IEA in 1970).

4 The rolling back of the welfare state, which was seen as stifling the potential vibrancy of a free-market economy, encouraging dependency and apathy instead of industry, innovation and entrepreneurialism; and which was also seen as a massive and unnecessary burden upon the taxpayer and thus a disincentive to investment and hence capitalist accumulation.[8]

Neo-liberalism, though perhaps the central influence upon the shaping of the Thatcherite policy agenda (King 1987: 8–9, 23–5; Jessop *et al.* 1988: 171–7; Durham 1991; Desai 1994; Cockett 1995; though compare Levitas 1986a; A. M. Smith 1994), is by no means the only body of thought on which the Thatcherite state and hegemonic project has drawn. In this respect Thatcherism is peculiarly Janus-faced. For the ideology of the new right is itself comprised of a flexible blend of neo-liberalism and neo-conservatism. Table 9 summarizes the influence of neo-liberalism upon the ideology of the new right.

Neo-conservatism

Working-class single mothers . . . are producing problem children, the future unmarried mothers, denizens of our borstals, subnormal educational establishments, prisons, hostels for drifters.

(Sir Keith Joseph in *The Times*, 22 October 1974,
cited in Somerville 1992: 99)

Table 9   Neo-liberalism and the new right

Intellectual gurus	Milton Friedman Friedrich von Hayek
Principal institutes	Institute of Economic Affairs (1957) Centre for Policy Studies (1974) Adam Smith Institute (1977)
Pressure groups	Aims of Industry Economic League Freedom Association Libertarian Alliance National Association for Freedom
Ideological precepts	The supremacy of the free market; freedom, individual autonomy and liberty; the rolling back of the frontiers of the state; the morality and sanctity of the market; the market as meritocratic; entrepreneurialism through incentive; libertarianism in place of egalitarianism.
Major policy objectives	Privatization of nationalized industries; curtailment of trade union power; rolling back of the welfare state; reductions in public expenditure; monetarism – control of the money supply; decreased taxation; 'supply-side economics'.

While possessing a similar intellectual and institutional history to that of neo-liberalism – in journals and more or less formalized think-tanks and discussion groups – the neo-conservatism of Thatcherism is much more closely associated with campaigning pressure groups. These include Mary White-house's National Viewers and Listeners Association, the anti-abortion lobby (Durham 1991: 16–38; Franklin 1991: 191–6), CARE (formerly the Festival of Light) and a host of groups concerned with the promotion of the patriarchal nuclear family (see David 1986; Abbott and Wallace 1992: 45–8; Somerville 1992: 100).

Intellectually, the neo-conservative resurgence is most closely associated with the Salisbury Group, its journal the *Salisbury Review*, the Conservative Philosophy Group and the more informal but no less significant Peterhouse School.[9] Thus, while the budding ideologues of the neo-liberal right were presumably dining in on Buxted Chickens at the IEA, those of the neo-conservative right were indulging their taste for good food and moral authoritarianism in the famous male-only dining clubs of Peterhouse (the oldest and most traditional of the Cambridge colleges).

Between the campaigning moral minority on the streets and the dizzy heights of conservative academe are an array of clubs and institutes oft-frequented by Conservative MPs, including Common Cause, the Monday Club, the Coalition for Peace and Security and the Institute for the Study of

Table 10   Neo-conservatism and the new right

Intellectual gurus	Edmund Burke Michael Oakeshott Roger Scruton
Intellectual groupings	Salisbury Group Peterhouse School Conservative Philosophy Group
Private political groups	Common Cause Monday Club Coalition for Peace and Security Institute for the Study of Conflict
Pressure groups	National Viewers and Listeners Association; Society for the Protection of the Unborn Child; Life; Festival of Light; Clean Up TV; Family Concern; National Family Trust; Conservative Family Campaign; Family and Youth Concern.
Ideological principles	Moral authoritarianism and traditional values; respect, discipline and moral decency; repressive/deterrent policing of deviance; reassertion of the nuclear family unit; defence of the 'British way of life'; patriotism, monarchism, nationalism; social hierarchy and tradition.
Major policy objectives	Increased expenditure on law-and-order; increased expenditure on defence; interventionist, authoritarian and coercive state; compulsory repatriation of ethnic minorities; curtailment of trade union power; dismantling of the 'dependency culture'; anti-pornography legislation.

Conflict. What this reveals is that if neo-liberalism had a much greater hold over the formulation of government policy, then neo-conservatism continues to exercise a corresponding hold over the 'hearts and minds' of many Tory MPs.

The central principles of neo-conservatism can be summarized as follows (see also Table 10):

1 A centrally imposed moral authoritarianism enforcing a return to 'traditional' values (on this reinvention of 'tradition' see Kaye 1987; cf. Hobsbawm and Ranger 1983; Pearson 1983; Wright 1985).
2 The reassertion of the values of respect, discipline, and moral decency (Casey 1978; Scruton 1980).
3 The active intervention of the state to police and coerce deviant miscreants, providing deterrence and re-instilling traditional values into those who have strayed from the path of moral fortitude at the alluring behest of the 'permissive society' (Scruton 1980).

4 The dismantling of the welfare state and the 'dependency culture' that it spawned;
5 The assertion and promotion of the institution of the patriarchal nuclear family unit (Scruton 1980; Mount 1982; Anderson and Dawson 1986; Kiernan and Wicks 1990).
6 The defence of the values of patriotism, nationalism, 'British identity' and the 'British way of life' against the alien ideologies of collectivism, compromise, consensus and cloying social welfarism (Casey 1982; Powell 1982; Honeyford 1983).
7 The restoration of social hierarchy and tradition (Berry 1983).

The potential lines of conflict between neo-liberalism and neo-conservatism become immediately apparent. For, in many respects, they propose antithetically opposed principles of social organization. While the former advocates a minimal role for the ('night-watchman') state in merely providing the conditions for the free play of the market, the latter requires a strong interventionist and authoritarian state prepared to impose a collective morality from the centre, thereby curtailing individual liberty. This central tension in new right ideology is well captured by Andrew Gamble (1988) in the paradox of 'the free economy [neo-liberalism] and the strong state [neo-conservatism]', which forms the title of his excellent study. Given this obvious and widely acknowledged contradiction (Gamble 1983; Levitas 1986a; King 1987; Jessop *et al.* 1988), it might be expected that the politics of the Thatcher years would be characterized by constant struggles between neo-liberal and neo-conservative tendencies.

However, such open ideological confrontation has in fact been rare. Moreover, it has tended to be restricted to areas of policy not crucial to the government's overall agenda. There are two striking examples of this potential tension: Sunday trading and the legalization of soft drugs. The ideological rift is detailed in Table 11. Interestingly, however, on many of the core components of the Thatcherite 'instinct' (Riddell 1983, 1991) neo-liberalism and neo-conservatism converge. For instance, both ideological sources target, though in rather different ways, the dismantling of the welfare state and the curtailment of trade union influence.

What emerges is a picture of new right ideology as the flexible synthesis of elements of neo-liberalism and neo-conservatism. Policies have generally being pursued as part of a neo-liberal project but often legitimated through the populist ideology of moral authoritarianism and a nostalgic re-imagination of 'tradition' which are characteristic themes of neo-conservatism. As Des King (1987: 8) notes, neo-conservative arguments have tended 'to constitute residual claims addressing the *political consequences* of liberal economic policies' (emphasis added). The desire to roll back the frontiers of the welfare state and the curtailment of union power, for instance, were central aspects of a broader neo-liberal *accumulation strategy*. Yet the ability to translate these strategic objectives into public policy was reliant upon a neo-conservative legitimating rhetoric (couched in terms of severing relations of dependency spawned by a 'nanny state') (see Table 12).

As I have suggested elsewhere, Thatcherism is perhaps best seen as 'a

Table 11   The contradictions of new right ideology

	Neo-liberalism	*Neo-conservatism*
Sunday trading	Favouring the free operation of the market wherever and whenever there is a demand	Defending the sanctity of the Sabbath from the encroachment of the market
Legalization of soft drugs	Favouring the freedom, liberty and autonomy of the subject to make unconstrained market choices	Seeing the legalization of soft drugs as the last stage on the inexorable road to permissiveness and moral decay from which the paternalistic state must defend its subjects

neo-liberal state project *camouflaged* in the rhetoric of moral conservatism' (Hay 1992b: 756).

'Authoritarian populism' and Thatcherism as a 'hegemonic project'

Still the most influential, and certainly one of the most sophisticated, provocative and perceptive, analyses of Thatcherism is that of Stuart Hall and Martin Jacques. Their work and the debate that it has generated has provided a central point of reference, and in many cases the starting point for subsequent critical interpretations of the legacy of the Thatcher years (see, for instance, O'Shea 1984; ten Tusscher 1986; Gamble 1988: 179–87, 203–7; Jessop *et al.* 1988, 1990; Leys 1990; Durham 1991: 161–78; Franklin *et al.* 1991: 22–5; McNeil 1991; Hay 1992a; A. M. Smith 1994).

Authoritarian populism, authoritarian statism

In a series of telling contributions, many of them first published in *Marxism Today* (and reproduced in Hall and Jacques 1983; Hall 1988a; see also Hall *et al.* 1978), they interpret the rise of Thatcherism and its enduring impact in terms of an 'authoritarian populism'.

In the Thatcherite state project they identify the blueprint for a distinctively new regime of the capitalist state in Britain. This regime, they suggest, is likely to be characterized by a tilting in the balance between coercion and consent (referred to in Chapter 2) towards the coercive or repressive pole. Yet this takes place within the confines of a state structure which maintains its democratic form. Indeed, it 'represents the new "democratic" form of the bourgeois republic in the current phase of capitalism' (Poulantzas 1978: 209). Here Hall and Jacques draw upon the work of Nicos Poulantzas and his 'courageous' and prophetic account of the tendency towards 'authoritarian statism' in Western Europe in the late 1970s (Hall *et al.* 1978: 273–323;

Table 12   The Thatcherite 'instinct'

	Neo-liberalism	Neo-conservatism
Dismantling of the welfare state	1 To eliminate the disincentive to entrepreneurialism of high taxation born of state welfare expenditure. 2 To promote fiscal austerity and stimulate the economy through reductions in PSBR. 3 To introduce the discipline and efficiency of the market to make services more responsive to the needs of 'consumers'.	1 To sever the relationships of dependency and moral frailty between the state and welfare 'scroungers' spawned by state welfare. 2 To reassert the 'traditional' (and patriarchal) values of charity, family support and care founded upon the unpaid domestic labour of women.
Curtailment of union influence	1 To put an end to overload, ungovernability and fiscal irresponsibility by minimizing the demands placed upon the state. 2 To roll back the frontiers of an overextended state and allow market mechanisms to determine outcomes. 3 To enhance the competitiveness of the domestic economy by removing this 'distortion' from the labour market.	1 To restore authority and respect for the state and the crown. 2 To eliminate the 'enemy within' who would dare to 'hold the country to ransom'. 3 To dismantle the structures of a creeping socialism born of post-war illusions. 4 To replace the consensual values of compromise and conciliation with the vigorous virtues of self-reliance and moral fortitude.

Poulantzas 1978: 203–65; Hall 1985: 151). Yet they are not uncritical of Poulantzas's interpretation of this new state regime as one characterized by 'intensive state control over every sphere of socio-economic life combined with a radical decline of the institutions of political democracy and with draconian and multiform curtailment of so-called "formal" liberties' (Poulantzas 1978: 203–4).

There are two major problems with simply superimposing this more generic evolutionary perspective on to the contemporary British experience. First, what for Poulantzas was an authoritarian *statism* is seemingly translated in Britain into an authoritarian *anti-statism* (Hall 1985: 152).[10] For one of the defining ideological precepts of Thatcherism is its retrenchment of the state from the economy, civil society and the private sphere. Yet this immediately requires some qualification. For, in Hall's conception, anti-statism does not refer to a strategy which refuses to make use of the resources of the state and extend them where possible, but rather to one which conceives for the state a limited role and which, 'for the purpose of popular mobilisation', represents itself as anti-statist.[11] Hall could not therefore simply equate Thatcherism with authoritarian statism, neat though this might have been.

Moreover, what for Hall is distinctive about Thatcherism is not merely its authoritarianism, startling and unprecedented (at least in the post-war period) though this is. Rather, the essence of Thatcherism lies in its paradoxical combination of authoritarianism *and populism*. Thus what Poulantzas neglects are

> the ways in which popular consent can be so constructed, by a historical bloc seeking hegemony, as to harness to its support some popular discontents, neutralise the opposing forces, desegregate the opposition and really incorporate some strategic elements of popular opinion into its own hegemonic project.
>
> (Hall 1985: 152)

The novelty and specificity of Thatcherism thus resides not so much in the drift towards a 'law-and-order society' (Hall 1979b), but rather in the fact that this has been complemented by a strengthening of consent among large sections of the population. 'Authoritarian populism', then, is a deliberately contradictory and paradoxical formulation reflecting the contradictory and paradoxical nature of this unique social, political and cultural phenomenon.

The perceptiveness of this analysis is most clearly revealed when it is considered that Stuart Hall and his co-authors initially used the term 'authoritarian populism' in 1978 to refer to the wide-scale moral backlash mobilized as a response to the mugging moral panic of the early 1970s (Hall *et al.* 1978). This they interpreted as symptomatic of an emerging crisis of the state. As they note, this crisis

> is experienced, first as a diffuse social unease . . . as an unlocated surge of social anxiety. This fastens on different phenomena: on the hedonistic culture of youth, on the disappearance of the traditional insignia of class, on the dangers of unbridled materialism, on change itself. Later, it appears to focus on more tangible targets: specifically, on the anti-social nature of youth movements, on the threat to British life [posed] by the black immigrant, and on the 'rising fever chart' of crime. Later still – as the major social upheavals of the counter-culture and the political student movements become more organised as social forces – it surges, in the form of a more focused 'social anxiety', around these points of disturbance . . . Finally, as the crisis deepens, and the forms of conflict and dissent assume a more explicitly political and a more clearly delineated class form, social anxiety also precipitates in its more political form. It is directed against the organised power of the working class; against political extremism; against trade-union blackmail; against the threat of anarchy, riot and terrorism . . . *Here the anxieties of the lay public and the perceived threats to the state coincide and converge.*
>
> (Hall *et al.* 1978: 321, emphasis added)

Rather like Poulantzas's account of 'authoritarian statism', this extraordinarily prescient analysis, in many respects predicts the phenomenon that was later to be labelled Thatcherism. The ultimate tribute to the sophistication of this account is the ease with which it has subsequently been extended to account for the origins and popular resonances of Thatcherism.

In the bleak mid-winter: authoritarian populism and the crisis of the state

As the above discussion suggests, the importance of Hall's contribution lies in its ability to reveal the mobilization of a popular social basis for Thatcherism out of crisis, and, indeed, the role of the new right in the very constitution of the moment of crisis itself (see also Chapter 5). As Hall perceptively notes in an article first published during the bleak mid-winter of discontent, 'the crisis has begun to be "lived" in *its* [Thatcherism's] terms. This is a new kind of taken-for-grantedness; a reactionary common sense, harnessed to the practices and solutions of the radical right and the class forces it now aspires to represent' (Hall 1979a: 30; see also Hay 1994b: 245–9). Once the Winter of Discontent was understood as a crisis of the state – a crisis of an over-extended, overloaded and ungovernable state 'held to ransom by the trade unions' – the victory of the new right was effectively secured. This was perhaps the only truly hegemonic moment of Thatcherism. It occurred well before Mrs Thatcher entered Number 10.

Accordingly, the initial success of Thatcherism was premised upon the ability of the new right to construct the moment of the late 1970s as a moment of crisis, in which a particular type of decisive intervention was required. In so doing it proved itself capable of changing, if not the hearts and minds of the electorate, then certainly the predominant perceptions of the political context, recruiting subjects to its vision of the 'necessary' response to a crisis of a monolithic state besieged by the trade unions.

It was in distorting and simplifying, but above all in *interpreting* and *giving meaning to*, the events of the Winter of Discontent that Thatcherism sowed the seeds of its hegemonic project and secured state power. In so doing it was to impose a new trajectory upon the institutions of the state. In the process, the very contours, boundaries, expectations and perceived responsibilities of the state, which had mapped out the terrain of the 'political' throughout the post-war period, became subject to redefinition. The stakes were raised from the 'conjunctural' politics of crisis management to the 'structural' politics of state transformation.

Thus, as Hall (1979a: 39) again suggests,

> Thatcherism's . . . success and effectivity does not lie in its capacity to dupe unsuspecting folk but in the way it addresses real problems, real and lived experiences, real contradictions – yet it is able to represent them within a logic of discourse which pulls them systematically into line with policies and class strategies of the right.

It was in this ability to resonate with the lived experiences of the crisis, to provide explanations, to attribute responsibility (to 'militant unionists' and an overextended state) and to propose a decisive response that Thatcherism's initial social base was forged. Thus, 'far from simply conjuring demons out

of the deep, [Thatcherism] operated directly on the real and manifestly contradictory experience of the popular classes under social-democratic corporatism' (Hall 1979a: 31).

In offering an account sufficiently flexible to 'narrate' a great variety of
'morbid symptoms' (Gramsci 1971: 276), yet sufficiently simple and abstract
to attribute responsibility unambiguously, the new right was able to win the
battle to define the crisis and hence the strategies appropriate for its resolution. In this way 'authoritarian populism' succeeded in co-opting broad sections of civil society into the moral authoritarian backlash that was to
characterize Thatcherism's rise to power. The principles of full employment,
an interventionist and universalist welfare state, equality of opportunity, the
caring society, Keynesianism and corporatism were all exposed to scathing
and public critique as the new canons of the right – the free market and the
Victorian social values of patriotism, patriarchy, racism, imperialist nostalgia,
tradition, respect and moral fortitude – were elevated in an authoritarian yet
populist backlash.

The Hall–Jessop debate: the 'monstrous monolith' and the 'gang of four'

Perceptive, provocative and prophetic as Hall's account certainly is, it is not
unproblematic. Indeed, it has generated one of the most important debates
in contemporary state theory. Hall's interpretation of Thatcherism and his
assessment of the strategic implications for the left has been challenged by
Bob Jessop and his co-authors, Kevin Bonnett, Simon Bromley and Tom Ling
(the self-styled alternative 'gang of four') in a series of telling interventions
(Jessop _et al._ 1984, 1985, 1987). Though their critique is constructive, broadly
sympathetic and similarly informed by the Marxist state theory of Gramsci
and Poulantzas, there is much at stake in this debate.

The gang of four's critique can be summarized as follows. First, the
term 'authoritarian populism' is unclear, confusing and confused. Hall and
his various co-authors are simply too ready to generalize from the ideological. The cost is to overstate the novelty of Thatcherism, implying that it has
been able to make a clean break with the past, when it has in fact been far
more heavily constrained by its social, political and economic inheritance
(Jessop _et al._ 1984: 70, 75, 77–8; cf. Marsh 1995; Marsh and Rhodes 1995).

Second, Hall tends to focus almost exclusively upon the _ideological_ at
the expense of the political and the economic. The result is a very partial
analysis of Thatcherism, and one that seems to imply that the realm of
discourse and ideology is free-floating and autonomous of political and economic determinations (Jessop _et al._ 1985: 112; Marsh 1995). Hall thus neglects 'the structural underpinnings of Thatcherism in the economic and
state systems and its specific economic and political bases of support among
both people and power bloc' (Jessop _et al._ 1984: 73; cf. 1985: 113–14).

Third, for an analysis which stresses the ideological, Hall perhaps surprisingly fails to look at the _reception_ of Thatcherite ideology within civil
society. As a consequence he tends to universalize the appeal of Thatcherism,
implying that it resonates in the same way with all sections of society.

Thatcherism becomes presented as an ideological monolith whose impact is thus homogenized (Jessop *et al.* 1984: 73–4; Hay 1992a: 44). This has the effect of further reinforcing the highly problematic undertone to the analysis – that Thatcherism has either become, or is becoming, hegemonic. What is instead required, Jessop and his co-authors argue, is a more nuanced account capable of asking: (a) which messages were accepted and by whom; (b) how the appeal to the electorate has evolved as the Thatcherite project has developed; and (c) to what extent this appeal has been socially differentiated (by class, gender and ethnicity, for instance). Hall's analysis 'tends to obscure the real sources of support for Thatcherism because they are subsumed indiscriminately under the rubric of authoritarian populism' (Jessop *et al.* 1984: 69).

Fourth, Thatcherite ideology cannot be both *hegemonic* and *authoritarian* simultaneously since the two are inherently contradictory. One effectively precludes the other. Hall talks of a coercion–consent axis yet apparently alternates between situating Thatcherism at either end of this spectrum. This makes a nonsense of the very distinction, or, more likely, of Hall's description of Thatcherism as an authoritarian populism (Jessop *et al.* 1984: 72; 1985: 111–12).

Fifth, the status of the term 'authoritarian populism' and thus the notion of 'Thatcherism' itself remain very unclear. Should the latter be seen as a strategic, calculating *imposition* of an ideology upon civil society from the top down; or a spontaneous, collective ground swell of popular resistance to the state and economic failure of the Keynesian welfare state? 'When emphasising its populist, popular, consensual aspects, Hall sees authoritarian populism as a passive revolution from below; when emphasising its authoritarian, disciplinary and coercive aspects, he regards it as a passive revolution from above' (Jessop *et al.* 1984: 71–2). Which is it to be?

Though these criticisms are far from devastating and are merely intended as constructive interventions in a debate of particular strategic significance for the left, Jessop and his co-authors do identify a number of weaknesses within Hall's overall approach. They do not necessitate a wholesale rejection of the authoritarian populism thesis (as the 'gang of four' would be the first to concede). What is required, however, is a partial reworking which emphasizes more the links between the political, the economic and the ideological in the constitution of Thatcherism as a hegemonic, state and economic project (cf. Hay 1994f: 352–4; Marsh 1995).

We will now take each of the above points in turn.

The confusions of authoritarianism populism

This is perhaps the weakest of the criticisms made by the gang of four and one which displays a certain misinterpretation and misunderstanding of Hall's work. The dispute is, in many respects, merely one of definitions. As we noted at the outset, Thatcherism means very many different things to a variety of different people. Though Hall and Jessop (both neo-Gramscian state theorists) agree on much, their emphases and corresponding definitions of Thatcherism diverge. Authoritarian populism appears confused and confusing to the gang of four largely because it does not reflect their chosen understanding of the term. For Hall, let us remember, Thatcherism is a term coined before 1979, a term which seeks to capture the novelty of this exceptional political and social phenomenon and its ability to mobilize civil society. For Jessop and his co-authors, Thatcherism is seen much more in terms of its *state* project and *accumulation strategy*. They are thus primarily concerned with Thatcher in power, and specifically with the impact of the Thatcher Governments upon Britain's languishing economy and crisis-ridden state apparatus. Similar theoretical concerns thus draw Hall and the 'gang of four' in rather different directions.

For Hall the 'ideological moment' is all important since it is in the 'battle for hearts and minds' that the novelty of Thatcherism lies. Given this focus, the term authoritarian populism is not particularly problematic since it stresses the populist appeal of a resurgent authoritarian moral conservatism couched in terms of tradition, authority, discipline, patriarchy and patriotism. It is a powerful and succinct description (if little more) of the distinctive appeal of Thatcherism in the late 1970s, and of the contradictory and paradoxical nature of this unique cultural–political phenomenon.

In challenging Hall's interpretation of Poulantzas, the gang of four are on a rather firmer footing.[12] They are certainly right to suggest that 'authoritarian populism' does represent a somewhat strange and unnecessary corruption of 'authoritarian statism' (Jessop *et al.* 1985: 112). For the latter refers to the 'political moment', to the state and the authoritarian form that it takes in contemporary capitalist societies. Yet once it is seen that Hall does not so much wish to correct Poulantzas as to complement his account by reapplying his description of the contemporary state form to the ideological plane, any confusion evaporates, and the term stands on its own.

Ideologism

This closely related critique reveals a certain failure on the part of the 'gang of four' to suspend temporarily their own distinctive agenda and to entertain the somewhat different concerns that animate Hall's contribution. For once again they really fail to consider what it was that initially stimulated Hall's interest in Thatcherism; they simply assume that he must share their own theoretical concerns and political motivations. Hall, with a degree of justification, is entirely unrepentant about his supposed ideologism, claiming that he: (a) asks a set of questions about the novelty and specificity of Thatcherism as a hegemonic project; (b) answers that what is distinctive and unique is its purchase upon the popular political imagination; (c) thus focuses upon Thatcherite discourse and rhetoric; and (d) correspondingly privileges an analysis of ideology over that of the political and the economic (Hall 1985: 156–8).

Hall's defence is completed by a reminder that all accounts are necessarily partial and that he never claimed to be writing the definitive word on Thatcherism anyway. He is thus quick to concede the importance of Jessop *et al.*'s more rounded and structural account of the economic and the political. Yet he then turns on the gang of four, suggesting that in their refusal to take the ideological moment sufficiently seriously, 'they have . . . robbed themselves of insights from which their own analysis might have profited' (Hall 1985: 156). There is a certain irony in this ill-tempered and unfortunate remark. For it is Hall, having backed himself into a particularly difficult corner, who repeatedly refuses to concede the political and economic mediation of ideological change (at least in anything other than a token fashion). Thus, despite numerous pretensions to the contrary (Hall 1985: 156, 157), it is his account which is guilty of reductionism in the form of a residual ideologism. If anything, Jessop *et al.*'s allegation seems to be borne out more by Hall's response than it is by the initial target itself.

The 'monstrous monolith' and the reception of new right ideology

Hall stands accused of: (a) a failure to consider the reception of Thatcherite ideology; (b) the universalization of the appeal of Thatcherism; (c) the homogenization of Thatcherism as a political project, implying the existence of a 'monstrous monolith' (Jessop *et al.* 1984: 73–4); and (d) a failure to consider the extent to which the appeal of Thatcherism was socially differentiated. Here at last the gang of four find themselves on a much firmer footing. For it is sadly ironic that Hall, in many respects the pioneer of Marxist accounts of ideological reception (see Hall 1980a, b), should, as Jessop *et al.* rightly observe, completely fail to analyse the differential appropriations, readings and interpretations of Thatcherite ideology within civil society. Moreover, this is an oversight which he has still failed to rectify.

The consequence is, as Jessop *et al.* again perceptively observe, to universalize and homogenize the appeal of Thatcherism, implying that new right imagery and ideology resonate in the same way with different sections of society. This in turn exaggerates the degree of hegemony that it has achieved, or is ever likely to.

Hegemonizing coercion?

Once again the proletariat has discredited itself terribly.
(Engels, in Marx and Engels 1962: 345)

Can a hegemonic project be authoritarian? This is an interesting and difficult question which perhaps suggests the need for a more differentiated conception of hegemony (see Hay 1992a: 31–43). Yet if there is a criticism to be made here the gang of four have not found it. For, in relation to Thatcherism and its ideological appeal Hall is surely correct – Thatcherism did seek to achieve an ideological dominance (albeit one restricted to certain sections of the population) on the basis of an initially authoritarian appeal. The gang of four seem to have difficulty with the suggestion that moral authoritarianism, discrimination and other forms of 'symbolic violence' (Bourdieu 1990, 1991) can be regarded as populist (Jessop *et al.* 1984: 71).[13] Yet here Hall's own research into the stigmatizing and vilification of the black urban proletariat (Hall *et al.* 1978; CCCS 1982) must surely have provided a constant and painful confirmation. As this example reveals, a very active if somewhat sadistic consent (perhaps even localized hegemony) can indeed be constructed on the basis of an ideology that criminalizes, marginalizes and systematically represses those sections of civil society that it labels 'deviant' or 'other' (Gilman 1985: 107, 214–15, 235–7; Sumner 1994: 134–8). The appeal of overtly racist ideology to the white urban proletariat, for instance, demonstrates the ability of authoritarianism to become almost pathologically hegemonic within certain sections of the population.

Authoritarian populism: top-down or bottom-up?

Here again Jessop and his co-authors display an uncharacteristic failure to appreciate the full significance of Hall's contribution and in fact to grasp fully the enterprise that Hall is engaged in. In asking him to plump for either a top-down or bottom-up conception of ideological change they are effectively implying that he is seeking to have his cake and eat it. This is to do him a grave disservice. For much of the originality and sophistication of his analysis lies in the ability to demonstrate how Thatcherism was able to draw upon the many spontaneous discourses of resistance to the disintegrating institutions of the Keynesian welfare state, and to co-opt them 'within a logic of discourse which pull[ed] them systematically into line with the policies and class strategies of the right' (Hall 1979a: 39).

This, after all, is the very subject matter of _Policing the Crisis_ (Hall _et al._ 1978). The strength of Thatcherism as an ideological onslaught on the structures and institutions of Britain's beleaguered Keynesian welfare state lay precisely in this ability to recruit existing expressions of dissatisfaction to the new right's diagnosis of crisis. The central achievement of Hall's account is the way in which he reveals this complementarity between the broadly articulated principles of authoritarian populism and a popular ground swell of resistance from below. In so doing he illustrates Régis Debray's (1973: 248) truism: 'the "moment of crisis" . . . is part of the new process that is growing out of it.' The moment of crisis as Hall (1979a: 30) himself notes, was 'lived in Thatcherism's terms'; in this moment it achieved state power.

Thatcherism as a 'two nation project'

> Thatcherism is neither a natural necessity nor a wilful contingency. It is a complex, contradictory, unstable, inchoate, and provisional product of social forces seeking to make their own history – but doing so in circumstances they have not chosen, cannot fully understand, and cannot hope to master.
>
> (Jessop _et al._ 1988: 13)

As we have seen, Jessop _et al._'s critique, though broadly sympathetic to Hall's Gramscian–Poulantzian perspective, certainly seeks to pack a few punches, many of which Hall succeeds in parrying rather successfully. Yet the gang of four's analysis is not exhausted by their critique of authoritarian populism. They develop a highly sophisticated and original interpretation of Thatcherism in their own right. Despite its origins in the 'conceptual gunfire' of theoretical dispute (Hall 1985: 159) it is in many respects complementary to that developed by Hall (Jessop *et al.* 1988, 1990; Jessop 1992).

Its two most significant contributions to the continuing debate are: (a) its analysis of Thatcherism's fragmented and socially differentiated social base; and (b) its periodization of Thatcherism. Both developments provide something of a corrective to Hall's homogenization of Thatcherism and his tendency to assume an ideologically motivated radicalism unchecked by pragmatism, opportunism and strategy (on which see Riddell 1983, 1991; Bulpitt 1986).

Thatcherism as a two nation project: the 'have nots' and the 'have lots'

As we have already noted, Hall's interpretation of Thatcherism as an authoritarian populism overstresses the universality of its ideological appeal. For, as Jessop *et al.* observe, though Thatcherism has certainly made inroads into the working class in securing a cross-class popular base, its appeal within classes has been far from universal. This is particularly visible within the working and lower-middle classes, where its appeal has been based upon the supposed route out of the proletarian impasse offered by the 'opportunity' of competing in the free market, structurally underpinned by a complex web of incentives and penalties (lucrative share offers and council house sales to name but two). This has established a clear split within the lower classes between: (a) the 'deserving poor' – those who have accepted Thatcherism's 'market logic', among whom new right ideology has found a captive audience; and (b) the 'undeserving poor' – those who have suffered disproportionately from the 'rolling back' of the welfare state, among whom passive acquiescence has given way to active discontent (Krieger 1986). The result has been an increasing resortion to coercive means of social control and a paramilitarization of the repressive apparatuses of the state (cf. Poulantzas 1978). This has in turn been legitimated by an appeal to 'moral authoritarianism' and the labelling of those unresponsive to the opportunities of the free market as 'parasitic' dependants of a 'nanny state' (McNeil 1991; cf. Hall 1988a: 227).[14] The 'parasitic' will suffer for their failure to contribute to the national economy whereas the 'worthy and productive' will be rewarded 'through the market'. The result is a 'two nation Toryism' (cf. Walker and Walker 1987; Oppenheim 1993).

Throughout the consolidation of Thatcherism, new right populism has consistently sought to unify the privileged nation of 'good citizens' and 'hard workers' against an increasingly subordinated and 'undeserving' nation, 'extending beyond the inner-cities and their ethnic minorities to include much of the non-skilled working class outside the South-East' (Jessop *et al.* 1984: 87).

Thatcherism has thus broken with the 'one nation' Toryism which characterized the post-war period. It has instead concerned itself with managing the political consequences of an emergent 'underclass' which it has spawned (Jessop *et al.* 1984: 87–8). Furthermore, as the above account demonstrates, Thatcherite rhetoric has increasingly been characterized by its appeal to discourses of inclusion and exclusion, notably the productive–parasitic distinction: the productive being rewarded through the market for their moral fibre, fortitude and entrepreneurialism; the parasitic correspondingly suffering the discipline of the market, which has become sanctified as the supreme arbiter of social justice. As a consequence of this subordination of the 'under nation', Thatcherism has increasingly had to resort to the politics of authoritarianism, though not so much on the basis of an authoritarian populism but rather on the necessities of economic and political crisis management. This would perhaps suggest that rather than resolving the structural weaknesses and crisis tendencies of the post-war settlement, Thatcherism has in fact merely displaced the symptoms, by: (a) passing the economic and social consequences on to certain marginalized sections of the population; and (b) socially stigmatizing this 'second nation' in an attempt to legitimate both their subordination and the repressive interventions of the state to quell the potential for unrest. Authoritarian populism thus represents an attempt to make a dubious virtue of a necessity born of such strategies of fragmentation and exclusion.

Different shades of blue: the periodization of Thatcherism

If Hall's account of authoritarian populism presents an unduly homogeneous picture of the appeal of Thatcherism to the electorate, then it is also guilty of extrapolating from the 'moment of crisis' itself. It thereby fails to take account of the *evolution* of the Thatcherite project after Thatcher's initial accession to power. If we are to move beyond this historically undifferentiated account then a periodization is required. Once again the gang of four provide us with the tools necessary to extend and develop Hall's account.

Yet as Jessop *et al.* (1988: 12–14) themselves note, there are many alternative *periodizations* and *chronologies* of Thatcherism that might be offered.[15] These are, in turn, likely to reflect different analytical concerns and problematics. The gang of four periodize (rather than 'chronologize') Thatcherism in terms of its evolving state and hegemonic project. For our purposes this is convenient, since their (state-theoretical) account of the genealogy of Thatcherism can provide the basis for an analysis of the impact of the Thatcher Governments upon the structures of the state – our central concern in this chapter. Such a periodization of Thatcherism as a state and hegemonic project is particularly important since the deployment of a *structural* mode of political rationality in response to crisis does not occur immediately. Although crisis is indeed an epoch-making transition between periods of politico-historical time and hence a strategic moment in the evolution of social and political systems, this is not to suggest that the structures and institutional configurations of the new (state) regime emerge instantaneously from the still smouldering embers of the former regime. Structural transformation takes times. Though a new trajectory may be imposed upon the state in the moment of crisis its translation into a new constellation of institutional relationships, boundaries and responsibilities is likely to be considerably more drawn out, contingent and cumulative. Our periodization must reflect this.

Thatcherism as a state and hegemonic project has changed significantly through time, a dynamism central to the character of the phenomenon itself. This renders Hall's initial description of it as an 'authoritarian populism' at best partial. Moreover, its impact and consequences – both intended and unintended – have been both spatially and temporally uneven. Thus if we are to interrogate the processes of social and political change in contemporary Britain in anything other than a purely token fashion, then we must first recognize the need both to distinguish specific stages and phases in the development of Thatcherism as a state project and 'to explore the timing and extent of its penetration into different areas of social life' (Jessop *et al.* 1988: 11–12). Accordingly we must consider the changing contours of the strategic terrain inhabited by the Thatcher Governments; their mappings of that terrain; the strategic calculations involved in the formulation and timing of policy; and the impact of such policy initiatives upon the landscape of future social and political change. In so doing we can extend, expand and update Jessop *et al.*'s periodization as follows (see Figure 12).

What this periodization suggests is that while authoritarian populism was crucial to the initial mobilization of support for Thatcherism, it was in fact almost wholly unrelated to the restructuring of the state which was to characterize the period of 'radical Thatcherism'.

Moreover, what emerges is a picture of Thatcherism slowly and strategically establishing a social basis within civil society. From this position it was to bid successfully for state power. The first Thatcher administration was characterized by a period of slow and again strategic consolidation in which the symptoms of a still unresolved state crisis were passed on to a proletarianized 'second nation'. This necessitated a certain paramilitarization of the repressive apparatuses of the state to deal with the growing disaffection of this new urban 'underclass'. During this period preparations were made for a fundamental structural transformation of the state and its relationship to both the economy and civil society. Yet this state project was only to be translated into policy following the re-election of Thatcher in 1987. Despite its obviously decisive impact upon the structures of the state, then, Thatcherism was characterized more by pragmatism, caution, strategy and timing than by radical ideologically driven fervour. The Thatcherite instinct, however strong, was always constrained by a coldly calculating and strategic 'statecraft' (Bulpitt 1986; Gamble 1988: 167–70).

Towards a synthesis

As the above discussion reveals, neither Hall's account of the initial appeal of Thatcherism as a hegemonic project nor Jessop *et al.*'s account of Thatcherism as a 'two nation project' can provide a complete analyses of the distinctiveness of Thatcherism as a social, political and cultural phenomenon. However, as the previous section suggests, they do provide the basis for formulating a more definitive account which draws upon the strengths of both. Such a synthetic account must prove itself capable of dealing with: (a) the strategic use of ideology made by the Thatcher Governments; and (b) the recomposition of the material interests of broad sections of civil society.

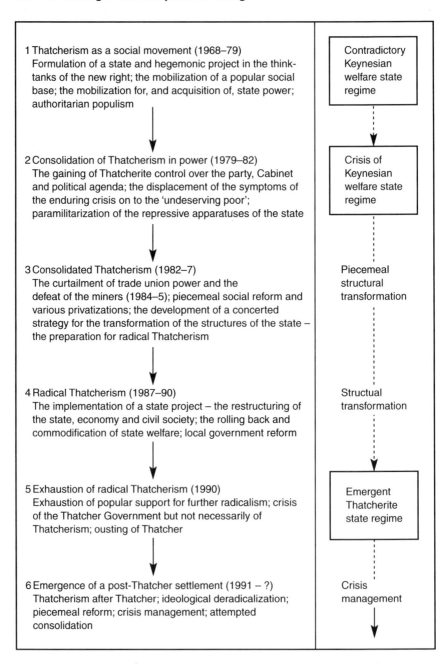

Figure 12   The periodization of Thatcherism.
Source: adapted, extended and updated from Jessop *et al.* (1988: 59–65).

Beyond ideologism: the strategic use of ideology

There is a considerable danger in any theoretically informed interpretation of Thatcherism (or of any other hegemonic project for that matter) in overstressing the ideological nature of political struggle and the homogeneity of ideological appeals. Hall's residual ideologism, as we have seen, leads him to credit new right ideology with an unjustified degree of unity. This is reflected in his rather one-dimensional description of Thatcherism as authoritarian populism, a paradoxical unity to which he ascribes its success. In fact the criteria that a potentially dominant ideology must satisfy are not those of unity or even consistency, but rather: (a) that the ideology is easily articulated and comprehended; (b) that it makes sense to individuals of their lived experiences and mediated understandings of events they have not directly witnessed; (c) that it provides a projected future which seems both attainable and desirable; and (d) that it legitimates the strategic policy objectives which might together comprise a coherent state project.[16] The *ad hoc* nature of new right ideology, combining neo-liberalism and neo-conservatism in a flexible synthesis, satisfies these criteria since either ideological base can be used to justify a particular policy objective. Thus, ironically, it is the very contradictions and inconsistencies of new right ideology that give Thatcherism its political strength and ideological vibrancy.

There is a certain polarization within the existing literature on Thatcherism between those accounts which emphasize strategy, statecraft and pragmatism on the one hand (Riddell 1983, 1991; Bulpitt 1986; Kavanagh 1987), and those which opt for an analysis couched in terms of ideological fervour on the other (Hall 1979a, 1983, 1988a; O'Shea 1984; Wolfe 1991; Moon 1994). Since these would appear mutually exclusive and irreconcilable interpretations (an observation seemingly confirmed by the vitriol to which such differences have given rise), it would appear that now is the time to declare our colours. Yet this would be to fail to consider the *strategic use of ideology*. For, as Jessop *et al.* (1984: 78) helpfully observe, 'it would be quite wrong to underestimate the pragmatism of Thatcher's strategy simply because she proclaims herself a conviction politician and appears to be ideologically motivated.'

Thatcherism both as a social movement and as a state project has made considerable strategic use of ideology. This is most clearly demonstrated in the attempts to extend its initial social base by building into Thatcherism's hegemonic project a strategic restructuring of the political agenda. Consecutive Thatcher Governments not only sought to secure the active consent of their many beneficiaries, but also engaged in strategic attempts to reconstruct the interests of large sections of the population. The (scarcely veiled) aim was to recast the material circumstances and conditions of targeted constituencies (principally potential home- and share-owners) such that their new interests coincided with those of the free market and a 'streamlined' state (rather than those of the public sector and the welfare state). This was achieved through a host of policies, the most prominent of which were the selling off of council housing and the privatization of nationalized industries (widening share ownership and decreasing public sector employment). From the vantage point of a former council tenant and now first-time home-owner, the ideological assault on the 'dependency culture' and the institutions of the 'nanny state' appears extremely palatable and resonates with her or his new material circumstances (Hay 1992a; Kennett 1994).

Seen in this light, the sale of council housing constitutes a thinly disguised restructuring of the political agenda and of civil society itself. For, in offering individual families a route out of their proletarian impasse and a corresponding 'status boost', the Thatcher Government succeeded in the recommodification of housing. In so doing, it replaced the interests of the family in the public sector and state welfare with those of the free market (albeit one distorted by mortgage interest tax relief) and the private sector.

The government, however, did not rely upon the direct appeal of home ownership to achieve its policy objectives. Rather, in what must be seen as a cynical and strategic attempt to imbue individuals in civil society with the material interests represented by Thatcherism, it offered council tenants their homes at reductions of up to 50 per cent on the estimated market value, while simultaneously withdrawing government rent subsidies (resulting in an average rent increase between 1980 and 1981 of 66 per cent). This is a clear example of the government penalizing those who refused to participate in the free market while appealing to the material interests of those who did. Such incentives and penalties were justified in terms of the freeing of council tenants from an unhealthy dependence upon the state, and in the moral supremacy of the traditional 'privatized' family unit. The logical fallacy of this argument is clearly exposed when it is considered that, with the privatization of council housing, this form of state dependency was merely replaced by a new reliance on mortgage interest tax relief. State-subsidized home ownership has now become the dominant form of public support for housing. So much for 'rolling back the frontiers of the state'.

Institutionalizing Thatcherism within civil society

As the above example would suggest, Thatcherism through a strategic use of ideology has redefined not only the boundaries of political discourse but also the very nature of the 'political' itself. This has been consolidated through a restructuring of the boundaries and responsibilities of the state. The effect has been to institutionalize the impact of policy objectives, making a reversal of the Thatcherite state project more difficult. Thus, from their very accession to power, consecutive Thatcher Governments have placed a very high priority on securing the structural underpinnings on which their hegemonic project[17] can be constructed. This move to reconstruct the state has been opportunistically presented as the 'rolling back of the welfare state'. In fact, as the above discussion reveals, although there has been a decisive disengagement of the state from 'welfarism', this has been balanced by a re-engagement of the state in other forms of intervention, creating new relations of dependency and thus new patterns of interest which may prove equally deeply entrenched. The result has been not so much a rolling back, but rather a rolling *right*-ward of the state (King 1987: 126; Overbeek 1990: 217–18; Riddell 1991: 245; Hay 1992a). Government intervention has shifted its point of focus from the public sector to the private sector (to the extent that council tenants now subsidize home-owners through mortgage interest tax relief, for instance).

Thatcherism and the structural transformation of the state

The above discussion would certainly appear to suggest that Thatcherism has effected a fundamental structural transformation of the institutions, practices, boundaries and perceived responsibilities of the state; a significant recasting of the very nature of the 'political'; and perhaps even a lasting impact on the 'hearts and minds' of the electorate. Yet herein lies a paradox. For despite its continuing (though apparently ever more fragile) electoral dominance, the Conservative Party in power now seems profoundly unpopular. Does this represent a profound threat to Thatcherism and its legacy, or have the parties converged to such an extent that a reinvigorated Labour Party under Tony Blair appears a more appropriate heir to the Thatcherite inheritance than the Major Government? We turn to this question in the final chapter, yet if we are to provide an answer it is crucial that we first consider the extent of the Thatcherite restructuring of the state, and the degree to which this transformation is likely to prove irreversible.

How should we interpret the Thatcherite legacy? What should our criteria of assessment be? Two candidates immediately present themselves.

Towards a Thatcherite state regime?

First, since our concern is with the structures of the state, we might compare the institutional form of the Keynesian welfare state regime with that which has emerged since 1979. Such a comparison would immediately reveal a fundamental structural transformation. What is more, it would suggest that such a transformation is likely to prove, at least for the foreseeable future, irreversible. The basic parameters of the emergent Thatcherite state regime, and thus the trajectory from the Keynesian welfare state regime, can be characterized as follows:

1 A systematic dismantling of all corporatist structures and tripartite bodies, a radical curtailment of the power and influence of the trade unions (both in national wage bargaining and in the broader political arena) and the removal of their status as 'governing institutions' (Middlemas 1979).
2 The abandonment of the expressed commitment to full employment and the promotion of price stability and tax reductions as the principal targets of government economic policy (Marquand 1988: 209–47; Anderson 1992c: 346; Jessop 1992: 35).
3 A dramatic tilting of the public–private sector balance decisively in favour of the latter with a host of privatizations and denationalizations and the imposition of compulsory competitive tendering within local government and the welfare state (Marsh 1991, 1995; Wolfe 1991); the displacement of responsibility for service provision from the state to the private sector, thus rolling back the frontiers of state.

4 The commodification of state welfare and the introduction of internal markets within the welfare state (King 1989); the transition from a universal welfare state free at the point of access to all to a residual 'social security state' (Jessop 1992: 32) increasingly characterized by means-testing and the subordination of welfare criteria to economic ends; and the establishment of an increasingly centralized welfare bureaucracy run from Whitehall yet which displaces responsibility for service provision directly to the local level in the name of 'local accountability' (Pollitt 1993).

5 The radical centralization of government power and a concerted erosion of the autonomy of local authorities; the replacement of many local government responsibilities by un-elected and scarcely accountable quangos; a residual role for local councils as service providers, agencies through which service-delivery contracts are awarded and 'enabling authorities' (R. Brooke 1989; Cochrane 1991, 1993; Stoker 1991).

Important and disturbing though much of this is, it is not so much an assessment as a description of the extent of change. Things certainly seemed to have been decisively altered. Yet how should we evaluate and assess that change?

Rhetoric, reality and strategy

The second option is to ask: 'Has Thatcherism proved successful in its own terms?' This might seem an obvious enough question to ask, yet it is not particularly easy to answer. For, perhaps unremarkably, much hinges on what we take to mean by 'in its own terms'. Once again two options immediately present themselves.

Rhetoric versus reality: the implementation gap

The first is to evaluate the successes and failures of Thatcherism in terms of the publicly stated aims and objectives of the Thatcher Governments – in terms of the explicit ideological justifications offered for particular reforms. Analyses of this sort have tended to discover something of an 'implementation gap' – a gulf between rhetoric and reality (Savage and Robins 1990; Marsh and Rhodes 1992: 170–87, 1995).

Given the Thatcher administration's highly strategic use of ideology this should perhaps come as no great surprise. For there is always likely to be something of a gap between what an incumbent government *would like to see* happen and the effects of legislation designed to bring about such desirable outcomes (see Hay 1995c). Far more significantly, however, we cannot assume a simple correspondence between the ideological justifications offered as aims and objectives on the one hand, and the underlying *strategic motivations* influencing the formulation of policy on the other.

What a government would like to see happen and what it presents as a desirable outcome are scarcely if ever identical. So, as well as an implementation gap we should also be on the look out for a 'strategy gap'. We should thus be extremely wary of the conclusion that David Marsh and R. A. W. Rhodes (1992: 187) are drawn to on the basis of such an investigation, that 'the Thatcherite revolution is more a product of rhetoric than of the reality of policy impact.'

Strategic motivations and policy outcomes

The alternative is to seek to discern an underlying and distinctly Thatcherite strategic agenda which may or may not correspond to the stated objectives of legislation in particular policy arenas. This type of analysis is outlined in Table 13, in which the achievements of the Thatcher Governments in four central areas of policy (privatization, trade union reform, local government reform and welfare reform) are considered in relation to ideological justifi-cations and strategic motivations. As assessment of the reversibility of struc-tural transformation in these areas is also provided.

What emerges is once again a picture of wholesale and fundamental institutional change, redefining the very contours of the state and setting in place the structures of a new state regime (whose characteristics are described further in the next chapter). Furthermore, it would appear that although there is quite a substantial gap between the Thatcherite policy record and the ideological justifications offered to legitimate particular policy initiatives: (a) this gap does not warrant Marsh and Rhodes's suggestion that the Thatcherite revolution is all rhetoric and no reality;[18] and (b) that the gap between strategic motivations and policy outcomes is considerably smaller. This in turn suggests that there has indeed been something of a Thatcherite revolution; that this revolution is characterized by far more than hollow rhetoric and ideological pronouncements; and that the Thatcher Govern-ments were indeed both cynical and strategic in their appropriation of new right ideology.

Above all, however, it would suggest that the Thatcher Governments presided over a period of profound structural transformation perhaps un-precedented in the post-war period, and certainly comparable in scope to that of the Attlee Governments. It is to this legacy, and to the structures of the post-Thatcher settlement, that we turn in the final chapter.

Notes

1 In turn defined by Jessop (1990: 198) as 'a specific economic "growth model" complete with its various extra-economic preconditions and . . . a general strategy appropriate to its realization'.
2 A second more methodological point should also be noted. In their studies of attitudinal changes, psephologists and political sociologists have, perhaps under-standably, used 1979 as their benchmark. Thus, when it comes to assessing the impact of Thatcherite housing policy upon voting patterns, analysts have tended to compare voting preferences in 1979 with those of 1983 or 1987. What they have observed is that while purchasers do tend to vote differently from non-purchasers, they were already more prone to vote Conservative in 1979; hence there is little evidence to suggest that the sale of council houses has produced new recruits for the Tories (Heath *et al.* 1985, 1991; Crewe 1989). Yet once the centrality of the 'right to buy' issue to the initial appeal of 'Thatcherism' and particularly to the

Table 13 Thatcherism and the structural transformation of the state: rhetoric, strategy and reality

	Ideological justifications	Strategic motivations	Policy record	Assessment and reversibility
Privatization and denationalization	Reassert market mechanisms; introduce the discipline of the market to promote competitiveness, efficiency and modernization; reduce PSBR and hence decrease taxation while increasing incentives; roll back the frontiers of an overextended state	Retrenchment of public sector trade unions; transform material interests of employees and consumers alike; transfer responsibility from the state; secure windfall revenues allowing tax cuts to the wealthy and reductions in the PSBR; create a 'share- and property-owning', Tory-voting democracy	Slow start with sale of assets and stakes in private companies; from 1984 privatization and denationalizations to include Jaguar, BT, BA, British Aerospace, British Gas, BAA, British Steel, Rover Group, regional electricity and electricity generating companies, water and sewerage companies	The crux of Thatcherite economic policy, providing a series of one-off windfall payments to the Exchequer; has destroyed the power of former public sector trade unions; displaced responsibility to the private sector; and disseminated share-ownership; almost completely irreversible in the medium term (revenue gained has been squandered)
Trade union reform	Regeneration of market mechanisms; end interference from trade unions capable of 'holding the country to ransom'; replace corporatism by democracy; modernize the economy; retrench the responsibilities of the overloaded state and cut demands placed upon it	Secure revenge for defeat of the Heath Government at the hands of the miners; weaken the trade unions before embarking upon a policy of labour market deregulation likely to result in a deterioration of pay and conditions and a rise in structural unemployment; link Labour with the militant extremists of the 'loony left'	Restriction of picketing and strike activity; tight constraints placed upon the closed shop; union assets rendered liable to sequestration; systematic preparation for a show-down with the NUM (planned since the 1978 Ridley Report) resulting in a year-long confrontation and ignominious defeat for the miners	Dramatic decrease in trade union influence and membership; delegitimation of the trade union movement; dismantling of corporatist structures; destruction of power of public sector unions; completely irreversible in the medium term

Local government reform	Increase the accountability and responsibility of local government to the electorate; decrease the political autonomy of 'loony left' local authorities to charge high rates at the behest of electors paying no rates; extend the free market by selling off local assets and contracting out services	Rolling back of the frontiers of the welfare state by increasing local responsibility for welfare provision yet imposing centralized fiscal controls; displace responsibility for welfare services where possible while increasing top-down control; impose universal charge/rate capping on all authorities	Initial pledge to abolish rates thwarted by the Treasury; rate support grant dramatically cut from 61 (1979) to 47% (1987); abolition of GLC and the six (Labour-controlled) metropolitan councils; rate-capping introduced and extended to all authorities with the Poll Tax and Council Tax; Poll Tax fiasco; Council Tax introduced in 1993	Contracting-out of local services has undermined public sector trade unions; responsibility displaced from central state to the local for service delivery increasingly constrained from the centre; Poll Tax seriously undermined legitimacy of the Thatcher Government; an irreversible restructuring but at the cost of delegitimation
Social welfare reform	Sever relationship of dependency created between the 'nanny state' and 'welfare scroungers'; reassert traditional values of family support, care and a patriarchal domestic division of labour; cut public spending to create incentives through decreased taxation; introduce discipline and efficiency of the market	Further erode the power of the public sector trade unions; encourage the population to take out private health cover; generate an internal market within the NHS; divest the state of responsibility for welfare where possible; subsidize private welfare creating a new Thatcherite constituency	Internal markets introduced throughout the welfare state (most notably in the NHS and education); creation of NHS Hospital Trusts, fund-holding GPs and an immense health care bureaucracy; care in the community (by unpaid women in the family) to replace state welfare; selling off of council housing	Commodification of welfare; stimulus to the private sector; displacement of responsibility to the local level; deterioration in the quality of care; transformation of the material interests of large sections of the population; again largely irreversible due to the costs of reorganization despite the nostalgia for the 'old' welfare state

1979 general election campaign is considered, the problems of this interpretation become all too apparent. For it would seem sensible to suggest that many of those who were eventually to buy their council houses voted for Mrs Thatcher in 1979 precisely because her election promised to provide them with this opportunity. By 1983, and certainly by 1987, most of these people had bought their homes. Given that the Labour Party was not committed to buying them back, we might in fact expect new home-owners to drift back to Labour after 1979. That this does not appear to be borne out by the evidence would in turn suggest that Thatcherism did manage to secure some long-term converts. Clearly a comparison of voting preferences which used 1974 (where the 'right to buy' was not on the political agenda) as a baseline would be much more useful. Yet even if this were to vindicate Crewe and Heath *et al.*'s interpretation it would not, in itself, provide a refutation of the 'hegemony thesis' for the reasons outlined above.

3 In a clear demonstration of the power and influence of the media, Fisher's introduction to Hayek came from reading the potted version of *The Road to Serfdom* published in the *Reader's Digest*. As Radhika Desai (1994: 45) observes, 'from the perspective of its Thatcherite apogee the IEA's beginnings are appropriately pedestrian' (see also Cockett 1995: 130–9, 306–8).

4 Established by Hayek himself in 1947, this was to become something of a European network for the new right (it included such notables as Karl Popper, Milton Friedman, Ludwig von Mises and Walter Lippman). Once tied into this prestigious network, the IEA rapidly took off.

5 Itself something of a collection of new right think-tanks.

6 Somewhat to the chagrin of its then director Chris Patten, who in a fit of pique is reputed to have compared Keith Joseph to Rasputin, describing him as 'the mad monk' – a label that was to stick.

7 The 'money supply' basically refers to the total pool of money (notes, coins and bank deposits) in circulation within the economy (Cobham 1985: 204–8). Unemployment, according to Friedman, has a 'natural' rate within a given political economy at a particular stage in its historical development. If government interventions keep unemployment artificially low then inflation will necessarily result. Friedman's diagnosis of the condition of the British economy during the 1970s, then, was that the rate of unemployment was simply too low and generating hyperinflation. If an increase in unemployment can be seen as one, albeit largely unacknowledged, policy goal of monetarism then it can be said to have had some success. Unfortunately, however, inflation was not curbed until the recession was over, reaching 22 per cent in May 1980 (King 1987: 113–18; Gamble 1988: 98–102; Jessop *et al.* 1988: 84–5).

8 Indeed, Arthur Laffer, an American economist, even went so far as to suggest that if governments were to reduce taxation they would increase revenue because of the boost to entrepreneurialism that this would stimulate. This convenient thesis was thankfully seized upon by the IEA (Harris and Seldon 1979; see Bosanquet 1983: 75–83) and Mrs Thatcher was even to make explicit reference to it during the 1979 general election campaign (Stephenson 1980: 49). Needless to say, when this so-called 'supply-side economics' was adopted by both Reagan and later Thatcher, decreasing taxation decreased revenue. None the less, it was to become a staple part of new right rhetoric, periodically dusted off to provide a convenient and popular justification for pre-election tax reductions.

9 A highly influential yet loose network of like-minded former graduates and current fellows, the Peterhouse School includes such bastions of conservatism, new racism and patriarchy as novelist Kingsley Amis; Thatcher's biographer Patrick Cosgrave; academics Maurice Cowling, Edward Norman, Roger Scruton (the editor of the *Salisbury Review* and regular participant in the BBC's *Moral Maze*) and John Vincent

(a regular contributor to *The Times*); and columnists George Gale (*Daily Express*), John Welch (*The Spectator* and the *Telegraph* group) and Peregrine Worsthorne (former associate editor of the *Sunday Telegraph*).

10 It is important to note that I am here merely reproducing Hall's distinctive interpretation of Poulantzas. This reading is not, however, uncontested. Indeed, much of the ensuing debate with Bob Jessop and his co-authors in the pages of *New Left Review* is concerned with this disputed interpretation of Poulantzas. We return to this question below.

11 This suggests that the difference between Hall's position and that of Poulantzas is merely one of emphasis – their foci are somewhat different yet the substance of their interpretations is very similar (cf. Jessop *et al.* 1984: 71–3; 1985: 111–13).

12 Given Jessop's widely acknowledged status as the foremost interpreter of Poulantzas's work in the English language, this should come as no great surprise (Jessop 1985).

13 The populism of systematic repression is most powerfully demonstrated by Poulantzas (1974) in his chilling description of the ideological appeal of Nazism to certain sections of civil society.

14 As Maureen McNeil (1991: 226) perceptively notes, 'the disdain for the "nanny state" conveyed the view that people should be "real men" [*sic*] and take care of themselves. It constructed a set of dichotomies: welfare state, socialism, femininity, dependence and indulgence versus the market, laissez-faire values, masculinity, independence and austerity.'

15 Jessop *et al.* (1988: 13–14) draw the extremely important distinction between chronology and periodization, arguing that 'whilst chronologies are essentially one-dimensional, focus on temporal coincidences and adopt a narrative approach, periodizations operate in several time dimensions, focus on conjunctures and presuppose an explanatory framework. Thus a chronology orders actions and events in a unilinear, calendrical time; classifies them into successive stages according to their occurrence in one or other time period . . . and thereby gives the basis for a simple narrative. Conversely a periodization orders actions and events in terms of multiple time horizons; classifies them into stages according to their conjunctural implications . . . for different social forces; and, since both these procedures involve consideration of how actions and events are generated as a complex result of multiple determinations, they operate with an explanatory framework as well as providing the basis for a complex narrative.' Accordingly, our concern is to formulate a theoretically informed periodization of *re-stated* social and political change as opposed to a simple narrative chronology (cf. Ricoeur 1984).

16 In short, a hegemonic project must be 'emplotted' (Czarniawska-Joerges 1995: 15–20) – providing a clear and resonant depiction of an original state ('where we are'), a projected end state ('where we should be') and a decisive intervention ('the means to get from there to here').

17 The Thatcherite hegemonic project has clearly been directed towards certain sections of the population (broadly speaking the 'upper nation' of the 'deserving poor' and the wealthy) and not others (the 'lower nation' of the undeserving poor and state dependants).

18 In a recent clarification of their earlier position Marsh and Rhodes qualify somewhat this claim. The result is a position that is not incompatible with the interpretation outlined above, though one that still does not take sufficient account of strategic motivations and which tends to use ideological justifications as the criteria against which policy outcomes should be measured (Marsh and Rhodes 1995; cf. Moon 1994).

8 *The* **state** *of the* **present:** *the* **consolidation** *of a* **post-Thatcher** **settlement**

In the previous chapter we considered the novelty, originality and specificity of Thatcherism as a state and hegemonic project. We examined the impact of the Thatcher years upon the institutional form, structures, boundaries and perceived responsibilities of the state, and began to assess the legacy of Thatcherism. We saw that the post-Thatcher inheritance was likely to be considerable. Indeed, the strategies and policies associated with Thatcherism have decisively reshaped the social, cultural and economic context within which processes of political struggle, ideological contestation and hence social and political change are likely to take place for some time to come. The *post-war settlement* has perhaps given way to a *post-Thatcher settlement* reflected in a new convergence between the principal parties around an agenda forged during the Thatcher years.

In this final chapter it is time to bring our analysis of the evolution of the state in post-war Britain up to date by considering in more detail the nature of the Thatcherite legacy, the form of the emerging state regime, its internal contradictions and crisis tendencies, and the future prospects for social and political change in contemporary Britain.

Thatcherism after Thatcher

[No one] has ever maintained that Thatcherism had discovered the secret of permanent electoral success. What may well be permanent, however, is the Thatcherite 'settlement' – at least as permanent as that of the post-war 'Keynesian welfare state'.

(Leys 1990: 119)

What of the present, what of the future? The analysis developed in Chapter 7 would suggest that the strategic context inhabited by the current Major Government and indeed by any future heirs to the Thatcherite inheritance has been decisively and perhaps irreversibly shaped by the strategies pursued by consecutive Thatcher Governments since 1979. Our task in this chapter is to map the contours of this strategic context. It is certainly tempting to suggest that with the ousting of Mrs Thatcher we have entered a distinctly post-Thatcherite era (Kavanagh 1994a; cf. Young 1994: 22–3).[1] Yet the state-theoretical periodization of social and political change thus far developed would suggest otherwise. If the argument of the previous chapters is correct, and the Winter of Discontent can be seen as a strategic moment in the transformation of the state – marking the transition between phases in politico-historical time and regimes of the state – then the new (Thatcherite) state regime is perhaps still very much in its infancy (cf. Leys 1990).

This would in turn suggest that in the absence of the *structural* politics of state-shaping and the sort of decisive intervention associated with moments of crisis, social and political change in contemporary Britain is likely to be characterized by the attempted consolidation and management of a post-Thatcher, yet Thatcherite, settlement.

Moreover, if, as is the argument of this chapter, such a settlement is in fact deeply contradictory and deleterious to Britain's economic competitiveness and social and political stability, then the consolidation of the post-Thatcher settlement threatens to ensnare Britain within a 'catastrophic equilibrium' in which 'the old is dying, yet the new cannot be born' (Gramsci 1971: 276). It is to the implications of such an assessment that we turn in the final section of this chapter. For the time being, however, it is important that we consider the grounds for making such bold if theoretically informed assertions.

The return to consensus?

In what follows I want to suggest that we follow Hugo Young in viewing 'Majorism' as 'the pursuit of Thatcherism by other means' (Young 1993), and that we interpret the re-election of the Major Government in 1992 as heralding the return to *consensus* politics in Britain (cf. Kavanagh 1994a: 13–17; Kavanagh and Morris 1994: 129–43).[2] This requires some immediate qualification and clarification, however. For it is important to stress that this is in no sense a return to the so-called 'Butskellite'[3] consensus of the post-war period. As we have been at pains to point out in previous chapters, much has changed in the intervening years. The new consensus represents the acceptance by all the principal parties of the profoundly transformed context of contemporary British politics and society – the legacy of well over a decade of Thatcherism.[4]

Neither is this consensus reflected in a happy camaraderie among the political elite. Indeed, in many respects it has been associated with a heightened politicization of personnel and personality – a legacy, perhaps, of the confrontational politics that characterized the Thatcher years and the contradictory nature of the Thatcherite inheritance. Yet this intensified politics of personality in fact masks a substantial degree of policy convergence, as the parties have increasingly accommodated themselves to the terms of the new settlement (Smyth 1991, 1994a, b; Anderson 1992c: 346; Elliott 1993; Dunleavy 1994; Hay 1994e; Shaw 1994; cf. M. J. Smith 1994).

Contemporary political competition in Britain would appear to present the electorate with the unenviable choice between different modes of consolidation of the post-Thatcher settlement. We live, then, not in a *one party state* as Tom Nairn (1994: 46–7) has recently suggested (see also A. King 1993; Dunleavy 1994; Hennessy 1994; O'Leary 1994; cf. Young 1994: 28), but, more crucially, in a *one vision democracy* (Hay 1995d).[5]

All of this, however, rests on a particular understanding of Thatcherism. For, whether the undeniably post-*Thatcher* political context also represents a post-*Thatcherite* context depends, perhaps unremarkably, on what one means by Thatcherism. Similarly, whether 'Majorism' represents continuity or change depends on the contexts with respect to which that change is assessed. If we chose to refer to the fleeting and ephemeral field of political style then Majorism might be viewed as the very antithesis of Thatcherism. Yet if we chose to contextualize contemporary political developments in terms of the structures of the state (the context in which political decisions are formulated and the subject of our reflections to date), then there are considerable elements of continuity.

Majorism and Thatcherism: continuity or change?

The initial problem, then, is one of definition and, in fact, one of selection of subject matter. In the previous chapter we made a case for conceiving of Thatcherism as a state project – a strategic project (not always coherent, and certainly not always coherently executed) to transform the boundaries, perceived responsibilities and legitimate expectations of the state, and its relationship to the economy, the public sphere and civil society. Conceptualizing Thatcherism in this way has the effect of emphasizing the considerable extent of the Thatcherite inheritance. For, if Thatcherism was indeed a project to transform the state and if, as we have suggested, it has had any more than a minimal degree of success, then its structural legacy is likely to be significant.

In conceiving of Thatcherism in this way, we can provide something of a corrective to the tendency within much of the existing literature to concentrate on the description of surface appearances – stressing the agency of elite political actors while failing to consider the dynamic social and political contexts which provide the setting for such action (Hay 1995c). By *re-stat(e)ing social and political change* we can begin to reveal the evolving contours of the always uneven playing field on which political strategies are formulated and compete for political ascendancy. Applying this approach to contemporary British politics we can see that the strategic context inhabited by government and opposition alike has been immeasurably altered as a consequence of the unfolding (however partial, however contradictory) of the Thatcherite project. It is to the contours of this fundamentally transformed context that the parties are now accommodating themselves.

Crisis management and consolidation

If Thatcherism means a variety of things to a variety of people (see Jessop *et al.* 1988: 22–56; Marsh 1995), then 'Majorism' is no less contested a term, though for somewhat different reasons. Indeed, though many theorists, commentators and political scientists are prepared to confer 'ism' status on the Thatcher Governments, rather fewer consider that the Major Government warrants this somewhat dubious accolade (see, for instance, Kavanagh 1994a: 4). None the less, given that the term has, perhaps inevitably, been coined within the media, it is useful to reflect on what, if anything, sets 'Majorism' apart as a distinctive social and political phenomenon. If, as seems likely, Majorism is an inevitable addition to the political lexicon, then we should attempt to reclaim it in such a way that it might shed some light on contemporary political dynamics.

Any attempt to do this reveals immediately that Majorism and Thatcherism are not analogous terms. Majorism belongs to an entirely different order of political concept. Hence, if the label is not to become merely one more piece of mystifying political jargon, then we must be able to conceive of Majorism as something other than the antithesis of Thatcherism. In fact there are two ways in which we might understand Majorism which can 'do some theoretical work' in informing a sophisticated account of the contemporary British social and political context.

Majorism as a stage in the evolution of Thatcherism

First, we might usefully conceive of Majorism as a stage in the periodization of Thatcherism, where Thatcherism is in turn viewed as a state and hegemonic project. Here we emphasize the first half of Hugo Young's couplet: Majorism is 'the pursuit of *Thatcherism* by other means'. As a stage in the evolution of the Thatcherite state and hegemonic project it is characterized by the attempted consolidation of the structures of the state, economy and civil society arising out of the period of structural transformation associated with radical Thatcherism. Majorism is thus a mode of political management, a mode of consolidation of the post-Thatcher settlement.

Majorism as the politics of crisis management

Alternatively we might chose to emphasize the second half of Young's couplet and conceive of Majorism as 'the pursuit of Thatcherism *by other means*', thereby emphasizing change. Majorism can here be viewed as the return to conjunctural politics, the return to the politics of state management – indeed crisis management – following the profound redrawing of the contours of the state in response to the crisis of the 1970s.

If we retain Young's entire aphorism, however, we can preserve the benefits of both insights, interpreting Majorism as an attempted consolidation of Thatcherism, which is characterized by the conjunctural politics of crisis management as opposed to the structural politics of institutional change (or 'state-shaping').[6] The current economic and political impasse suggests that the repertoire of crisis management techniques available to managerial governments (like Major's or, conceivably Blair's) within a post-Thatcher settlement is severely limited and has, perhaps, already been exceeded. The attempted politics of crisis management has thus degenerated somewhat inevitably into the politics of crisis *mis*management and retribution. This is reflected not only in parliamentary bickering and the unprecedented unpopularity of the Government but also in an accelerating tide of disaffection with party politics altogether (cf. Mulgan 1994: esp. 7–36).

If we were to summarize the argument presented in Parts II and III then we might suggest that the evolution and transformation of the state be periodized and broken down into four stages (see also Figure 13).

1 The moment of *crisis* itself – the moment, marking the transition between periods of political–historical time, in which a new trajectory is imposed upon the state discursively unified in crisis.
2 *Restructuring* – the structural transformation of the system in response to crisis, ushering in a new state regime.
3 The *consolidation* of the new state regime – a period which tends to be characterized by relative social and political stability, indeed tranquillity, reflecting the absence of obvious internal contradictions.
4 Conjunctural *crisis management* – the period in which the internal contradictions of the state regime are exposed by domestic political struggles and changes in the global political–economic context – the accumulation of unresolved steering problems and the condensation of contradictions. If this phase is drawn out over a long period of political time we might identify a condition of 'catastrophic equilibrium'.

The above discussion would, however, suggest that the contradictions of the emergent post-Thatcher settlement are so profound that the phase of 'happy consensus' (stage 3) that characterized the period following the initial post-war reconstruction[7] has been by-passed altogether in the post-Thatcher era. The post-Thatcher settlement and, paradoxically, the new politics of *consensus* would thus appear to be characterized by factionalism, retribution (both between and within parties) and crisis mismanagement (see Figure 13).

What is perhaps required, then, is a new *structural* politics capable of addressing the contradictions and crisis tendencies of a post-Thatcher settlement which appears to be disintegrating even as it is being consolidated (cf. Gamble 1994b; Rustin 1994). We return to the prospects of, and conditions for, such a politics emerging later.

Majorism, plagiarism and Blaijorism: the politics of flattery

The above discussion once again reveals the importance of distinguishing between periods of *structural* change during which the very contours of the state regime are subject to transformation at the hands of governments with *state* power (such as the Attlee and Thatcher administrations); and periods of *conjunctural*, piecemeal, iterative change and consolidation during which governments lacking *state* power (such as the administrations of Macmillan, Heath, Wilson and Major) seek to manage the institutions of a state regime inherited from the past and bequeathed to the future.

Periods of structural politics thus represent *strategic moments* in the evolution of the state, ushering in new state regimes; while periods of conjunctural politics represent the routine management of such regimes in the 'slower moving political time in which the contradictions are ripening' (Debray 1973: 102).

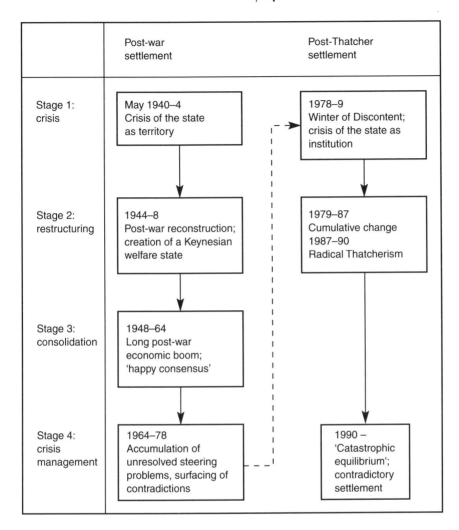

Figure 13   Periodizing settlements in post-war Britain.

Majorism is distinctive in marking the return to managerial or consensual politics: *Majorism is to Thatcherism what Butskellism was to the post-war reconstruction.* If Butskellism represented the politics of consolidation of the post-war settlement, then Majorism represents the politics of consolidation of the post-Thatcher settlement. The specificity of the contemporary political context in Britain therefore lies in the return to managerial politics, which has increasingly involved *both* Conservative and Labour in an accommodation to the new contours of the state regime. If a political neologism – 'Butskellism' – was required to capture such a phenomenon in the post-war period, then perhaps its analogue – 'Blaijorism' (the Blair–Major hybrid) – best reflects the nature of the current context (see Figure 14).

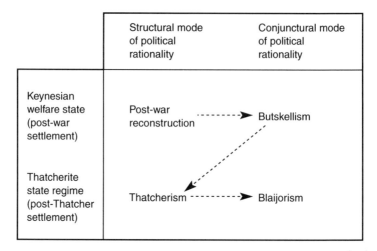

Figure 14   Modes of political rationality in post-war Britain.

If we map this simple periodization on to the account of the evolution of the British state that we began to develop in Chapter 6, then we can chart the emergence of the post-Thatcher settlement characterized by the broadly consensual politics of Blaijorism. This model is schematically outlined in Figure 15.

The Butskellite consensus existing from the 1950s to the mid-1970s is seen as a period of conjunctural politics in which periodic operational difficulties, tensions and contradictions were dealt with by making use of available crisis management techniques (such as corporatist conciliation and incomes policies). During this era, the parameters of state activity remained basically unchallenged and institutional change, where enacted, took the form of minor tinkering by governments lacking the vision, opportunity and indeed capacity for decisive structural intervention.

With the slump into global economic recession following the Oil Crisis of 1973, this cosy stability was threatened as the accumulated and unresolved contradictions of the post-war period began to surface and the repertoire of crisis management techniques available for coping with such eventualities was finally exhausted. Though the social contract between the trade unions and their 'fraternal' allies in the Wilson/Callaghan Government succeeded in delaying the inevitable, the crisis when it came was to shatter the fragile settlement. With it went the Butskellite consensus.

In the wake of the crisis, the Thatcher Government assumed the mantle of governmental and state power, embarking upon a strategic, cautious and yet ultimately comprehensive overhaul of the structures, institutions, practices and above all responsibilities of the state. By 1990 the discernible form of a new state regime was taking shape. It bore little resemblance to that inherited in 1979. From here on Thatcher's radical zeal was to give way to an ideologically deradicalized consolidation of Thatcherism behind the superficially bland exterior of Majorite managerialism. With Labour's *Policy*

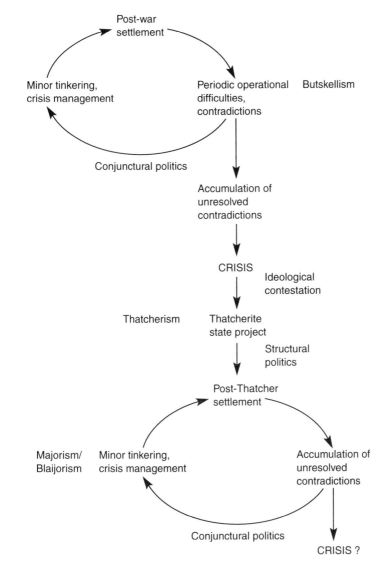

Figure 15   The politics of consensus: from Butskellism to Blaijorism.

Review (initiated in 1987 following the party's third consecutive election defeat), and the media-groomed modernization of first John Smith's 'New Model Party' (Hughes and Wintour 1990) and subsequently Tony Blair's 'New Labour', the terms of the Blaijorite consensus and the structures of the post-Thatcher settlement appear to have been accepted by all serious political contenders for the legacy of Thatcherism (Leys 1990; Anderson 1992c;

Crewe 1993; Elliott 1993: 152–67; Heath and Jowell 1994; Kavanagh 1994b: 153; Shaw 1994; Smyth 1994a, b).

The pursuit of Thatcherism by other means

Majorism thus represents *continuity in terms of the inherited structures of the state precisely because it represents change in terms of its mode of political rationality*. Majorism is Thatcherite in its inheritance, because it is not Thatcherite in its practice. This allows us to identify both continuity and change, and to contrast Thatcherism *à la* Thatcher with Thatcherism *à la* Major (see Table 14).

None the less, the ideologically deradicalized appearance of Thatcherism *à la* Major can be misleading. We should not allow ourselves to be entirely drawn in by Major's politics of constant readjustment. If the Lady was not for turning, then appearances would suggest that Major is indulging a desire for the politics of the perpetual pirouette. Yet looks can be deceptive. For, as the policy record reveals, Majorism is still characterized by a subterranean radicalism (Savage *et al.* 1994: xi), albeit one born more of economic pragmatism within the neo-liberal straitjacket than of ideological fervour or the realization of a coherent project.[8]

Structural politics, though in a much less highly vaunted form, is still very much the order of the day within certain policy arenas. As a consequence, we cannot yet speak of the post-Thatcher settlement as truly consolidated. None the less, contemporary party political struggle in Britain is concerned not with the competition between alternative state projects and conceptions of social justice, but with different modes of consolidation of the post-Thatcher settlement.

Major's managerial and bureaucratic mask in fact hides a more radical series of policy initiatives. The current phase of structural politics within specific policy fields is distinctive in that it is associated with an ideologically deradicalized appearance – policies are justified to the electorate not in terms of their ideological cogency as part of a broad strategy to transform state and society and 'change the hearts and minds of the electorate', but out of a parochial political expediency. Yet the policy initiatives thrown up by the Major Government are no less radical for their conservative presentation. A flurry of scandals, speculation and 'sleaze' allegations has merely averted public gaze and critical scrutiny from the subterranean continuation of neo-liberal, free-market radicalism.[9] This somewhat paradoxical phenomenon of *radical pragmatism* is perhaps best exemplified in the Government's flirtation with workfare schemes and in its reinvigorated, if defensively driven, privatization programme. It is to such initiatives that we now turn.

Towards a workfare state?

Though a popular idea among some of the neo-liberal think-tanks for a considerable period of time, workfare was never closely associated with Thatcher, or indeed the phase of radical Thatcherism, since it was seen as

Table 14   The pursuit of Thatcherism by other means

	Thatcherism à la Thatcher	Thatcherism à la Major
Ideology	Crusading ideology of the new right (a flexible synthesis of neo-liberalism and neo-conservatism); policies often pursued as strategic components of a neo-liberal state project and accumulation strategy, yet legitimated by appeal to a neo-conservative moral authoritarianism.	Ideologically deradicalized Thatcherism; appeal to neo-liberal ideology softened with the collectivist and communitarian tone of the 'classless society'; 'one nation' ideology; neo-conservatism largely abandoned as an ideological legitimation for strategic policy objectives; consensual tone.
Accumulation strategy	Neo-liberal attempt to transform the mode of intervention of the state, opportunistically presented in terms of the 'rolling back' of the frontiers of the state; reassertion of the 'primacy' of the market through privatization and deregulation; undermining of the (negative) power of the public sector trades unions.	Consolidation: neo-liberal project largely inherited from the Thatcher years – extended and consolidated through the privatization of rail and coal and attempts to cut the public sector borrowing requirement; strategy of 'social dumping in one country' within the European Union.
Welfare reform	Destruction of welfare; dismantling of Keynesian welfare state.	Tentative subordination of welfare to workfare; tendential emergence of a neo-liberal workfare state.
Political competition	Structural politics – clash of different conceptions of the political; period of disharmony with a sharp polarization between the parties; adversarial politics opening a space for the centre parties.	Personality/personnel politics; return to new consensus politics following the Labour Party's Policy Review; space for centre parties squeezed – left to scrabble around the margins for votes.
Political style	Aggressive politics of state-shaping and preference-shaping; dissensus.	Defensive politics of consolidation and stabilization; consensus.
Mode of political rationality	Structural with respect to the state regime (state-shaping); restructuring in response to crisis.	Conjunctural with respect to the state regime; structural within specific policy fields; crisis management and crisis displacement.
Project	Creation of structures of a Thatcherite settlement.	Consolidation of the structures of a Thatcherite, post-Thatcher settlement.

involving too great a role for the state (Peck and Tickell 1995: 30; cf. Breheny 1989: 15).[10] In its narrow sense, 'workfare' involves making unemployment benefit dependent upon the performance of menial labour in the local community paid at subsistence income levels. Within the British context, this was initially somewhat tentatively proposed by John Major in two speeches in February 1993 (Major 1993: 26–34).[11] The scheme would be supplemented by a variety of buttressing measures and supply-side initiatives designed to promote 'permanent innovation' and labour market flexibility by subordinating social policy to the (perceived) exigencies of structural competitiveness (cf. Jessop 1993, 1994a, b; Peck and Jones 1995).[12] This emergent post-neo-liberal workfarism threatens to sound the final death-knell of any residual collectivist ethic within an already far less than universalist welfare state. The *subordination of welfare to workfare* would appear, at least rhetorically, to be the defining motif of Major's pursuit of Thatcherism by other means, modifying the neo-liberal desire simply to withdraw from state welfare altogether (cf. Finn 1987; Harris 1988; King and Ward 1992; King 1993, 1994; King and Rothstein 1994; Peck and Jones 1995). This form of *modified* Thatcherism suggests important elements of discontinuity in the transition from Thatcherism *à la* Thatcher to Thatcherism *à la* Major (Evans 1992, 1993; Farnham and Lupton 1994).

Yet once again we must proceed with a certain degree of caution. Workfare rhetoric there may well have been. But what is clear is that where this discursive shift has been translated into policy – as in the recent Jobseeker's Allowance[13] – this has been driven more by a neo-liberal desire to cut welfare expenditure than by a genuine strategy to promote labour market flexibility and the structural competitiveness of the economy (see especially Hay 1994g: 26–8; Peck and Jones 1995: 30).

The 'Toll Tax': widening the road from serfdom

Though far less significant in its own right, the introduction of private finance on a routine basis into transport infrastructural expenditure through the proposed levying of motorway tolls represents a considerable extension of the privatization and denationalization schemes of the Thatcher Governments (HMSO 1993, 1994b). Direct charging, it is argued, 'could provide another source of finance for improving roads, help to make more efficient use of the existing network and facilitate more private sector involvement in road developments' (HMSO 1994b: 31). The commodification and marketization of road transport would be further extended by proposals for new contracts under which the private sector will design, build, finance and operate ('DBFO') new or upgraded roads in return for 'shadow tolls' (the government pays the road builder/improver a fee for each vehicle choosing to use the new/upgraded road). However, as Peter Jones (1993: 237) observes, where this scheme has been tried, it has failed to generate much enthusiasm from the private sector. Thus, for example,

> plans announced by the government for a private sector road between Birmingham and Manchester, paralleling the M6 motorway, had to be

abandoned because of lack of private sector response, and instead the government has announced the widening of the existing motorway route.

Once again it must be noted that such attempts to introduce private finance into the road-building programme, however unsuccessful, are driven more by fiscal expediency at a time when the government is running out of things to sell off than by ideological fervour or a clearly identifiable strategic vision. This is despite the hollow rhetorical pretensions to environmental consciousness displayed in the government's vague and tentative linking of such policies to the introduction of road-use taxation in urban areas – technological developments permitting (HMSO 1994a: 175, para. 26.35; 1994b; cf. Whitelegg 1993: 127–8). That such policies are not in any sense driven by environmental considerations becomes immediately apparent when other aspects of the government's transport policy are considered: (a) the proposed privatization and disintegration of British Rail; (b) the proposed widening of the M25 (now likely to be shelved owing to a combination of cost and public protest); and (c) the suggestion that the private sector be given licence to charge tolls on new private motorways that they build (Whitelegg 1992; Potter 1993; Potter and Cole 1993; Roberts 1993; Salveson 1993; HMSO 1994a: 175, para. 26.34).

At the same time, however, it does represent the return to a structural mode of political rationality within this particular policy arena. The Major Government may well be characterized by a *conjunctural* politics *with respect to the state regime*; yet we should be extremely careful not to understate its radicalism in pursuit of a series of *structural* reforms within particular policy fields.

The privatization of rail and coal

The plans to strip down and despatch the profitable core of British Rail and British Coal to the private sector represent a clear extension of the privatization and denationalization programme of the Thatcher Governments, though, interestingly, in industries that it was initially thought would prove impossible to privatize. Again, such policies are driven less by ideological fervour and, indeed, any innate desire to privatize rail or coal than by the simple fact that consecutive Conservative Governments since 1979 have: (a) failed to cut public spending (owing largely to increased social security expenditure in a time of mass unemployment); and (b) thus become reliant upon windfall revenues from privatization and a diminishing stock of North Sea oil to service the public sector borrowing requirement (which, at the time of writing, stands at over £50 billion). They have currently run out of items on the neo-liberal think-tanks' lists of contenders for privatization and are now having to look towards 'rationalizing' industries and services in preparation for privatization. Moreover, as Dennis Kavanagh (1994a: 9) notes, once British Rail, British Coal and parts of the Post Office[14] have been despatched to the private sector, 'this effectively ends the list of utilities which can be sold off'. 'Rationalization' is here a euphemism for closing down non-profit making component parts that no one would be likely to bid for (such as the bulk of the coal industry, for instance)[15] in order to produce a profitable core to be rapidly despatched to the private sector at an attractive price. The 'rationalization' and privatization of British Coal is a case in point.

In March 1991 British Coal had 74,000 employees and a turnover of over £3.95 billion. Yet, as Neil Walden (1993: 220) notes, 'its future size was unclear because most of its output went to the English electricity generating companies.' These contracts expired in March 1993. None the less, on 22 July 1992 British Coal was still able to declare profits of £170 million, the highest in its history. Moreover, between 1980 and 1990, productivity within the coal industry rose by 8.1 per cent (Bishop and Thompson 1992: 1187; cited in Crafts 1994: 208). Despite such indicators of apparent success, however, on 18 September 1992 a leaked Department of Trade and Industry document was published in the *Guardian*. It indicated that the government intended to shut thirty pits and sack 25,000 miners as soon as possible. This was to prove a conservative estimate. For, less than a month later, the President of the Board of Trade, Michael Heseltine, announced that the government would support British Coal's decision to close thirty-one pits with the projected loss of 30,000 jobs to take effect in March 1993 (sixteen pits had already been closed in the previous year with the loss of 16,000 jobs: Walden 1992). This would represent 'the most savage redundancy programme ever inflicted on British industry' (Walden 1993: 221). The announcement stimulated a wave of public protest, a series of local demonstrations across the country on 18 October and a temporary reprieve to prevent another Tory back-bench revolt in the Commons. It was finally to put paid to Michael Heseltine's prospects of succeeding John Major as Prime Minister. Yet within a week of the government's statement, ten of the pits had been closed, and as Robert Taylor (1994: 258) notes, by the time the resulting review of the coal industry was published in March 1993, 'the mood of national defiance had ebbed away and the closures took place amidst apathy and despair on the coalfields. By the beginning of 1994 there was hardly anything left of the mining industry to privatise.' Though likely to be somewhat more protracted, a similar process of 'rationalization' is currently underway in the marketized, but not yet fully privatized, rail system (HMSO 1992).

As the above discussion again suggests, much of the Major Government's continued radicalism can be interpreted as the product of economic expediency when contextualized in relation to: (a) the conceptual constraints imposed by a neo-liberal, free-market view of the 'economic' (which dramatically restricts the range of strategic options available to the government); and (b) the substantive constraints imposed by the institutional architecture of a state stripped of the capacity for the degree of economic intervention necessary to restore industrial competitiveness.

The contradictions of the Thatcherite project

Thatcherism, as we saw in Chapter 7, was a response not so much to the contradictions of the post-war settlement, as to the narrative of crisis placed upon those contradictions during the Winter of Discontent. This is a crucial point. For, if true, it would suggest that the very strength of its ideological appeal may well have derived from its *distortion* of the contradictions of the post-war settlement and not from any real purchase on the condition afflicting the state in the late 1970s. As a consequence, Thatcherism as a project may well have responded to the construction of *crisis* by in fact more deeply entrenching the persistent *failures* of the British state and economy. This is an important conclusion, since it sensitizes our analysis to the contradictions of the post-Thatcher settlement.

If we examine the nature of the Thatcherite project in some detail what we find is the co-existence of two very different conceptions of state and economic restructuring: the first, a regressive, ideologically driven, neo-liberal project; the second a more pragmatically oriented, modernizing strategy. This latter project is referred to by Bob Jessop as 'Schumpeterian' (after the Austrian economist) and refers to the strategy of promoting permanent innovation and the 'structural competitiveness' of the economy (Jessop 1993, 1994a, b).

Closer scrutiny reveals that these twin conceptions of social and economic change are found to be both mutually incompatible and internally contradictory. The former neo-liberal project is characterized by the notion of an unsteered economy and a minimal state. Any stable mode of economic growth can thus only arise contingently out of the uncoordinated and un-regulated interplay of the decisions of individual capitals. This is reflected in the somewhat opportunistic faith that the 'discipline of the market' can overcome the structural weaknesses of the British economy. State power is, ironically, reserved for the rolling back of the frontiers of the state and the replacement of areas of democratic political responsibility with the discipline and freedom of the market. The problem with such a strategy is that the state is effectively stripped of the strategic capacity to intervene to address the persistent frailty and backwardness of the British economy (which can be traced, as in Chapter 3, to imperial preference and the economic inheritance of the post-war period). If the market fails to regenerate the British economy, then the latter is effectively consigned to permanent stagnation (cf. Leys 1985; Anderson 1987; Gamble 1988: 229).

The latter Schumpeterian state project is characterized by a somewhat different set of strategic targets and an antithetically opposed conception of the role of the state. The economy, within this framework, must be steered by the state in search of a stable mode of insertion within global and supra-national economic dynamics. It must be positioned or inserted into a growth niche within the global economy through social and political regulation. The state must therefore be interventionist, acting in some respects as an 'ideal collective capitalist' (*pace* Engels 1878), disciplining the market and the social market for labour (as opposed to responding to the '*discipline* of the market') and seeking to position the national economy favourably within the dynamics of global capitalism. The state must thus promote innovation, competition and structural competitiveness. Furthermore, it must do so by intervening on the supply side, promoting a flexible and highly skilled labour force through training and reskilling policies that subordinate welfare

Table 15   Thatcherism and economic restructuring: the role of the state

	State–economy relationship	*State-civil society relationship*
Neo-liberal state project	Deregulation, free market mechanisms, privatization, *laissez-faire*, night-watchman state	Minimalist welfare provision, internal markets, promotion of private sector provision through tax incentives
Schumpeterian state project	Innovation, competition, structural competitiveness, labour market flexibility, supply-side intervention to enhance competitiveness	Subordination of welfare to the exigencies of competitiveness and flexibility, stimulation of flexibility and skills/technology diversity, workfare state

to the perceived requirements of economic policy. Thus, instead of a minimal welfare state, welfare becomes reoriented and restructured as *workfare* – as a mechanism for disciplining the labour market and promoting economic competitiveness (see Table 15).

To periodize the evolution of the Thatcherite project somewhat crudely, under Thatcher the rhetoric of the Schumpeterian conception was subordinated (if not absent altogether)[16] and a dominant ideologically driven regressive inflection was given to the project. By contrast, under the ideologically deradicalized 'pursuit of Thatcherism by other means' characteristic of the Major Government, the Schumpeterian project has increasingly come to prominence, at least in the government's own rhetoric. Yet, despite such rhetorical posturing, an immense £50 billion public sector borrowing requirement has had the effect of driving the government further down the neo-liberal road towards further rounds of 'rationalization' and privatization in search of windfall revenues. Though there seems some recognition of the need for consistent supply-side intervention to rectify the persistent structural weaknesses of the British economy, this has been consistently subordinated to the short-term exigencies of neo-liberal crisis management.

What this suggests is that the Thatcherite project was, from its inception, deeply problematic and contradictory, suffering from what might be termed a permanent *Schumpeterian deficit* (Hay 1994g: 27). None the less, as we have already seen, it has effected a profound structural transformation of the state, economy and civil society, redefining the very context within which contemporary political struggles are played out. For the purposes of our argument, the principal constituents of the emerging settlement can be summarized as: a marketized and residual welfare–workfare state; a largely deregulated labour market; a displacement of responsibility to the local level for the delivery of services increasingly tightly constrained from the centre; an associated diminution of local autonomy; the ravaging of the influence of the public sector trade unions; a neo-liberal accumulation strategy (premised on privatization, deregulation and recommodification) driving Britain towards a hire-and-fire, sweatshop, low-skill, low-wage, assembly plant economy on the periphery of Europe; and a state increasingly stripped of the strategic capacities for economic intervention (see Jessop 1988; Jessop *et al.* 1990: 92–5; Leys 1990: 119, 127; Anderson 1992c).

The Major Government has thus marked a return to managerial politics, representing an attempt to consolidate the structures of an emergent post-Thatcher, yet none the less *Thatcherite* settlement. Moreover, Labour's *Policy Review*, initiated in 1987, represents a belated attempt to come to terms with the impact of Thatcherism on the structures of the state and economy. Yet, rather than leading the party towards a consistent alternative based upon a critique of the Thatcherite project, its Schumpeterian deficit and its deleterious impact on Britain's economic competitiveness and social fabric, the review has in fact marked the symbolic return of Labour to consensus politics as the party has increasingly accommodated itself to the terms of this post-Thatcher settlement (Hay 1994e; see also Leys 1990; Anderson 1992c: 346; Crewe 1993; Elliott 1993; Sanders 1993; Shaw 1994: 103–7; Smyth 1994a, b; cf. Smith and Spear 1992; M. J. Smith 1994). This is particularly ironic since Labour's accommodation to 'adulterated conservatism' and the economic nostrums of the new right (see J. Smith 1993) has come at precisely the moment in which the contradictions of the Thatcherite project are becoming most apparent.

Social dumping in one country

That Britain is indeed witnessing the consolidation of a post-Thatcher settlement reflected in the return to consensus politics, the depoliticization of policy and the corresponding repoliticization of personnel may well be apparent. However, it is important to stress that this does not mean that differences in the inflection given by the parties to the management of the structures of this settlement are insignificant. The most obvious of these is Labour's attachment to the Social Protocol of the Maastricht Treaty, which commits signatories to a transnational, European social wage and to a degree of unified labour market regulation to protect workers' rights (Rosamund 1992: 97–8). This was introduced as an attempt to alleviate the tendency towards 'social dumping' in a largely unregulated, neo-liberal single European market (Teague 1989; Grahl and Teague 1990: 195–6).

'Social dumping' refers to the consequences of the internal competition likely to emerge within a liberalized European market. In such a situation, it is widely feared, national economies (and regional sectors therein) would be prone to compete to attract inward investment from footloose multinational capital on the basis of a 'burning' of national and local structures of labour market regulation. Thus Britain and Italy might compete to attract Japanese investment by effectively offering more and more exploitative labour relations in an accelerating 'race for the bottom'. Major's opt-out of the Social Protocol is thus an attempt to construct a *niche* for Britain on the periphery of the European market as a low-wage, low-skill, flexi-time, sweat-shop economy – an assembly plant for non-European products that wish to penetrate the European market. It is, as David Marquand (1994a: 18) rightly observes, a classic example of free-rider politics. In effect, Britain has been allowed to escape her share of the social costs of the single market. She is riding free on the backs of the other member states, in an attempt to make herself that much more attractive to inward investment, and that much more competitive in the cheap and shoddy end of the global market place.

Britain is thus attempting to pull a fast one on its European competitors at the cost of trapping industrial labour within a deskilled, low wage, hire-and-fire ratchet. Such manoeuvrings, though a logical extension of the inherited neo-liberal accumulation strategy, are not, however, uncontradictory. Put simply, if Major's strategy proves successful and Britain becomes a pole for inward investment within the Single Market, it will, inevitably, be followed. The consequence will be the social dumping that the Social Protocol was initially designed to prevent. Furthermore, if, as seems likely, the Community progressively reduces its barriers to trade with countries beyond the single market, then, as Peter Lange (1993: 21) observes, 'low-technology, labour-intensive industries in Europe will increasingly be out-competed by Third World and NIC producers. To survive, it would appear, the poorer countries and regions of the EC must upgrade their products and production techniques.' (Lange 1993: 21).

It might, therefore, appear that Labour's commitment to the Social Chapter represents economic pragmatism. Things are, however, somewhat more complicated. The problem for Labour is that, having effectively committed itself to a neo-liberal accumulation strategy and a desire to compete against the Tories on the basis of lower taxation, short-term structural competitiveness can only be achieved on the basis of an unregulated labour market and a low-skill, low-wage employment strategy. Yet this is clearly inherently antithetical to a commitment to the Social Protocol. Unless Labour is to reject the tenets of Thatcherite neo-liberalism altogether and opt for a more interventionist and developmental role for the state (of which the Social Chapter might then be an integral part), it is in great danger of accommodating itself to a set of neo-liberal orthodoxies which (a) are proving increasingly contradictory in Britain and (b) are likely to be further compromised by Labour's commitment to a social Europe.

Alternative scenarios: beyond Thatcherite revisionism?

> The future for British politics looks depressingly similar to the immediate past – disruptive rather than creative conservatism; slow but persistent and unmanaged economic decline; and a further loosening of the ties that bind British society.
>
> (Dunleavy 1994: 156)

Thatcherism's success, as we have already noted, was premised upon the ability of the new right to construct the moment of the late 1970s as a moment of crisis. In so doing it proved itself capable of changing, if not the hearts and minds of the electorate, then certainly the predominant perceptions of the political context, recruiting subjects to its vision of the 'necessary' response to the crisis of an 'overextended' state. However unhegemonic Thatcherism now is in terms of the popularity of a residual welfare state and the moral discipline of the market, the initial success of its hegemonic project surely lay in its ability to mould perceptions of the nature of the crisis of the 1970s, and the 'painful' though 'necessary' remedies.

There is much that the opposition parties can learn from this. Indeed, the similarities between the late 1970s and the early 1990s are considerable. Both contexts can be seen as providing ideal and rare opportunities for the successful pursuit of *preference-* and *state-shaping* (as opposed to accommodating) strategies for opposition parties which prove themselves capable of successfully distancing themselves from the dominant political and economic orthodoxies of the time (Dunleavy and Ward 1991: 112–27). What applied to Thatcherism[17] in the mid to late 1970s applies equally well to the position of the Labour Party today. The current context, like that of the 1970s, is one of profound and protracted state failure and economic recession. What is more, the symptoms of such state and economic dislocation are widely perceived and experienced. This provides a considerable opportunity for the mobilization of a populist political and economic project based on a diagnosis of the crisis of the Thatcherite state and a coherent vision of a realistic alternative.

Though the crisis might be narrated in a number of different ways, all capable of finding resonance with individuals' various experiences of state and economic failure, some of the core *economic* contradictions of the Thatcherite project can be summarized as follows:

1 By pursuing both the deregulation of banking and monetarist counterinflationary strategies, the Thatcherite project has created conditions discouraging investment in the 'real' economy, thus exacerbating a persistent structural weakness. This has resulted in a situation in which the UK invests more of its available resources overseas than does any of its competitors.
2 The rolling back of the frontiers of the social democratic state has persistently been pursued for political advantage to the detriment of economic responsibility. This can be seen in the short-term asset stripping of the public sector for the sake of a 'share- and property-owning democracy' and cosmetic reductions in the public sector borrowing requirement at the expense of long-term improvements in competitiveness and industrial performance; and the government's preferred strategy of maximizing revenues by selling off monopolies rather than promoting competition by dissolving them. Furthermore, there is little evidence to substantiate the government's claim that off-loading firms into the private sector has improved their competitiveness and performance.
3 The government's broader economic strategy has been directed towards securing tax cuts instead of channelling tax incentives and public expenditure towards industrial investment, research and development, training, innovation and reskilling. This has resulted in a consumer boom and import penetration undermining the prospects of economic recovery.

4 The policy of selective disengagement from economic intervention has resulted in the disintegration of both private and public sector training initiatives, leading to a situation in which Britain's training system is 'just about the worst of our international competitors' in an economic context which places a premium on industrial flexibility and skill diversity (Ashton *et al.* 1989: 137). As Bob Jessop and Rob Stones (1992: 187) observe, 'at a time when high-grade flexibility depends on polyvalent skills, the government sponsors flexibility through hire-and-fire industrial relations legislation and adopts a low-cost, low-skill training policy. This has reinforced the low-skill, low-wage, low-productivity character of British industry.'

5 The persistent failure of the government to develop a coherent industrial strategy has led to the deterioration of many of the previous incentives and mechanisms for stimulating investment. This has resulted in a situation in which, as Jessop (1992: 37) again notes, 'Britain is fast losing the last vestiges of an independent and coherent manufacturing base which could serve as the basis for an effective national economic strategy' (cf. Glyn 1989: 65–79; Rowthorn 1989: 281–9).

6 The systematic stripping of the strategic capacities of the state for intervention on the supply side has compromised its ability to address the persistent weaknesses of the British economy and to promote labour market flexibility, skill diversity and the enhanced structural competitiveness necessary for sustained economic growth (Marquand 1988; Ashton *et al.* 1989; Rubery 1989; Jessop *et al.* 1990: 89–92; Jessop 1992: 35–7; Jessop and Stones 1992: 185–9; Ling 1993).

This list is certainly not exhaustive, but it does illustrate the profound nature of Britain's current economic impasse and its association with the neo-liberal orthodoxies of Thatcherism (cf. Campbell *et al.* 1994). When we consider that a multitude of related contradictions in Thatcherite social policy can also be identified[18] it becomes clear not only that there is an alternative to Labour's Thatcherite revisionism, but that the construction of an alternative vision based on an understanding of the contradictions of Thatcherism is a necessary (though not in itself sufficient) condition (however unlikely) of Britain's emergence from persistent economic decline.

Conclusion: stat(e)ing the future

> The country is in a mess, and many of the solutions [*sic*] of the 1980s have been discredited. Labour has an opportunity to relaunch itself and become the focus of a new radical politics. Will it take it?
>
> (Gamble 1994b: 44)

The current deep dissatisfaction with the policies and, above all, personnel of the Major Government demonstrates the potential susceptibility of the electorate to an attempt to identify and account for such experiences in terms of crisis. This is a *crisis of the state regime*. Furthermore, this crisis of the state arises out of the contradictions of the Thatcherite project. If the crisis of the 1970s was a crisis of ungovernability and overload, a crisis of an overextended state, then today's crisis is that of an under-extended, re-trenched and debilitated state stripped of the strategic capacities for economic intervention.

The adoption of a *preference*-shaping and *state*-shaping strategy might, therefore, provide Labour with the basis from which to construct a populist political project premised upon a rejection of Thatcherite neo-liberalism and on the need for the construction of a 'developmental state' capable of providing the modernizing role that the free play of the market has consistently failed to deliver (Leys 1985; Marquand 1988; Ling 1993: 273–5).

What is certain is that this alternative cannot be constructed out of a nostalgia for a past to which there can be no return. The Keynesian welfare state is gone. The post-war settlement cannot be resurrected like a phoenix to arise from the smouldering embers of the current impasse. An alternative vision, an alternative project, is required. But like all realistic visions, this must be grounded in a tightly focused analysis of the current context. This presents a considerable challenge to those who would like to see themselves as the 'organic intellectuals' of a resurgent (new) left. The contradictions of the Thatcherite project are all too apparent. The crisis of the Thatcherite state regime is almost upon us. Yet, without an alternative project, an alternative vision, we will remain ensnared within this 'catastrophic equilibrium' in which the 'old is dying and the new cannot be born' (Gramsci 1971: 276). If Labour continues to seek electability by default then, as David Marquand (1994b) observes, 'Britain will be locked into the downward spiral of the new right. And by the election after next, it will be too late.'

If the Labour Party cannot take us back to the post-war settlement then it can, and must, ensure that the post-Thatcher settlement is short-lived, a merely transitional phase in the movement towards a truly *post-Thatcherite* settlement. If, in all likelihood, the British left cannot find the voice to project such an alternative history and to project an alternative future then there will soon be nothing left but to stare back in rueful retrospect. *Après nous le déluge.*

Notes

1 Though Dennis Kavanagh refers to the post-Thatcher period as post-Thatcherite, his analysis is in many respects similar to that developed below, demonstrating that much hinges on what the term 'Thatcherism' is understood to imply.

2 In Chapter 3 we suggested that 'consensus' might usefully be conceived of as an epiphenomenon of settlement. We also noted that consensus is, above all, a *relative* and *comparative* concept. Though we will concentrate principally upon the former use of the term (on consensus as an epiphenomenon of settlement) in this chapter, it is none the less instructive to reflect upon the essentially comparative nature of the concept in describing the contemporary British political context as one characterized by an emergent consensus. The notion of a *return* to consensus immediately implies a series of historical comparisons, indeed a historical narrative: a prior consensus phase; a departure from consensus; and a return to consensus. The argument presented in this chapter is thus part of a broader narrative linking moments of crisis to the structural transformation of the state, and the resulting

phases of comparative settlement to periods of elite political consensus. It is important to note that such a narrative makes no *a priori* assumptions about the content of such periods of consensus.

3 The term was coined by *The Economist* (on 13 February 1954) to capture the continuity in economic policy between the outgoing Labour Government (with Gaitskell as Chancellor) and the incoming Conservative administration (with Butler as Chancellor) in 1951. It has since become synonymous with consensus (see Kavanagh 1987: 4; Dutton 1991: 41–5; Pierson 1991: 125–6). Though, as we have seen, only a handful of political historians and political scientists openly question the notion of a post-war consensus (though its dates continue to be hotly contested), rather more dissent from the view that 'Butskellism' provides an appropriate label for such a consensus (see, for instance, Perkin 1991: 203; Rollings 1994).

4 To suggest such an accommodation to the new contours of the state regime on the part of the principal parties is not to imply that Labour and the Tories would not give rather different inflections to the settlement, nor that they would not seek to impose different (however incremental) trajectories of *reform* within the broad architecture of the settlement. Rather, it is to argue that such strategies of reform and adaptation to changing circumstances (however radical they may prove within particular policy fields) are not motivated by alternative state projects.

5 To some extent the notions of 'consensus' and 'one vision democracy' are synonymous. However, in this context I prefer to use the deliberately pejorative label 'one vision democracy' since it implies that there is an alternative in the current context, and that Labour's strategy of accommodation to an emergent Thatcherite settlement has had the unnecessarily and unfortunate effect of narrowing the range of alternatives presented to the electorate (see also Hay 1994e, 1995d).

6 At this point it is important to clear up a potential misperception, and to emphasize that the structural/conjunctural distinction is not a distinction between the radical and the pragmatic. Thus, to argue that Majorism is characterized by a conjunctural mode of political rationality with respect to the state regime is not to imply that the policies that it has pursued are not radical. Indeed, it is the argument of this chapter that although the Major Government may well be regarded as pragmatic, what passes for pragmatism within a disintegrating post-Thatcher settlement and within the neo-liberal straitjacket inherited from the Thatcher years is a series of ever more radical attempts at crisis management. Majorism might thus be seen as the politics of *radical pragmatism* or, perhaps better still, *pragmatic radicalism* (for a similar argument see Kerr 1995). Furthermore, to suggest that Majorism is not engaged in the politics of state-shaping (pursuing policies that are *conjunctural* with respect to the state regime) is in no sense to imply that its policies are also conjunctural with respect to particular modes of policy-making within particular policy fields (a point to which we return below). The politics of crisis management has involved the Major Government in radical policies that have increasingly proved structural in specific policy fields. Indeed, crisis management within the constraints imposed by an existing state regime is always likely to be associated with structural responses within specific policy fields. Yet such policies, in so far as they are driven by the attempt to *manage* the contradictions of the state regime, are conjunctural with respect to the state regime. The policies of the current government are not oriented to recasting the state regime, but to the task of consolidating the state regime through a combination of conjunctural and structural responses within particular policy fields. That such a task is proving increasingly impossible is driving the government in pursuit of ever more radical initiatives.

7 Itself largely the product of the immediate post-war boom and its ability to hide temporarily the persistent structural weaknesses of the British economy.

8 The perceived need to sell off the few wares still left in the cupboard in order to

service the PSBR has, for instance, had a far greater impact on economic policy than the desire to complete the 'rolling back of the frontiers of the state'.

9 A rash of ministerial resignations has plagued the Major Government since 1993 (the most prominent candidates being David Mellor, Tim Yeo, Michael Mates, Tim Smith, and Neil Hamilton). This has created the embarrassing situation where competent replacements for departing ministers are proving increasingly difficult to find, much to the delight of the opposition. Moreover, it has seemingly confirmed the tabloid's portrayal of 'Tory sleaze' within a corrupt one party state. Perhaps the most damaging of these scandals for the Government was the unholy muddle which surrounded the long-drawn-out departure of Neil Hamilton following allegations that he had received a free holiday at the Ritz Hotel in Paris (owned by Mohammed Al-Fayed) in return for 'political favours'. This episode revealed deep divisions within the Cabinet as Michael Portillo manoeuvred to prevent John Major from sacking his Minister for Corporate Affairs (or 'financial propriety' as the tabloid press insisted) by openly declaring that Hamilton was innocent until proven guilty and that he should be encouraged to use his ministerial position to defend these 'unsubstantiated' allegations. Major insisted on his resignation regardless. Hamilton's fate was probably sealed when he linked the clearing of his own name with that of the Prime Minister (whom, it had previously been alleged, had been having an affair with a cleaning lady in the House of Commons). Understandably Major did not take kindly to this analogy. Shortly afterwards similar allegations were made against Jonathan Aitken, the Chief Secretary to the Treasury, who, it emerged, had also been interviewed by Sir Robin Butler in his inquiry into the 'cash for questions' affair. Normal service was now resumed as John Major, who had previously backed David Mellor, Tim Yeo and Michael Mates, yet had sacked Neil Hamilton, came to Aitken's defence. The impression of a hapless, sleaze-ridden and above all indecisive government lurching from scandal to scandal was merely reinforced, as was the perception that fifteen years of government by the same party had bred corruption within a new Tory Establishment.

10 On earlier supply-side strategies for labour market deregulation see HM Treasury (1984, 1986). See also Robertson (1986), Johnson (1991), Peck and Tickell (1995: 30–1).

11 In the second (and more confident) of these speeches (to the Carlton Club in London), John Major openly pondered on the theme of workfare when he commented: 'increasingly, I wonder whether paying unemployment benefit, without offering or requiring any activity in return, serves unemployed people or society well' (Major 1993: 34). Yet it was not until October 1994 that Peter Lilley took the first substantive step on the road to a 'workfare state' when he announced proposals to replace Unemployment Benefit with the somewhat euphemistically entitled Jobseeker's Allowance, and to introduce a 'Back to Work Bonus'. Under the former scheme, the 'workshy jobseeker' will be required to sign an agreement accepting her or his 'availability for any work which they can reasonably be expected to do' at pain of severance of benefit. Under the latter initiative, unemployment claimants who take part-time work while officially 'seeking work' will be able to accumulate a maximum of £1000 worth of 'credits', to be drawn in cash once if, and only if, a full-time job is subsequently secured. Fifty per cent of any earnings above £5 per week is immediately siphoned off by the Treasury.

12 Around this latter and more inclusive conception of workfare there is a certain convergence between the parties. Blaijorism should perhaps be associated with workfarism (see Commission on Social Justice 1994: 151–265).

13 In apparent confirmation of this interpretation, the White Paper on Unemployment which launched the Jobseeker's Allowance estimated a reduction in the net expenditure on the 'workshy' of £100 million in the first year of implementation

(April 1996 to April 1997). This figure would rise to £200 million in each subsequent year. The *Daily Mail* captured the ethos of the reforms well, suggesting that
'special attention will be given to jolting the long-term unemployed out of their
slough of despair. If all else fails, some of them could be directed to do socially
useful work. And why not? It should be good for them and good for the community' (25 October 1994).

14 The privatization of the Post Office was put on permanent hold in October 1994
to prevent the threatened Tory back-bench revolt in the Commons – discretion
presumably proving the better part of valour.

15 That much of the former coal industry became unprofitable was a direct consequence of the government's attempt to deregulate the market for fuel. Until 1991
government restrictions prevented gas from being burned in power stations, since,
it was argued, it was too valuable a fuel to be squandered in this way, especially
given Britain's abundant coal reserves (Aubrey 1992; Fothergill and Witt 1992a).
Deregulation combined with electricity privatization, however, resulted in the 'dash
for gas' as the electricity generating and distributing companies in England and
Wales announced plans to build gas-fired power stations to replace their coal-fired
predecessors (Fothergill and Witt 1992b; Walden 1992). This, as the House of
Commons Energy Select Committee pointed out (1993) was despite the fact that
electricity generated from coal was, by PowerGen's own figures, much cheaper than
that generated from gas (£2.20 per unit as opposed to £2.73 per unit, or £2.64 as
opposed to £2.89 per unit after flue gas desulphurization). Such a situation could
only arise, as Neil Walden (1993: 220) notes, by virtue of 'the duopoly power
wielded by PowerGen and National Power, which enabled them to pass on any
extra costs; and the monopoly power of the twelve regional electricity companies
and their financial stakes in independent power producers, which gave them the
ability to pass on higher costs to the consumers and the incentive to build new
power stations.'

16 A neo-liberal version of workfare was clearly hinted at by Thatcher in her speech
to the General Assembly of the Church of Scotland in 1989: 'If a man shall not
work he shall not eat.'

17 Itself perhaps the boldest and most self-conscious attempt at preference-shaping in
the history of British electoral competition.

18 Many of them relating to the impact of neo-liberal economic strictures upon Thatcher's 'second nation' (Walker and Walker 1987; Jessop *et al.* 1988; Oppenheim 1993).

Bibliography

Aaronovitch, S. *et al.* (1981) *The Political Economy of British Capitalism.* London: McGraw-Hill.

Abbott, P. and Wallace, C. (1992) *The Family and the New Right.* London: Pluto.

Abrams, P. (1963) 'The failure of social reform, 1918–20', *Past and Present*, 24, 43–64.

Addison, P. (1977) *The Road to 1945.* London: Quartet.

Addison, P. (1991) 'The intellectual origins of the Keynesian revolution', *Twentieth Century British History*, 2 (2), 201–6.

Addison, P. (1993) 'Churchill and social reform', in R. Blake and W.R. Louis (eds) *Churchill.* Oxford: Oxford University Press.

Aglietta, M. (1979) *A Theory of Capitalist Regulation.* London: New Left Books.

Agnew, J. and Corbridge, S. (1995) *Mastering Space: Hegemony, Territory and International Political Economy.* London: Routledge.

Alford, R.R. and Friedland, R. (1985) *Powers of Theory: Capitalism, the State and Democracy.* Cambridge: Cambridge University Press.

Allen, V.L. (1960) *Trade Unions and the Government.* London: Longman.

Almond, G. and Verba, S. (1963) *The Civic Culture: Political Attitudes and Democracy in Five Nations.* Princeton, NJ: Princeton University Press.

Althusser, L. (1968/71) 'Ideology and ideological state apparatuses', in *Lenin and Philosophy and Other Essays.* London: New Left Books.

Altvater, E. (1984) 'The double character of the current crisis of the capitalist world system', *Socialism in the World*, 8, 42.

Anderson, B. (1983) *Imagined Communities: Reflections on the Origin and Spread of Nationalism.* London: Verso.

Anderson, D. and Dawson, G. (1986) *Family Portraits.* London: Social Affairs Unit.

Anderson, P. (1977) 'The antinomies of Antonio Gramsci', *New Left Review*, 100, 5–80.

Anderson, P. (1987) 'The figures of dissent', *New Left Review*, 161, 20–77.

Anderson, P. (1992a) *English Questions.* London: Verso.

Anderson, P. (1992b) 'Figures of descent', in *English Questions.* London: Verso.

Anderson, P. (1992c) 'The light of Europe', in *English Questions.* London: Verso.

Andrzewski, S. (1954) *Military Organisation and Society.* London: Routledge.

Anthias, F. and Yuval-Davis, N. (1992) *Racialized Boundaries: Race, Nation, Gender, Colour and Class and the Anti-racist Struggle.* London: Routledge.

Aristotle (1948) *Politics*, translated by E. Barker. Oxford: Clarendon Press.

Armstrong, P., Glyn, A. and Harrison, J. (1991) *Capitalism Since 1945.* Oxford: Blackwell.

Ashton, D. *et al.* (1989) 'The training system of British capitalism', in F. Green (ed.) *The Restructuring of the UK Economy.* London: Harvester Wheatsheaf.

Atkins, F. (1986) 'Thatcherism, populist authoritarianism and the search for a new left political strategy', *Capital and Class*, 28, 25–48.

Atkinson, R. and Savage, S.P. (1994) 'The Conservatives and public policy', in S.P. Savage *et al.* (eds) *Public Policy in Britain*. London: Macmillan.

Aubrey, C. (1992) 'The power and the Tory', *Guardian*, 31 January.

Bagguley, P. (1991) *From Protest to Acquiescence? Political Movements of the Unemployed*. London: Macmillan.

Balbo, L. (1987) 'Crazy quilts: rethinking the welfare state debate from the woman's point of view', in A. Showstack-Sassoon (ed.) *Women and the State*. London: Routledge.

Balibar, E. (1991) 'Racism and nationalism', in E. Balibar and I. Wallerstein (eds) *Race, Nation and Class: Ambiguous Identities*. London: New Left Books.

Baran, P. and Sweezy, P. (1966) *Monopoly Capital*. New York: Monthly Review Press.

Barbalet, J.M. (1988) *Citizenship*. Milton Keynes: Open University Press.

Barnett, C. (1986) *The Audit of War: the Illusion and Reality of Britain as a Great Nation*. London: Macmillan.

Barrow, C.W. (1993) *Critical Theories of the State*. Madison: University of Wisconsin Press.

Bartholemew, A. (1990) 'Should Marxists believe in Marx on rights?', in R. Miliband and L. Panitch (eds) *Socialist Register 1990*. London: Merlin.

Beer, S. (1965) *Modern British Politics*. London: Faber.

Beer, S. (1982) *Britain Against Itself*. London: Faber.

Bell, D. (1960) *The End of Ideology*. Glencoe, IL: Free Press.

Berry, C. (1983) 'Conservatism and human nature', in I. Forbes and S. Smith (eds) *Politics and Human Nature*. London: Frances Pinter.

Bertramsen, R. *et al.* (1991) *State, Economy and Society*. London: Unwin Hyman.

Beveridge, J. (1954) *Beveridge and His Plan*. London: Hodder & Stoughton.

Beveridge, W. (1942) *Social Insurance and Allied Services*. London: HMSO, Cmd 6404.

Billig, M. (1992) *Talking of the Royal Family*. London: Routledge.

Birch, A.H. (1984) 'Overload, ungovernability and delegitimation: the theories and the British case', *British Journal of Political Science*, 14, 135–60.

Bishop, M. and Thompson, D. (1992) 'Regulatory reform and productivity growth in the UK's public utilities', *Applied Economics*, 24 (11), 1181–90.

Blackwell, T. and Seabrook, J. (1988) *The Politics of Hope*. London: Faber.

Block, F. (1987a) *Revising State Theory: Essays in Politics and Post-industrialism*. Philadelphia: Temple University Press.

Block, F. (1987b) 'Beyond relative autonomy: state managers as historical subjects', in *Revising State Theory: Essays in Politics and Postindustrialism*. Philadelphia: Temple University Press.

Bonefeld, W. (1993) *The Recomposition of the British State during the 1980s*. Aldershot: Dartmouth.

Booth, A. (1983) 'The Keynesian revolution in economic policy-making', *Economic History Review*, XXXVI, 103–23.

Booth, A. (1984) 'Defining the "Keynesian revolution"', *Economic History Review*, XXXVII, 263–7.

Booth, A. (1989) 'Britain in the 1930s: a managed economy?', *Economic History Review*, XLII, 548–56.

Bosanquet, N. (1983) *After the New Right*. Aldershot: Dartmouth.

Bottomore, T. (1992) 'Citizenship and social class, forty years on', in T.H. Marshall and T. Bottomore (eds) *Citizenship and Social Class*. London: Pluto.

Bourdieu, P. (1990) 'Social space and symbolic power', in *In Other Words*. Cambridge: Polity.

Bourdieu, P. (1991) *Language and Symbolic Power*. Cambridge: Polity.

Bowles, S. (1981) 'The Keynesian welfare state and the post-Keynesian containment of the working class', unpublished manuscript.

Bowles, S. and Gintis, H. (1982) 'The crisis of liberal democracy: the case of the United States', *Politics and Society*, 11 (1), 51–93.

Bowles, S. and Gintis, H. (1987) *Democracy and Capitalism*. New York: Basic Books.

Breheny, M. (1989) 'Southern discomfort: the costs of success in the south east', *The Planner*, May, 14–15.

Brittan, S. (1975) 'The economic contradictions of democracy', *British Journal of Political Science*, 5 (2), 129–59.

Brittan, S. (1979) *Participation without Politics*. London: The Institute of Economic Affairs.

Brooke, R. (1989) *Managing the Enabling Authority*. London: Longman.

Brooke, S. (1989) 'Revisionists and fundamentalists: the Labour Party and economic policy during the Second World War', *The Historical Journal*, 32 (1), 157–75.

Brown, W. (1992) 'Finding the man in the state', *Feminist Studies*, 18 (1), 7–34.

Bryson, L. (1992) *Welfare and the State*. London: Macmillan.

Buci-Glucksmann, C. (1980) *Gramsci and the State*. London: Lawrence & Wishart.

Bulpitt, J. (1986) 'The discipline of the new democracy: Mrs Thatcher's domestic statecraft', *Political Studies*, 34, 19–39.

Burnham, P. (1990) *The Political Economy of Postwar Reconstruction*. London: Macmillan.

Butler, D. *et al.* (1994) *Failure in British Government: the Politics of the Poll Tax*. Oxford: Oxford University Press.

Cain, P.J. and Hopkins, A.G. (1993) *British Imperialism: Crisis and Deconstruction 1914–90*. London: Longman.

Cairncross, A. (1992) *The British Economy Since 1945: Economic Policy and Performance, 1945–90*. Oxford: Blackwell.

Calder, A. (1969) *The People's War*. London: Jonathan Cape.

Callaghan, J. (1985) *Time and Chance*. London: Collins.

Campbell, A. *et al.* (1994) 'Back to basics', in H. Margetts and G. Smyth (eds) *Turning Japanese? Britain with a Permanent Party of Government*. London: Lawrence & Wishart.

Carnoy, M. (1984) *The State and Political Theory*. Princeton, NJ: Princeton University Press.

Casey, J. (1978) 'Tradition and authority', in M. Cowling (ed.) *Conservative Essays*. London: Cassell.

Casey, J. (1982) 'One nation: the politics of race', *The Salisbury Review*, 1, 23–8.

Cashmore, E. (1979) *Rastaman: the Rastafarian Movement in England*. London: Allen & Unwin.

CCCS (1982) *The Empire Strikes Back*. London: Hutchinson.

Chester, D.N. *et al.* (1968) *The Organisation of British Central Government, 1914–64*. London: Allen & Unwin.

Chick, M. (1991) 'Competition, competitiveness and nationalisation, 1945–51', in G. Jones and M. Kirby (eds) *Competitiveness and the State: Government and Business in the Twentieth Century*. Manchester: Manchester University Press.

Clarke, P. (1988) *The Keynesian Revolution in the Making, 1924–36*. Oxford: Clarendon.

Clarke, S. (1987) 'Capitalist crisis and the rise of monetarism', *Socialist Register*, 393–427.

Clarke, S. (1988) *Keynesianism, Monetarism and the Crisis of the State*. London: Edward Elgar.

Clarke, S. (1994) *Marx's Theory of Crisis*. London: Macmillan.

Coates, D. (1980) *Labour in Power*. London: Longman.

Coates, D. (1989) *The Crisis of Labour: Industrial Relations and the State in Contemporary Britain*. London: Philip Allen.

Coates, D. (1991) *Running the Country*. London: Hodder & Stoughton.

Coates, D. (1994) *The Question of UK Decline: the Economy, State and Society*. London: Harvester Wheatsheaf.

Cobham, D. (1985) 'Controlling the money supply', in G. Thompson *et al.* (eds) *Managing the UK Economy: Current Controversies*. Cambridge: Polity.

Cochrane, A. (1991) 'The changing state of local government: restructuring for the 1990s', *Public Administration*, 69, 281–302.

Cochrane, A. (1993) *Whatever Happened to Local Government?* Buckingham: Open University Press.

Cockett, R. (1995) *Thinking the Unthinkable: Think-tanks and the Economic Counter-revolution, 1931–83*. London: Fontana.

Cohen, S. (1980) *Folk Devils and Moral Panics: the Creation of the Mods and Rockers*, 2nd edn. Oxford: Blackwell.

Cohen, S. (1985) *Visions of Social Control: Punishment and Classification*. Cambridge: Polity.

Cohen, S. and Scull, A. (eds) (1985) *Social Control and the State: Historical and Comparative Essays*. Oxford: Blackwell.

Colletti, L. (1972) *From Rousseau to Lenin*. London: New Left Books.

Colletti, L. (1975) 'Marxism and the dialectic', *New Left Review*, 93, 2–29.

Commission on Social Justice (1994) *Social Justice*. London: Institute for Public Policy Research.

Connell, R.W. (1990) 'The state, gender and sexual politics: theory and appraisal', *Theory and Society*, 19 (5), 507–44.

Connolly, W.E. (1993) *The Terms of Political Discourse*, 3rd edn. Oxford: Blackwell.

Cooper, D. (1994) 'Productive, relational and everywhere? Power and resistance within Foucauldian feminism', *Sociology*, 28 (2), 435–54.

Crafts, N.F.R. (1994) 'Industry', in D. Kavanagh and A. Seldon (eds) *The Major Effect*. London: Macmillan.

Crewe, I. (1989) 'Has the electorate become Thatcherite?', in R. Skidelsky (ed.) *Thatcherism*. Oxford; Blackwell.

Crewe, I. (1993) 'The Thatcher legacy', in A. King *et al.* (eds) *Britain at the Polls 1992*. Chatham, NJ: Chatham House.

Cronin, J. (1988) 'The British state and the structure of political opportunity', *Journal of British Studies*, 27 (3), 199–231.

Cronin, J. (1991) *The Politics of State Expansion: War, State and Society in Twentieth-century Britain*. London: Routledge.

Crosland, C.A.R. (1956) *The Future of Socialism*. London: Jonathan Cape.

Crozier, M. (1975) 'Are European democracies becoming ungovernable?', in M. Crozier *et al.*, *The Crisis of Democracy*. New York: New York University Press.

Crozier, M. *et al.* (1975) *The Crisis of Democracy*. New York: New York University Press.

Czarniawska-Joerges, B. (1995) 'Narration or science? Collapsing the division in organization studies', *Organization*, 2 (1), 11–33.

Dandeker, C. (1990) *Surveillance, Power and Modernity: Bureaucracy and Discipline from 1700 to the Present Day*. Cambridge: Polity.

David, M. (1986) 'Moral and maternal: the family in the right', in R. Levitas (ed.) *The Ideology of the New Right*. Cambridge: Polity.

Deacon, A. (1982) 'An end to the means test? Social security and the Attlee Government', *Journal of Social Policy*, 9, 289–306.

Debray, R. (1973) 'Time and politics', in *Prison Writings*. London: Allen Lane.

Desai, R. (1994) 'Second-hand dealers in ideas: think-tanks and Thatcherite hegemony', *New Left Review*, 203, 27–64.

Dietz, M. (1992) 'Context is all: feminism and theories of citizenship', in C. Mouffe (ed.) *Dimensions of Radical Democracy: Pluralism, Citizenship, Community*. London: Verso.

Dillon, G.M. and Everard, J. (1992) 'Stat(e)ing Australia: squid jigging and the masque of state', *Alternatives*, 17, 281–312.

Dorfman, G.A. (1983) *British Trade Unionism Against the Trade Union Congress*. London: Macmillan.

Douglas, J. (1976) 'The overloaded crown', *British Journal of Political Science*, 6 (4), 483–505.

Doyal, L. *et al.* (1981) 'Your life in their hands: migrant workers in the National Health Service', *Critical Social Policy*, 1 (2), 54–71.

Dunleavy, P. (1981) *The Politics of Mass Housing, 1945–75*. Oxford: Oxford University Press.

Dunleavy, P. (1994) 'British politics in the doldrums', in H. Margetts and G. Smyth (eds) *Turning Japanese? Britain with a Permanent Party of Government*. London: Lawrence & Wishart.

Dunleavy, P. and Ward, H. (1991) 'Party competition – the preference-shaping model', in P. Dunleavy, *Democracy, Bureaucracy and Public Choice*. Hemel Hempstead: Harvester Wheatsheaf.

Durham, M. (1991) *Sex and Politics: the Family and Morality in the Thatcher Years*. London: Macmillan.

Dutton, D. (1991) *British Politics Since 1945: the Rise and Fall of Consensus*. Oxford: Blackwell.

Edgerton, D. (1991) 'The prophet militant and industrial: the peculiarities of Corelli Barnett', *Twentieth Century British History*, 2 (3), 360–79.

Eisenstein, Z. (1980) 'The state, the patriarchal family and working mothers', *Kapitalistate*, 8, 43–66.

Elliott, F.R. (1989) 'The family: private arena or adjunct of the state', *Journal of Law and Society*, 16 (4), 443–63.

Elliott, G. (1993) *Labourism and the English Genius: the Strange Death of Labour England?* London: Verso.

Engels, F. (1878) *Anti-Dühring*, in K. Marx and F. Engels, *Collected Works, Volume 25*. London: Lawrence & Wishart (1987).

Esping-Ånderson, G. (1990) *The Three Worlds of Welfare Capitalism*. Cambridge: Polity.

Evans, B.J. (1992) *The Politics of the Training Market: from Manpower Services Commission to Training and Enterprise Councils*. London: Routledge.

Evans, B.J. (1993) 'Employment Policy', in P. Catterrall (eds) *Contemporary Britain: an Annual Review 1993*. Oxford: Blackwell.

Farnham, D. and Lupton, C. (1994) 'Employment relations and training policy', in S.P. Savage *et al.* (eds) *Public Policy in Britain*. London: Macmillan.

Fielding, S. (1991) 'Don't know and don't care: popular political attitudes in Labour's Britain, 1945–51', in N. Tiratsoo (ed.) *The Attlee Years*. London: Pinter Press.

Fine, B. and Harris, L. (1985) *The Peculiarities of the British Economy*. London: Lawrence and Wishart.

Finn, D. (1987) *Training without Jobs: New Deals and Broken Promises*. London: Macmillan.

Flanaghan, R.J. *et al.* (1983) *Unionism, Economic Stabilization and Incomes Policies*. Washington, DC: The Brookings Institute.

Forgács, D. (1989) 'Gramsci and Marxism in Britain', *New Left Review*, 176, 70–88.

Foster, J. (1974) *Class Struggle and the Industrial Revolution*. London: Weidenfeld & Nicolson.

Fothergill, S. and Witt, S. (1992a) *The Case against Gas*. London: Coalfield Communities Campaign, January.

Fothergill, S. and Witt, S. (1992b) *The End of Coal? The Impact of the Dash for Gas on UK Electricity Privatisation*. London: Coalfield Communities Campaign, October.

Franklin, S. (1991) 'Fetal fascinations: new dimensions to the medical-scientific construction of fetal personhood', in S. Franklin *et al.* (eds) *Off-centre: Feminism and Cultural Studies*. London: Harper Collins.

Franklin, S. *et al.* (1991) 'Feminism, Marxism and Thatcherism', in S. Franklin (eds) *Off-centre: Feminism and Cultural Studies*. London: Harper Collins.

Fraser, N. (1989) 'Women, welfare and the politics of need interpretation', in P. Lassmann (eds) *Politics and Social Theory*. London: Routledge.

Fraser, N. (1993) 'Clintonism, welfare, and the antisocial wage: the emergence of a neoliberal political imaginery', *Rethinking Marxism*, 6 (1), 9–23.

Fraser, N. and Gordon, L. (1994) 'Civil citizenship against social citizenship? On the ideology of contract-versus-charity', in B. van Steenbergen (ed.) *The Condition of Citizenship*. London: Sage.

Gallie, W.B. (1956) 'Essentially contested concepts', *Proceedings of the Aristotelian Society*, 56, 167–98.

Gamble, A. (1974) *The Conservative Nation*. London: Routledge.

Gamble, A. (1983) 'Thatcherism and Conservative politics', in S. Hall and M. Jacques (eds) *The Politics of Thatcherism*. London: Lawrence & Wishart.

Gamble, A. (1988) *The Free Economy and the Strong State*. London: Macmillan.

Gamble, A. (1990) *Britain in Decline: Economic Policy, Political Strategy and the British State*. London: Macmillan.

Gamble, A. (1994a) *Britain in Decline: Economic Policy, Political Strategy and the State*, 4th edn. London: Macmillan.

Gamble, A. (1994b) 'Loves labour lost', in M. Perryman (ed.) *Altered States: Postmodernism, Politics, Culture*. London: Lawrence & Wishart.

Giddens, A. (1982) 'Class division, class conflict and citizenship rights', in *Profiles and Critiques in Social Theory*. London: Macmillan.

Giddens, A. (1985) *The Nation-state and Violence*. Cambridge: Polity.

Gilman, S.L. (1985) *Difference and Pathology: Stereotypes of Sexuality, Race and Madness*. Ithaca, NY: Cornell University Press.

Gilroy, P. (1982) 'Steppin' out of Babylon – race, class and autonomy', in Centre for Contemporary Cultural Studies, *The Empire Strikes Back*. London: Hutchinson.

Gilroy, P. (1987) *There Ain't No Black in the Union Jack*. London: Hutchinson.

Gingrich, N. *et al.* (1994) *Contract with America*. New York: Times Books.

Ginsburg, N. (1992) *Social Divisions of Welfare*. London: Sage.

Glyn, A. (1989) 'The macro-anatomy of the Thatcher years', in F. Green (ed.) *The Restructuring of the UK Economy*. London: Harvester Wheatsheaf.

Godfrey, M. (1986) *Global Unemployment: the New Challenge of Economic Theory*. London: Harvester Wheatsheaf.

Gold, D. *et al.* (1975/6) 'Recent developments in Marxist theories of the capitalist state', *Monthly Review*, 27 (5), 29–43, and 27 (6), 36–51.

Goode, E. and Ben-Yehuda, N. (1994) *Moral Panics: the Social Construction of Deviance*. Oxford: Blackwell.

Goodin, R.E. and Dryzek, J.S. (1995) 'Justice deferred: wartime rationing and postwar welfare policy', *Politics and Society*, 23 (1), 49–73.

Goodin R.E. *et al.* (1987) *Not Only the Poor: the Middle Classes and the Welfare State*. London: Allen & Unwin.

Gordon, L. (1990a) 'The new feminist scholarship on the welfare state', in L. Gordon (ed.) *Women, the State and Welfare*. Madison: University of Wisconsin Press.

Gordon, L. (1990b) 'The welfare state: towards a socialist-feminist perspective', in R. Miliband and L. Panitch (eds) *Socialist Register 1990*. London: Merlin.

Gough, I. (1979) *The Political Economy of the Welfare State*. London: Macmillan.

Gourevitch, P. *et al.* (1984) *Unions and Economic Crisis: Britain, West Germany and Sweden*. London: Allen & Unwin.

Grahl, J. and Teague, P. (1990) *1992 – the Big Market: the Future of the European Community*. London: Lawrence & Wishart.

Gramsci, A. (1971) *Selections from Prison Notebooks*. London: Lawrence & Wishart.

Green, H. (1985) *Informal Carers*. London: OPCS/HMSO.

Groves, D. (1992) 'Occupational pension provision and women's poverty in old age', in C. Glendinning and J. Millar (eds) W*omen and Poverty in Britain: the 1990s*. London: Harvester Wheatsheaf.

Habermas, J. (1975) *Legitimation Crisis*. London: Heinemann.

Habermas, J. (1979) 'Legitimation problems in the modern state', in *Communication and the Evolution of Society*. London: Heinemann.

Habermas, J. (1992) 'Conservatism and capitalist crisis', in P. Dews (ed.) *Autonomy and Solidarity: Interviews with Jürgen Habermas*, 2nd edn. London: Verso.

Hall, J.A. and Ikenberry, G.J. (1989) *The State*. Milton Keynes: Open University Press.

Hall, P. (1986) *Governing the Economy: the Politics of State Intervention in Britain and France*. Cambridge: Polity.

Hall, S. (1979a) 'The great moving right show', *Marxism Today*, January, reprinted in S. Hall and M. Jacques (eds) *The Politics of Thatcherism*, pp. 19–39. London: Lawrence & Wishart.

Hall, S. (1979b) 'Drifting into a law-and-order society', *The Cobden Lecture*. London: The Cobden Trust.

Hall, S. (1980a) 'Encoding/decoding', in S. Hall *et al*. (eds) *Culture, Media, Language*. London: Unwin Hyman.

Hall, S. (1980b) 'Recent developments in theories of language and ideology', in S. Hall *et al*. (eds) *Culture, Media, Language*. London: Unwin Hyman.

Hall, S. (1983) 'Popular democratic vs. authoritarian populism: two ways of "taking democracy seriously"', in A. Hunt (ed.) *Marxism and Democracy*. London: Lawrence & Wishart.

Hall, S. (1985) 'Authoritarian populism: a reply', *New Left Review*, 151, reprinted in *idem., The Hard Road to Renewal: Thatcherism and the Crisis of the Left*, pp. 112–24. London: Lawrence & Wishart.

Hall, S. (1988a) *The Hard Road to Renewal: Thatcherism and the Crisis of the Left*. London: Lawrence & Wishart.

Hall, S. (1988b) 'The state: socialism's old caretaker', in *The Hard Road to Renewal: Thatcherism and the Crisis of the Left*. London: Verso.

Hall, S. and Jacques, M. (eds) (1983) *The Politics of Thatcherism*. London: Lawrence & Wishart.

Hall, S. and Schwarz, B. (1985) 'State and society, 1880–1929', in M. Langan and B. Schwarz (eds) *Crises in the British State, 1880 to 1930*. London: Hutchinson.

Hall, S. *et al*. (1978) *Policing the Crisis: Mugging, the State, and Law and Order*. London: Macmillan.

Harris, J. (1977) *William Beveridge: a Bibliography*. Oxford: Oxford University Press.

Harris, J. (1986) 'Political ideas and the debate on state welfare, 1940–45', in H.L. Smith (ed.) *War and Social Change*. Manchester: Manchester University Press.

Harris, J. (1990) 'Enterprise and welfare states: a comparative perspective', *Transactions of the Royal Historical Society*, 40, 175–95.

Harris, R. (1988) *Beyond the Welfare State*. London: Institute of Economic Affairs.

Harris, R. and Seldon, A. (1979) *Overruled on Welfare*. London: Institute of Economic Affairs.

Harvie, C. (1994) *Scotland and Nationalism: Scottish Society and Politics, 1707–1994*, 2nd edn. London: Routledge.

Hay, C. (1992a) 'Housing policy in transition: from the post-war settlement towards a Thatcherite hegemony', *Capital and Class*, 46, 25–64.

Hay, C. (1992b) Review of M. Durham's Sex and Politics, *Sociology*, 26 (4), 755–6.

Hay, C. (1994a) 'The structural and ideological contradictions of Britain's post-war reconstruction', *Capital and Class*, 54, 25–60.

Hay, C. (1994b) 'Crisis and the discursive unification of the state', in P. Dunleavy and J. Stanyer (eds) *Contemporary Political Science 1994*. Belfast: Political Studies Association.

Hay, C. (1994c) 'Environmental security and state legitimacy', *Capitalism, Nature, Socialism*, 5 (1), 83–97. Reprinted in M. O'Connor (ed.) *Is Capitalism Sustainable? Political Economy and the Politics of Ecology*. New York: Guilford.

Hay, C. (1994d) 'The political sociology of voting behaviour', in A. Warde and N. Abercrombie (eds) *Stratification and Social Inequality: Studies in British Society*. Lancaster: Framework.

Hay, C. (1994e) 'Labour's Thatcherite revisionism: playing the politics of catch-up', *Political Studies*, 42 (4), 700–8.

Hay, C. (1994f) 'Werner in Wunderland', in F. Sebaï and C. Vercellone (eds) *École de la Régulation et Critique de la Raison Économique*. Special issue of *Futur Antérieur*. Paris: Editions L'Harmattan.

Hay, C. (1994g) *Moving and Shaking to the Rhythm of Local Economic Development: towards a Local Schumpeterian Workfare State?* Lancaster Working Papers in Political Economy, 49.

Hay, C. (1995a) 'Mobilisation through interpellation: James Bulger, juvenile crime and the construction of a moral panic', *Social and Legal Studies*, 4 (2), 197–223.

Hay, C. (1995b) 'Rethinking crisis: narratives of the new right and constructions of crisis', *Rethinking Marxism*, 8 (2), 7–24.

Hay, C. (1995c) 'Structure and agency', in D. Marsh and G. Stoker (eds) *Theories and Method in Political Science*. London: Macmillan.

Hay, C. (1995d) 'Re-stating crisis: strategic moments in the structural transformation of the state in post-war Britain', unpublished PhD thesis, Lancaster University.

Hay, C. (1995e) 'Narrating crisis: the discursive construction of the Winter of Discontent', *Sociology*, 30 (in press).

Heath, A. and Jowell, R. (1994) 'Labour's policy review', in A. Heath *et al.* (eds) *Labour's Last Chance? The 1992 Election and Beyond*. London: Dartmouth.

Heath, A. *et al.* (1985) *How Britain Votes*. London: Pergamon.

Heath, A. *et al.* (1991) *Understanding Political Change: the British Voter 1964–87*. Oxford: Pergamon.

Heath, A. *et al.* (eds) (1994) *Labour's Last Chance? The 1992 Election and Beyond*. London: Dartmouth.

Heffernan, R. and Marqusee, M. (1992) *Defeat from the Jaws of Victory: inside Kinnock's Labour Party*. London: Verso.

Held, D. (1982) 'Crisis tendencies, legitimation and the state', in J.B. Thompson and D. Held (eds) *Habermas: Critical Debates*. London: Macmillan.

Held, D. (1984) 'Power and legitimacy in contemporary Britain', in G. McLellan *et al.* (eds) *State and Society in Contemporary Britain*. Cambridge: Polity.

Held, D. (1989) 'Citizenship and autonomy', in *Political Theory and the Modern State*. Cambridge: Polity.

Hennessy, P. (1993) 'Never again', in B. Brivati and H. Jones (eds) *What Difference Did the War Make?* Leicester: Leicester University Press.

Hennessy, P. (1994) 'Bluehall? The British Civil Service since 1979', in H. Margetts and G. Smyth (eds) *Turning Japanese? Britain with a Permanent Party of Government*. London: Lawrence & Wishart.

Hernes, H.M. (1987) 'Women and the welfare state: the transition from private to public dependence', in A. Showstack-Sassoon (ed.) *Women and the State*. London: Routledge.

Himmelstrand, U. and Lundberg, L. (1981) 'The interventionist state and the contradictions of capitalism', in U. Himmelstrand *et al.*, *Beyond Welfare Capitalism*. London: Heinemann.

Hindess, B. (1987) *Freedom, Equality and the Market: Arguments on Social Policy.* London: Tavistock.

Hitchens, C. (1979) 'Strange death of a social contract', *New Statesman*, 26 January.

HMSO (1944) *White Paper on Employment Policy.* London: HMSO (Cmnd 6527).

HMSO (1990) *This Common Inheritance: Britain's Environmental Strategy.* London: HMSO (Cm 1200).

HMSO (1992) *New Opportunities for the Railways: the Privatisation of British Rail.* London: HMSO (Cm 2012).

HMSO (1993) *Paying for Better Motorways: Issues for Discussion.* London: HMSO (Cm 2200).

HMSO (1994a) *Sustainable Development: the UK Strategy.* London: HMSO (Cm 2426).

HMSO (1994b) *Transport Report 1994: Government Expenditure Plans, 1994–5 to 1996–7.* London: HMSO (Cm 2506).

HM Treasury (1984) 'Helping markets work better', *Economic Progress Report*, 173, 1–5.

HM Treasury (1986) 'A more flexible labour market', *Economic Progress Report*, 182, 1–4.

Hobsbawm, E. (1993) 'Britain: a comparative view', in B. Brivati and H. Jones (eds) *What Difference Did the War Make?* Leicester: Leicester University Press.

Hobsbawm, E. and Ranger, T. (1983) *The Invention of Tradition.* Cambridge: Cambridge University Press.

Hoffman, J. (1995) *Beyond the State: an Introductory Critique.* Cambridge: Polity.

Hogwood, B. (1992) *Trends in British Public Policy: Do Governments Make a Difference?* Buckingham: Open University Press.

Holmes, M. (1985a) *The Labour Government, 1974–79.* London: Macmillan.

Holmes, M. (1985b) *The First Thatcher Government 1979–83: Contemporary Conservatism and Economic Change.* Brighton: Wheatsheaf.

Honeyford, R. (1983) 'Multi-ethnic intolerance', *The Salisbury Review*, 4, 12–13.

Hughes, C. and Wintour, P. (1990) *Labour Rebuilt: the New Model Party.* London: Fourth Estate.

Ingham, B. (1991) *Kill the Messenger.* London: Harper Collins.

Ingham, G. (1982) 'Divisions within the dominant class and British "exceptionalism"', in A. Giddens and G. Mackenzie (eds) *Social Class and the Division of Labour.* Cambridge: Cambridge University Press.

Ingham, G. (1984) *Capitalism Divided? The City and Industry in British Social Development.* London: Macmillan.

Ingham, G. (1988) 'Commercial capital and British development', *New Left Review*, 172, 45–66.

Jacobs, S. (1985) 'Race, Empire and the welfare state: council housing and racism', *Critical Social Policy*, 5, 6–28.

Jacques, M. (1979) 'Breaking out of the impasse', *Marxism Today*, October.

Jänicke, M. (1990) *State Failure: the Impotence of Politics in Industrial Policy.* Cambridge: Polity.

Jay, P. (1977) 'Enlanditis', in R.E. Tyrell (ed.) *The Future that Doesn't Work.* New York: Doubleday.

Jeffreys, K. (1987) 'British politics and social policy during the Second World War', *Historical Journal*, 30 (1), 123–44.

Jenkins, P. (1988) *The Thatcher Revolution: the Post-socialist Era.* London: Cape.

Jenson, J. (1989) '"Different" but not "exceptional": Canada's permeable Fordism', *Canadian Review of Sociology and Anthropology*, 26 (1), 69–94.

Jenson, J. (1993) 'De-constructing dualities: making rights claims in political institutions', in G. Drover and P. Kerans (eds) *New Approaches to Welfare Theory.* London: Edward Elgar.

Jessop, B. (1980) 'The transformation of the state in post-war Britain', in R. Scase (ed.) *The State in Western Europe*. New York: St Martin's Press.

Jessop, B. (1982) *The Capitalist State*. Oxford: Blackwell.

Jessop, B. (1985) *Nicos Poulantzas: Marxist Theory and Political Strategy*. London: Macmillan.

Jessop, B. (1988) 'Thatcherism: the British road to post-Fordism?', *Essex Papers in Politics and Government*, 68.

Jessop, B. (1989) 'Regulation theories in prospect and retrospect', *Economies et Sociétés*, 4.

Jessop, B. (1990) *State Theory: Putting the Capitalist State in Its Place*. Cambridge: Polity.

Jessop, B. (1992) 'From social democracy to Thatcherism. Twenty-five years of British politics', in N. Abercrombie and A. Warde (eds) *Social Change in Contemporary Britain*. Cambridge: Polity.

Jessop, B. (1993) 'Towards a Schumpeterian workfare state? Preliminary remarks on post-Fordist political economy', *Studies in Political Economy*, 40, 7–40.

Jessop, B. (1994a) 'The transition to post-Fordism and the Schumpeterian workfare state', in R. Burrows and B. Loader (eds) *Towards a Post-Fordist Welfare State?* London: Routledge.

Jessop, B. (1994b) 'Post-Fordism and the state', in A. Amin (ed.) *Post-Fordism: a Reader*. Oxford: Blackwell.

Jessop, B. and Stones, R. (1992) 'Old city and new times, in L. Budd and S. Whimster (eds) *Global Finance and Urban Living*. London: Routledge.

Jessop, B. *et al.* (1984) 'Authoritarian populism, "two nations" and Thatcherism', *New Left Review*, 147, reprinted in *Thatcherism: A Tale of Two Nations*, pp. 32–60. Cambridge: Polity.

Jessop, B. *et al.* (1985) 'Thatcherism and the politics of hegemony: a reply to Stuart Hall', *New Left Review*, 153, reprinted in *Thatcherism: A Tale of Two Nations*, pp. 87–101. Cambridge: Polity.

Jessop, B. *et al.* (1987) 'Popular capitalism, flexible accumulation and left strategy', *New Left Review*, 165, reprinted in *Thatcherism: A Tale of Two Nations*. Cambridge: Polity.

Jessop, B., Bonnett, K., Bromley, S. and Ling, T. (1988) *Thatcherism: a Tale of Two Nations*. Cambridge: Polity.

Jessop, B., Bonnett, K. and Bromley, S. (1990) 'Farewell to Thatcherism? Neo-liberalism and new times', *New Left Review*, 179, 81–102.

Johnmann, L. (1991) 'Labour and private industry, 1945–51', in N. Tiratsoo (ed.) *The Attlee Years*. London: Pinter.

Johnson, C. (1991) *The Economy Under Mrs Thatcher, 1979–1990*. Harmandsworth: Penguin.

Jones, P.M. (1993) 'Transport', in P. Catterall (ed.) *Contemporary Britain: an Annual Review 1993*. Oxford: Blackwell.

Joseph, K. (1975) *Reversing the Trend*. London: Barry Rose.

Joseph, K. (1976) *Stranded in the Middle Ground*. London: Institute for Economic Affairs.

Kautsky, K. (1892) *The Class Struggle*. Chicago: Charles Kerr (1910).

Kavanagh, D. (1987) *Thatcherism and British Politics: the End of Consensus?* Oxford: Oxford University Press.

Kavanagh, D. (1992) 'The postwar consensus', *Twentieth Century British History*, 3 (2), 175–90.

Kavanagh, D. (1994a) 'A Major agenda?', in D. Kavanagh and A. Seldon (eds) *The Major Effect*. London: Macmillan.

Kavanagh, D. (1994b) 'Opposition', in D. Kavanagh and A. Seldon (eds) *The Major Effect*. London: Macmillan.

Kavanagh, D. and Morris, P. (1994) *Consensus Politics: from Attlee to Major*, 2nd edn. London: Institute of Contemporary British History/Blackwell.

Kaye, H.J. (1987) 'The use and abuse of the past: the new right and the crisis of history', *Socialist Register*, 332–64.

Keane, J. (1978) 'The legacy of political economy: thinking with and against Claus Offe', *Canadian Journal of Political and Sociological Theory*, 2 (3), 49–92.

Keane, J. (1984) *Public Life and Late Capitalism*. Cambridge: Cambridge University Press.

Keegan, W. (1984) *Mrs Thatcher's Economic Experiment*. Harmondsworth: Penguin.

Keith, M. (1993a) *Race, Riots and Policing: Lore and Disorder in a Multi-racist Society*. London: University College London Press.

Keith, M. (1993b) 'From punishment to discipline? Racism, racialisation and the policing of social control', in M. Cross and M. Keith (eds) *Racism, the City and the State*. London: Routledge.

Kellner, D. (1989) *Critical Theory, Marxism and Modernity*. Cambridge: Polity.

Kennett, P. (1994) 'Modes of regulation and the urban poor', *Urban Studies*, 31 (7), 1017–31.

Kerr, P. (1995) 'Why the Conservatives are heading towards the goal with no-one marking them', paper presented at the Political Studies Association annual conference, University of York, April.

Kiernan, K. and Wicks, M. (1990) *Family Change and Future Policy*. London: Family Policy Studies Centre.

King, A. (1975) 'Overload: problems of governing in the 1970s', *Political Studies*, 23 (2/3), 284–96.

King, A. (1993) 'The implications of one-party goverment', in A. King *et al.*, *Britain at the Polls 1992*. Chatham, NJ: Chatham House.

King, D.S. (1987) *The New Right: Politics, Markets and Citizenship*. London: Macmillan.

King, D.S. (1989) 'Economic crisis and welfare state recommodification: a comparative analysis of the United States and Britain', in M. Gottdiener and N. Komninos (eds) *Capitalist Development and Crisis Theory*. London: Macmillan.

King, D.S. (1993) 'The Conservatives and training policy 1979–92: from a tripartite to a neo-liberal regime', *Political Studies*, 41, 214–35.

King, D.S. (1994) 'The new right and public policy', *Political Studies*, 42, 486–91.

King, D.S. (1995) *Actively Seeking Work: the Politics of Unemployment and Welfare Policy in the United States and Great Britain*. Chicago: Chicago University Press.

King, D.S. and Rothstein, B. (1994) 'Government legitimacy and the Labour market: a comparative analysis of employment exchanges', *Public Administration*, 72 (2), 291–308.

King, D.S. and Ward, H. (1992) 'Working for benefits: rational choice and the rise of work–welfare programmes', *Political Studies*, 40 (3), 479–97.

King, P. (1991) *The Channel Islands War 1940–45*. London: Robert Hale.

Kingdom, J. (1992) *No Such Thing as Society? Individualism and Community*. Buckingham: Open University Press.

Koselleck, R. (1988) *Critique and Crisis: Enlightenment and the Pathogenesis of Modern Society*. Oxford: Berg.

Krieger, J. (1986) *Reagan, Thatcher and the Politics of Decline*. Cambridge: Polity.

Laclau, E. and Mouffe, C. (1985) *Hegemony and Socialist Strategy*. London: Verso.

Lange, P. (1993) 'Maastricht and the Social Protocol', *Politics and Society*, 21 (2), 5–36.

Le Grand, J. (1982) *The Strategy of Equality*. London: Allen & Unwin.

Lenin, V.I. (1917) 'State and revolution', in *Selected Works, Volume II*. Moscow: Progress (1970).

Lereuz, J. (1979) *Economic Planning and Politics in Britain*. London: Martin Robertson.

Levitas, R. (ed.) (1986a) *The Ideology of the New Right*. Cambridge: Polity.

Levitas, R. (1986b) 'Competition and compliance: the utopias of the new right', in R. Levitas (ed.) *The Ideology of the New Right*. Cambridge: Polity.

Lewis, J. (1992) *Women in Britain Since 1945*. Oxford: Blackwell.

Leys, C. (1983) *Politics in Britain*, 2nd edn. London: Verso.

Leys, C. (1985) 'Thatcherism and manufacturing', *New Left Review*, 151, 5–25.

Leys, C. (1986) 'The formation of British capital', *New Left Review*, 160, 114–20.

Leys, C. (1989) *Politics in Britain*, revised edition. London: Verso.

Leys, C. (1990) 'Still a question of hegemony', *New Left Review*, 181, 119–28.

Ling, T. (1993) 'Overview and conclusion', in R. Maidment and G. Thompson (eds) *Managing the United Kingdom: an Introduction to Political Economy and Public Policy*. London: Sage.

Lipset, S.M. (1960) *Political Man*. New York: Free Press.

Lowe, R. (1990) 'The Second World War, consensus and the foundation of the welfare state', *Twentieth Century British History*, 1 (2), 152–82.

Lyon, D. (1988) *The Information Society: Issues and Illusions*. Cambridge: Polity.

Lyon, D. (1994) *The Electronic Eye: The Rise of Surveillance Society*. Cambridge: Polity.

McCrone, D. (1992) *Understanding Scotland: the Sociology of a Stateless Nation*. London: Routledge.

McEachern, D. (1990) *The Extended State*. London: Croom Helm.

McIntosh, M. (1978) 'The state and the oppression of women', in A. Kuhn and A.-M. Wolpe (eds) *Feminism and Materialism*. London: Routledge.

MacIver, R.M. (1926) *The Modern State*. Oxford: Oxford University Press.

Macmillan, H. (1938) *The Middle Way*. London: Macmillan.

McNeil, M. (1991) 'Making and not making a difference: the gender politics of Thatcherism', in S. Franklin *et al*. (eds) *Off-centre: Feminism and Cultural Studies*. London: Harper Collins.

Macpherson, C.B. (1962) *The Political Theory of Possessive Individualism*. Oxford: Oxford University Press.

McRobbie, A. (1994) 'Folk devils fight back', *New Left Review*, 203, 107–16.

Maier, C.S. (1987) 'The two postwar eras and the conditions for stability in twentieth-century Western Europe', in *In Search of Stability: Explorations in Historical Political Economy*. Cambridge: Cambridge University Press.

Major, J. (1993) *Conservatism in the 1990s: Our Common Purpose*. London: Carlton Club Political Committee/Conservative Political Centre.

Mann, M. (1985) *The Sources of Social Power, Volume 1*. Cambridge: Cambridge University Press.

Mann, M. (1987) 'Ruling class strategies and citizenship', *Sociology*, 21, 339–54.

Mann, M. (1988) *States, War and Capitalism*. Oxford: Blackwell.

Marin, L. (1988) *The Portrait of the King*. London: Macmillan.

Marquand, D. (1988) *The Unprincipled Society: New Demands and Old Politics*. London: Fontana.

Marquand, D. (1989) 'The decline of the post-war consensus', in T. Gorst *et al*. (eds) *Post-war Britain, 1945–64: Themes and Perspectives*. London: Pinter.

Marquand, D. (1994a) 'Reinventing Federalism: Europe and the Left', *New Left Review*, 203, 17–26.

Marquand, D. (1994b) 'Two heads and a tale', *Guardian*, 14 February.

Marsh, D. (1991) 'Privatisation under Mrs Thatcher', *Public Administration*, 69, 459–80.

Marsh, D. (1992) *The New Politics of British Trade Unionism: Union Power and the Thatcher Legacy*. London: Macmillan.

Marsh, D. (forthcoming) 'Explaining "Thatcherite" policies: beyond uni-dimensional explanation', *Political Studies*, 43.

Marsh, D. and Rhodes, R.A.W. (eds) (1992) *Implementing Thatcherite Policies: Audit of an Era.* Buckingham: Open University Press.

Marsh, D. and Rhodes, R.A.W. (1995) 'Evaluating Thatcherism: over the moon or as sick as a parrot?', *Politics,* 15 (1), 49–54.

Marshall, B.L. (1994) *Engendering Modernity: Feminism, Social Theory and Social Change.* Cambridge: Polity.

Marshall, T.H. (1950) 'Citizenship and social class', in T.H. Marshall and T. Bottomore, *Citizenship and Social Class.* London: Pluto.

Marshall, T.H. (1981) *The Right to Welfare and Other Societies.* London: Heinemann.

Marwick, A. (1968) *Britain in the Century of Total War.* London: The Bodley Head.

Marwick, A. (1974) *War and Social Change in the Twentieth Century.* London: Macmillan.

Marwick, A. (1976) *The Home Front: the British and the Second World War.* London: Thames Hudson.

Marwick, A. (1979) 'Great Britain: society in flux', in A.J.P. Taylor and J.M. Roberts (eds) *The Twentieth Century, XIV.* Oxford: Oxford University Press.

Marwick, A. (1984) 'Total war and social change: myths and misunderstandings', *Social History Science Newsletter,* 9 (2), 4–5.

Marx, K. (1843) 'On the Jewish question', in *Early Writings.* Harmondsworth: Penguin (1975).

Marx, K. (1867) *Capital. Volume 1.* London: Lawrence & Wishart (1967).

Marx, K. and Engels, F. (1962) *On Britain.* Moscow: Progress Publishers.

Mason, T. and Thompson, P. (1991) 'Reflections on a revolution? The political mood in wartime Britain', in N. Tiratsoo (ed.) *The Attlee Years.* London: Pinter.

Mercer, H. (1991) 'The Labour Governments of 1945–51 and private industry', in N. Tiratsoo (ed.) *The Attlee Years.* London: Pinter.

Middlemas, K. (1979) *Politics in Industrial Society.* London: André Deutsch.

Middlemas, K. (1986) *Power, Competition and the State, Volume 1: Britain in Search of Balance, 1940–61.* London: Macmillan.

Middlemas, K. (1990) *Power, Campetition and the State, Volume 2: Threats to the Postwar Settlement, 1961–74.* London: Macmillan.

Middlemas, K. (1991) *Power, Competition and the State, Volume 3: the End of the Post-war Era.* London: Macmillan.

Miliband, R. (1969) *The State in Capitalist Society.* London: Merlin.

Miliband, R. (1970) *Parliamentary Socialism,* 2nd edn. London: Merlin.

Minkin, L. (1974) 'The British Labour Party and the trade unions: crisis and compact', *Industrial and Labour Relations Review,* October, 9–37.

Minkin, L. (1991) *The Contentious Alliance: Trade Unions and the Labour Party.* Edinburgh: Edinburgh University Press.

Mitchell, J. (1974) *Psychoanalysis and Feminism.* Harmondsworth: Penguin.

Mitchell, T. (1991) 'The limits of the state', *Americal Political Science Review,* 85 (1), 77–96.

Mooers, C. (1991) *The Making of Bourgeois Europe.* London: Verso.

Moon, J. (1994) 'Evaluating Thatcherism: sceptical versus synthetic approaches', *Politics,* 14 (2), 43–9.

Morgan, D. and Evans, M. (1993a) 'The road to *Nineteen Eighty-Four:* Orwell and the post-war reconstruction of citizenship', in B. Brivati and H. Jones (eds) *What Difference Did the War Make?* Leicester: Leicester University Press.

Morgan, D. and Evans, M. (1993b) *The Battle for Britain: Citizenship and Ideology in the Second World War.* London: Routledge.

Morgan, K.O. (1984) *Labour in Power, 1945–51.* Oxford: Oxford University Press.

Mouffe, C. (1993) *The Return to the Political.* London: Verso.

Mount, F. (1982) *The Subversive Family.* London: Jonathan Cape.

Mulgan, G. (1994) *Politics in an Anti-political Age*. Cambridge: Polity.

Murray, R. (1989) 'Fordism and post-Fordism', in S. Hall and M. Jacques (eds) *New Times: the Changing Face of Politics in the 1990s*. London: Lawrence & Wishart.

Myrdal, A. and Klein, V. (1968) *Women's Two Roles: Home and Work*, 2nd edn. London: Routledge.

Nairn, T. (1964) 'The anatomy of the Labour Party', *New Left Review*, 27, 38–65, and 28, 33–62.

Nairn, T. (1976) 'The twilight of the British state', *New Left Review*, 101/2, 3–61.

Nairn, T. (1981) *The Break-up of Britain*. London: Verso.

Nairn, T. (1988) *The Enchanted Glass*. London: Radius.

Nairn, T. (1994) 'The sole survivor', *New Left Review*, 200, 41–8.

Newton, S. (1991) 'The Keynesian revolution debate: time for a new approach?', in A. Gorst *et al*. (eds) *Contemporary British History, 1931–61*. London: Pinter.

Newton, S. and Porter, D. (1988) *Modernisation Frustrated: the Politics of Industrial Decline in Britain Since 1900*. London: Unwin Hyman.

O'Connor, J. (1973) *The Fiscal Crisis of the State*. New York: St Martin's Press.

O'Connor, J. (1987) *The Meaning of Crisis*. Oxford: Blackwell.

Offe, C. (1975) 'The theory of the capitalist state and the problem of policy formation', in L. Lindberg *et al*. (eds) *Stress and Contradiction in Modern Capitalism*. Lexington, MA: Lexington Press.

Offe, C. (1979) 'Ungovernability: the renaissance of conservative theories of crisis', in *Contradictions of the Welfare State*. London: Hutchinson. Originally in J. Habermas (ed.) *Stichworte zur 'Geistigen Situation der Zeit'*. Frankfurt: Surkhampf Verlag.

Offe, C. (1983) 'Competitive party democracy and the Keynesian welfare state', in S. Clegg *et al*. (eds) *The State, Class and Recession*. London: Croom Helm.

Offe, C. (1984) *The Contradictions of the Welfare State*. London: Hutchinson.

Offe, C. (1985) *Disorganized Capitalism*. Cambridge: Polity.

O'Leary, B. (1994) 'Britain's Japanese question: is there a dominant party?', in H. Margetts and G. Smyth (eds) *Turning Japanese? Britain with a Permanent Party of Government*. London: Lawrence & Wishart.

Oliver, D. and Heater, D. (1994) *The Foundations of Citizenship*. London: Harvester Wheatsheaf.

Oppenheim, C. (1993) *Poverty: the Facts*. London: Child Poverty Action Group.

Orwell, G. (1941) 'The lion and the unicorn', in *Collected Essays, Journalism and Letters, Volume 2*. Harmondsworth: Penguin (1970).

O'Shea, A. (1984) 'Trusting the people: how does Thatcherism work?, in *Formations of Nation and People*. London: Routledge.

Overbeek, H. (1990) *Global Capitalism and National Decline: the Thatcher Decade in Perspective*. London: Unwin Hyman.

Panitch, L. (1976) *Social Democracy and Industrial Militancy*. Cambridge: Cambridge University Press.

Papadakis, E. and Taylor-Gooby, P. (1987) *The Private Provision of Public Welfare*. London: Harvester Wheatsheaf.

Parsons, W. (1982) 'Politics without promises: the crisis of "overload" and "governability"', *Parliamentary Affairs*, 35 (4), 421–35.

Pascall, G. (1993) 'Citizenship – a feminist analysis', in G. Drover and P. Kerans (eds) *New Approaches to Welfare Theory*. London: Edward Elgar.

Pateman, C. (1989a) 'The Civic Culture: a philosophic critique', in *The Disorder of Women*. Cambridge: Polity.

Pateman, C. (1989b) 'The patriarchal welfare state', in *The Disorder of Women*. Cambridge: Polity.

Pearson, G. (1983) *Hooligan: a History of Respectable Fears*. London: Macmillan.

Peck, J. and Jones, M. (1995) 'TECs: Schumpeterian workfare state, or what?', *Environment and Planning A*, 27 (9), 1361–96.

Peck, J. and Tickell, A. (1994) 'Searching for a new institutional fix: the *after*-Fordist crisis and the global–local disorder', in A. Amin (ed.) *Post-Fordism: a Reader*. Oxford: Blackwell.

Peck, J. and Tickell, A. (1995) 'The social regulation of uneven development: "regulatory deficit", England's south east, and the collapse of Thatcherism', *Environment and Planning A*, 27, 15–40.

Peden, G.C. (1990) 'Old dogs and new tricks: the British Treasury and Keynesian economics in the 1940s and 1950s', in M.O. Furner and B. Supple (eds) *The State and Economic Knowledge*. Cambridge: Cambridge University Press.

Perkin, H. (1991) 'Postwar Britain', *Twentieth Century British History*, 2 (2), 201–6.

Pierson, C. (1991) *Beyond the Welfare State?* Cambridge: Polity.

Pimlott, B. (1988) 'The myth of consensus', in L.M. Smith (ed.) *The Making of Britain: Echoes of Greatness*. London: LWT/Macmillan.

Pimlott, B. (1989) 'Is the postwar consensus a myth?', *Contemporary Record*, 2 (6), 12–14.

Pirie, M. (1993) 'More Thatcherite than Thatcher', *Spectator*, 10 April, 14–16.

Pollard, S. (1982) *The Wasting of the British Economy*. London: Croom Helm.

Pollard, S. (1992) *The Development of the British Economy*, 2nd edn. London: Edward Arnold.

Pollitt, C. (1993) 'Running hospitals', in R. Maidment and G. Thompson (eds) *Managing the United Kingdom*. London: Sage.

Porter, D. (1993) 'Downhill all the way: thirteen Tory years 1951–64', in R. Coopey *et al.* (eds) *The Wilson Government 1964–70*. London: Pinter.

Poster, M. (1990) *The Mode of Information: Poststructuralism and Social Control*. Cambridge: Polity.

Potter, S. (1993) 'Integrating fiscal and transport policies', in J. Roberts *et al.* (eds) *Travel Sickness: the Need for a Sustainable Transport Policy for Britain*. London: Lawrence & Wishart.

Potter, S. and Cole, S. (1993) 'Funding an integrated transport policy', in J. Roberts *et al.* (eds) *Travel Sickness: the Need for a Sustainable Transport Policy for Britain*. London: Lawrence & Wishart.

Poulantzas, N. (1970) *Fascism and Dictatorship*. London: New Left Books.

Poulantzas, N. (1973) *Political Power and Social Classes*. London: New Left Books.

Poulantzas, N. (1976) *Crisis of the Dictatorships*. London: New Left Books.

Poulantzas, N. (1978) *State, Power, Socialism*. London: New Left Books.

Powell, J. Enoch (1982) 'Our loss of sovereignty', *The Salisbury Review*, 4, 28–9.

Przeworski, A. (1985) *Capitalism and Social Democracy*. Cambridge: Cambridge University Press.

Rand, A. (1957) *Atlas Shrugged*. New York: Random House.

Rand, A. (1964) *The Virtue of Selfishness: a New Concept of Egoism*. New York: New American Library.

Ranelagh, J. (1991) *Thatcher's People*. London: Harper Collins.

Reeves, F. (1983) *British Racial Discourse*. Cambridge: Cambridge University Press.

Resnick, S. and Wolff, R. (1987) *Knowledge and Class: a Marxian Critique of Political Economy*. Chicago: University of Chicago Press.

Ricoeur, P. (1984) *Time and Narrative, Volume 1*. Chicago: University of Chicago Press.

Riddell, P. (1983) *The Thatcher Government*. Oxford: Martin Robertson.

Riddell, P. (1989) *The Thatcher Decade*. Oxford: Blackwell.

Riddell, P. (1991) *The Thatcher Era and Its Legacy*. Oxford: Blackwell.

Riley, D. (1983) *War in the Nursery*. London: Virago.

Roberts, J. (1993) 'The problem of British transport', in J. Roberts *et al.* (eds) *Travel Sickness: the Need for a Sustainable Transport Policy for Britain*. London: Lawrence & Wishart.

Robertson, D.B. (1986) 'Mrs Thatcher's employment prescription: an active neo-liberal labour market policy', *Journal of Public Policy*, 6, 275–96.

Roche, M. (1992) *Rethinking Citizenship: Welfare, Ideology and Change in Modern Society*. Cambridge: Polity.

Rollings, N. (1988) 'British budgetary policy, 1945–54: a "Keynesian revolution"?', *Economic History Review*, XLI, 283–98.

Rollings, N. (1994) 'Poor Mr Butskell: a short life, wrecked by schizophrenia', *Twentieth Century British History*, 5 (2), 183–205.

Rosamund, B. (1992) 'The Labour Party, trade unions and industrial relations', in M.J. Smith and J. Spear (eds) *The Changing Labour Party*. London: Routledge.

Rose, R. (1979) 'Ungovernability; is there fire behind the smoke?', *Political Studies*, 27 (3), 351–70.

Rose, R. and Peters, G. (1978) *Can Government Go Bankrupt?* London: Macmillan.

Rosenthal, U. (1983) 'Welfare state or state of welfare? Repression and welfare in the modern state', *Comparative Social Research*, 6, 279–97.

Rothbart, M. (1978) *For a New Liberty: the Libertarian Manifesto*. New York: Collier Books.

Rowthorn, B. (1989) 'The Thatcher revolution', in F. Green (ed.) *The Restructuring of the UK Economy*. London: Harvester Wheatsheaf.

Rubery, J. (1989) 'Labour market flexibility in Britain', in F. Green (ed.) *The Restructuring of the UK Economy*. London: Harvester Wheatsheaf.

Rustin, M. (1994) 'Unfinished business: from Thatcherite modernisation to incomplete modernity', in M. Perryman (ed.) *Altered States: Postmodernism, Politics, Culture*. London: Lawrence & Wishart.

Salveson, P. (1993) 'Playing trains', in J. Roberts *et al.* (eds) *Travel Sickness: the Need for a Sustainable Transport Policy for Britain*. London: Lawrence & Wishart.

Sanders, D. (1993) 'Why the Conservative Party won – again', in A. King *et al.* (eds) *Britain at the Polls 1992*. Chatham, NJ: Chatham House.

Sassoon, A.S. (1980) *Gramsci's Politics*. New York: St Martin's Press.

Savage, S.P. and Robins, L. (eds) (1990) *Public Policy under Thatcher*. London: Macmillan.

Savage, S.P. *et al.* (eds) (1994) *Public Policy in Britain*. London: Macmillan.

Saville, J. (1988) *The Labour Movement in Britain*. London: Faber.

Sayer, D. (1987) *The Violence of Abstraction: the Analytic Foundations of Historical Materialism*. Oxford: Blackwell.

Scase, R. (ed.) (1980) *The State in Western Europe*. London: Croom Helm.

Schlesinger, P. (1987) 'On national identity: some conceptions and misconceptions', *Social Science Information*, 26 (2), 219–64.

Schlesinger, P. (1991) 'On national identity: collective identity in social theory', in *Media, State and Nation: Political Violence and Collective Identities*. London: Sage.

Schmitter, P. (1985) 'Neo-corporatism and the state', in W. Grant (ed.) *The Political Economy of Corporatism*. London: Macmillan.

Schwarz, B. (1991) 'The tide of history: the reconstruction of Conservatism, 1945–51', in N. Tiratsoo (ed.) *The Attlee Years*. London: Pinter.

Scott, J. (1994) *Poverty and Wealth: Citizenship, Deprivation and Privilege*. London: Longman.

Scruton, R. (1980) *The Meaning of Conservatism*. Harmondsworth: Penguin.

Seldon, A. (1994) 'Consensus: a debate too long?', *Parliamentary Affairs*, 47 (4), 501–14.

Shaw, E. (1994) *The Labour Party Since 1979: Crisis and Transformation*. London: Routledge.

Shaw, M. (ed.) (1984) *War, State and Society*. London: Macmillan.

Skocpol, T. (1995) *Social Policy in the United States: Future Possibilities in Historical Perspective*. Princeton, NJ: Princeton University Press.

Small, S. (1994) *Racialised Barriers: the Black Experience in the United States and England in the 1980s*. London: Routledge.

Smith, A.M. (1994) *New Right Discourse on Race and Sexuality: Britain 1968–1990*. Cambridge: Cambridge University Press.

Smith, H.L. (1986) 'The effects of the war on the status of women', in H.L. Smith (ed.) *War and Social Change*. Manchester: Manchester University Press.

Smith, J. (1993) 'Reclaiming the ground', in C. Bryant (ed.) *Reclaiming the Ground*. London: Spire.

Smith, M.J. (1994) 'Understanding the "politics of catch-up": the modernization of the Labour Party', *Political Studies*, 42 (4), 708–15.

Smith, M.J. and Spear, J. (eds) (1992) *The Changing Labour Party*. London: Routledge.

Smyth, G. (1991) 'The meaning of Major', in G. Smyth (ed.) *Can the Tories Lose?* London: Lawrence & Wishart.

Smyth, G. (1993) *The Trade Union Question in British Politics: Government and Unions Since 1945*. Oxford: Blackwell.

Smyth, G. (1994a) 'Clinging to the wreckage', in H. Margetts and G. Smyth (eds) *Turning Japanese? Britain with a Permanent Party of Government*. London: Lawrence & Wishart.

Smyth, G. (1994b) 'Employment and industrial relations policy', in D. Kavanagh and A. Seldon (eds) *The Major Effect*. London: Macmillan.

Solomos, J. (1985) 'Problems, but whose problems? The social construction of black youth unemployment', *Journal of Social Policy*, 14 (4), 527–54.

Solomos, J. (1988) 'Black youth, crime and the ghetto: common sense images and law and order', in *Black Youth, Racism and the State: the Politics of Ideology and Policy*. Cambridge: Cambridge University Press.

Somerville, J. (1992) 'The new right and family politics', *Economy & Society*, 21 (2), 93–128.

Stedman-Jones, G. (1983) *Languages of Class: Studies in Working-class History 1832–1982*. Cambridge: Cambridge University Press.

Stephenson, H. (1980) *Mrs Thatcher's First Year*. London: Jill Norman.

Stevenson, J. (1988) 'The New Jerusalem', in L.M. Smith (ed.) *The Making of Britain: Echoes of Greatness*. London: LWT/Macmillan.

Stoker, G. (1991) *The Politics of Local Government*, 2nd edn. London: Macmillan.

Stones, R. (1990) 'Government-finance relations in Britain 1964–7: a tale of three cities', *Economy and Society*, 19 (1), 32–55.

Strange, S. (1971) *Sterling and British Policy*. London: Royal Institute of International Affairs.

Summerfield, P. (1988) 'Women, war and social change: women in Britain in World War II', in A. Marwick (ed.) *Total War and Social Change*. London: Macmillan.

Summerfield, P. (1993) 'Approaches to women and social change in the Second World War', in B. Brivati and H. Jones (eds) *What Difference Did the War Make?* Leicester: Leicester University Press.

Sumner, C. (1994) *The Sociology of Deviance: An Obituary*. Buckingham: Open University Press.

t'Hart, P. (1993) 'Symbols, rituals and power: the lost dimension of crisis-management', *Journal of Contingencies and Crisis Management*, 1 (1), 36–50.

Taylor, I. (1991) 'Labour and the impact of the war, 1939–45', in N. Tiratsoo (ed.) *The Attlee Years*. London: Pinter.

Taylor, P. (1989) 'Britain's changing role in the world economy', in J. Mohan (ed.) *The Political Geography of Contemporary Britain*. London: Macmillan.

Taylor, P. (1992) 'Changing political relations', in P. Cloke (ed.) *Policy and Change in Thatcher's Britain*. Oxford: Pergamon.

Taylor, R. (1982) 'The trade union "problem" in British politics', in B. Pimlott and C. Cook (eds) *Trade Unions in British Politics*. London: Longman.

Taylor, R. (1993) *The Trade Union Question in British Politics: Government and Unions Since 1945*. Oxford: Blackwell.

Taylor, R. (1994) 'Employment and industrial relations policy', in D. Kavanagh and A. Seldon (eds) *The Major Effect*. London: Macmillan.

Taylor-Gooby, P. (1985) *Public Opinion, Ideology and State Welfare*. London: Routledge.

Teague, P. (1989) *The European Community: the Social Dimension*. London: Kogan Page.

ten Tusscher, T. (1986) 'Patriarchy, capitalism and the new right', in J. Evans *et al.* (eds) *Feminism and Political Theory*. London: Sage.

Thain, C. (1984) 'The Treasury and Britain's decline', *Political Studies*, 32, 581–95.

Thatcher, M. (1993) *The Downing Street Years*. London: Harper Collins.

Thompson, E.P. (1984) 'Mr Attlee and the Gardarene Swine', *The Guardian*, 3 March.

Thompson, G. (1977) 'The relationship between the financial and industrial sector in the UK economy', *Economy and Society*, 6 (3), 235–83.

Thompson, G. (1987) 'Objectives and instruments of economic management', in G. Thompson *et al.* (eds) *Managing the UK Economy*. Cambridge: Polity.

Tilly, C. (1973) *The Formation of the National States in Western Europe*. Princeton, NJ: Princeton University Press.

Tiratsoo, N. (ed.) (1991a) *The Attlee Years*. London: Pinter.

Tiratsoo, N. (1991b) 'Introduction', in N. Tiratsoo (ed.) *The Attlee Years*. London: Pinter.

Tiratsoo, N. and Tomlinson, J. (1993) *Industrial Efficiency and State Intervention: Labour 1939–51*. London: LSE/Routledge.

Titmuss, R. (1950) *Problems of Social Policy*. London: Allen & Unwin.

Titmuss, R. (1958) *Essays on the Welfare State*. London: Allen & Unwin.

Titmuss, R. (1964) 'Goals of today's welfare state', in P. Anderson and R. Blackburn (eds) *Towards Socialism*. London: Fontana.

Tomlinson, J. (1981) 'Why was there never a "Keynesian revolution" in economic policy?', *Economy & Society*, 10 (1), 72–87.

Tomlinson, J. (1984) 'A "Keynesian revolution" in economic policy-making?', *Economic History Review*, XXXVII, 258–62.

Tomlinson, J. (1991) 'A missed opportunity? Labour and the productivity problem 1945–51', in G. Jones and M. Kirby (eds) *Competitiveness and the State: Government and Business in Twentieth Century Britain*. Manchester: Manchester University Press.

Tomlinson, J. (1992) 'Planning: debate and policy in the 1940s', *Twentieth Century British History*, 3 (2), 154–74.

Tomlinson, J. (1993) 'Mr Attlee's supply-side socialism', *Economic History Review*, XLVI, 1–22.

Tomlinson, J. (1994) *Government and the Enterprise Since 1900*. Oxford: Clarendon.

Tomlinson, J. (1995) 'The iron quadrilateral: political obstacles to economic reform under the Attlee Government', *Journal of British Studies*, 34 (1), 90–111.

Townsend, P. and Davidson, N. (eds) (1982) *Inequalities in Health*. Harmondsworth: Penguin.

Turner, B. (1986) *Citizenship and Capitalism: the Debate over Reformism*. London: Allen & Unwin.

Turner, B. (1990) 'Outline of a theory of citizenship', *Sociology*, 24 (2), 189–217.

Turner, B. (1993) 'Preface', in B. Turner (ed.), *Citizenship and Social Theory*. London: Sage.

Turner, J. (1992) *British Politics and the Great War: Coalition and Conflict 1915–18*. New Haven, CT: Yale University Press.

Twine, F. (1994) *Citizenship and Social Rights: the Interdependence of Self and Society.* London: Sage.

Usher, D. (1981) *The Economic Prerequisite to Democracy.* New York: Columbia University Press.

van Stenbergen, B. (1994) 'Towards a global ecological citizen', in B. van Stenbergen (ed.) *The Condition of Citizenship.* London: Sage.

Walden, N. (1992) 'Energy policy', in P. Catterall (ed.) *Contemporary Britain: an Annual Review 1992.* Oxford: Blackwell.

Walden, N. (1993) 'Energy policy', in P. Catterall (ed.) *Contemporary Britain: an Annual Review 1993.* Oxford: Blackwell.

Walker, A. and Walker, C. (eds) (1987) *The Growing Divide: a Social Audit 1979–87.* London: Child Poverty Action Group.

Walzer, M. (1985) *Spheres of Justice.* Oxford: Blackwell.

Warde, A. (1982) *Consensus and Beyond: the Development of Labour Party Strategy Since the Second World War.* Manchester: Manchester University Press.

Weber, M. (1978) *Economy and Society: an Outline of Interpretative Sociology.* Berkeley: University of California Press.

Webster, C. (1990) 'Conflict and consensus: explaining the British health service', *Twentieth Century British History*, 1 (2), 115–51.

Weiner, M. (1981) *English Culture and the Decline of the Industrial Spirit.* Cambridge: Cambridge University Press.

Whitaker, R. (1987) 'Neo-conservatism and the state', *Socialist Register*, 1–31.

Whitelegg, J. (1992) 'Rail's contribution to improving transport and the environment', in J. Roberts *et al.* (eds) *Travel Sickness: the Need for a Sustainable Transport Policy for Britain.* London: Lawrence & Wishart.

Whitelegg, J. (1993) *Transport for a Sustainable Future: the Case for Europe.* London: Belhaven.

Williams, F. (1989a) *Social Policy: a Critical Introduction. Issues of Race, Gender and Class.* Cambridge: Polity.

Williams, F. (1989b) 'The welfare state as part of a racially structured and patriarchal capitalism', in *Social Policy.* Cambridge: Polity.

Wolfe, A. (1977) *The Limits of Legitimacy: Political Contradictions of Contemporary Capitalism.* New York: Free Press.

Wolfe, J. (1991) 'State, power and ideology in Britain: Mrs Thatcher's privatisation programme', *Political Studies*, 39, 237–52.

Wootton, G. (1980) 'The impact of organized interests', in W.B. Gwyn and R. Rose (eds) *Britain: Progress and Decline.* London: Macmillan.

Wright, G. (1968) *The Ordeal of Total War, 1939–45.* New York: Free Press.

Wright, P. (1985) *On Living in an Old Country: the National Past in Contemporary Britain.* London: Verso.

Young, H. (1993) 'You clap, I'll sing', *Guardian*, 12 June.

Young, H. (1994) 'The Prime Minister', in D. Kavanagh and A. Seldon (eds) *The Major Effect.* London: Macmillan.

Yuval-Davis, N. (1990) 'The citizenship debate: women, ethnic processes and the state', *Feminist Review*, 39, 58–68.

Index